The
Social
Christian
Novel

The Social Christian Novel

ROBERT GLENN WRIGHT

Contributions in American Studies, Number 93

GREENWOOD PRESS
New York • Westport, Connecticut • London

890226

Library of Congress Cataloging-in-Publication Data

Wright, R. Glenn (Robert Glenn)
   The social Christian novel / Robert Glenn Wright.
      p.   cm.   —   (Contributions in American studies, ISSN 0084–9227 ;
   no. 93)
   Bibliography: p.
   Includes index.
   ISBN 0–313–24661–0 (lib. bdg. : alk. paper)
   1. Christian fiction, American—History and criticism.   2. Church
and social problems in literature.   3. Sociology, Christian, in
literature.   4. Social problems in literature.   5. Social gospel in
literature.   I. Title.   II. Series.
PS374.C48W7   1989
813′.009355—dc19   88–25106

British Library Cataloguing in Publication Data is available.

Library of Congress Catalog Card Number: 88–25106
ISBN: 0–313–24661–0
ISSN: 0084–9227

First published in 1989

Greenwood Press, Inc.
88 Post Road West, Westport, Connecticut   06881

Printed in the United States of America

∞

The paper used in this book complies with the
Permanent Paper Standard issued by the National
Information Standards Organization (Z39.48–1984).

10 9 8 7 6 5 4 3 2 1

To Muriel Hope McClanahan,
with Love and Friendship

Contents

Foreword

While Robert Glenn Wright was a candidate for the doctorate in American civilization at The George Washington University, we acquired the manuscript bibliography of the recently deceased Lisle Abbott Rose. Rose, whose University of Chicago dissertation had dealt with protest fiction, went on to compile an enormous bibliography dealing with reform issues between the Civil War and World War I. The Rose Bibliography, which I brought to Washington from Illinois, became the immediate subject of a seminar of which Wright was a member. It was here, in the context of protest fiction, that Bob Wright began to explore some of Rose's citations, becoming gradually convinced that there was more to social Christian fiction than had been theretofore recognized.

Wright began to suspect that even the indefatigable Rose had not covered the subject. Consequently he shelf-read the Library of Congress holdings in the PZ 3 classification, pulling from 168,000 titles some 1,300 of apparent relevance and which, on closer examination, were narrowed to the 145 novels on which Wright based his research. On May 15, 1968, he defended this research against examiners who included Daniel Aaron, Wallace E. Davies, and Muriel McClanahan.

Neither Wright nor I, who had directed the dissertation, felt any need to rush the work into publication. He, in fact, had become much more entranced with shelf-reading than with protest fiction. His major scholarly legacy is a set of bibliographies that come close to cataloguing the universe of fiction in English.

For my own part, I have sustained an interest in social change and in the relation between literature and that process. I watched as numerous works appeared on muckraking, naturalism, utopianism, and other genres that comprise the nexus of literature and politics. No one made a direct attack, as Wright had done, on this one particular and recognizable part of the spectrum. I kept citing his dissertation as the best—and in many ways the only—comprehensive treatment of the subject.

For this reason I undertook to persuade Bob Wright to return to his dissertation to revise and update it for publication in "Contributions in American Studies." He agreed and set to work.

Soon thereafter misfortune struck. To the dismay of his many friends and colleagues, Bob Wright was diagnosed as carrying an elusive but virulent cancer. As he searched for a more lucid diagnosis and began his fight against the malignancy, he also attempted to meet his professional obligations. There were, however, too many commitments to be matched by his waning energy. Although he devoted considerable time and effort to bringing the former dissertation into publishable condition, he was not able to complete the work.

Disappointed at having lost a friend and former student, I was determined not to have this effort wasted. The same justifications that had led me to approach Wright months before were still valid. I therefore took counsel with my colleague in the Department of Religion, Dewey Wallace, who had served as a reader of the dissertation. He agreed that the basic research was too valuable to remain unpublished. To both of us these novels—as discovered, described, and categorized by Wright—remain an important chapter in the conjunction of religion, literature, and social questions. Professor Wallace—without whose help I would not have proceeded—agreed to join me in writing an introduction that would identify the context in which to place this work.

For better or worse neither Wallace nor I would have presented the material as Wright has done. Aside from compressing the text and quotations, however, we have made very few changes. While we may not agree with everything Wright has written, we have refrained from imposing our own sense of interpretive priorities. It was Bob Wright who read through the shelves, found and examined these novels, worked out their typologies, and presented them to the reader. This work and these judgments have been preserved. Our introduction is a tribute to the value of the basic research and, by extension, to the life and career of Robert Glenn Wright.

Robert H. Walker

Introduction

Out of the Civil War came two visions of America. One placed the nation's future in the hands of those who had already industrialized the North, stringing telegraph wires, laying railroad tracks, mining coal and iron in order to manufacture a new secondary environment. The other vision drew on emancipation as a large step toward a social evolution that would eventually produce true equality of opportunity and equitable distribution of the national product.

In the conflict between these two visions lay the fundamental dynamic of Victorian America. This dynamic permeated politics, economics, and diplomacy. Much of the literature of this era was devoted to promoting one vision or the other and occasionally mediating between the two. The involvement of the creative imagination in this dynamic was so palpable as to demand a new vocabulary featuring such terms as "realism," "muckraking," and "the ashcan school." The social histories and anthologies of this era have paid homage to the cartoonists (like Thomas Nast), the exposé journalists (like Lincoln Steffens and Ida Tarbell), and the utopian romancers (like Edward Bellamy). If they have noted the presence of Christian social fiction at all, it has usually been with a slight nod of the head to an idiosyncratic best seller, *In His Steps*.

The most apparent contribution of Robert Glenn Wright's study is to document the existence of a sizable body of what he reasonably calls "social Christian fiction." Although he does not claim for it high literary quality, it is clear that many of these works were popular (one of them unprecedentedly so) and that a few were written by individuals who were important in the context of religion, journalism, and other fields. Almost regardless of its quality, this body of material claims recognition as a missing piece in the full story of the rise of a category of socially conscious literature within which was debated the merits of the competing American visions. Along with the naturalists, the proletarian novelists, the journalistic muckrakers, and the creators of literary utopias, there must be—Wright demonstrates—a place for these social moralists who chose fiction as their vehicle.

For those rare few (like Wallace Davies) who took this literary category as a serious part of social history, there was a temptation to oversimplify the genre. *In His Steps* does not represent all social Christian fiction. Wright, in fact, is able to identify no fewer than four attitudinal categories which align these authors on both sides of the basic debate that occupied their generation. Some defended entrepreneurship. Some took a patrician view that depended on generosity from above. At the other extreme were those who outlined a Christian radicalism and, at the center, were those whose advocacy of institutional change makes it easy to identify them with the emerging progressive movement.

Political philosophy was not the only element that characterized and distinguished the authors of this fiction. At least as important was the interaction between the church and society and the related questions of Christian and denominational doctrine. The social gospel did not monopolize this fiction; but the issues related to it were the very issues that then preoccupied the novelists.

The social gospel was a movement within the American Protestant churches that called for the application of Christian principles to the solution of social problems, particularly those problems related to matters generated by the clash of labor and capital; by the early twentieth century it had significantly transformed large segments of American Protestant life and thought. The social gospel was clearly related to progressivism, as evidenced by the importance of it to such progressive thinkers as Henry George or Edward Bellamy; like the progressives, the social gospellers were reacting to the rapid industrialization and urbanization of the United States that occurred in the generations after the Civil War. As was the case with the progressives, they believed that the promise of democracy and equality was being defeated by industrial greed, the growth of urban slums, and governmental corruption.

Nor were these American Protestants unique in Christendom in responding in this way. Thomas Chalmers in Scotland and F. D. Maurice and Charles Kingsley in England (the latter two with a program they called Christian socialism) had pioneered earlier with such concerns and influenced many Americans—the influence of Kingsley and Maurice on American Episcopalians was especially notable. Pope Leo XIII issued many important encyclicals dealing with the problems of capital and labor that were concurrent with Protestant social gospel efforts, though scarcely of much influence upon them. The work of the novelist Leo Tolstoy was another example of the widespread concern about the un-Christian character of society, and even though he was reacting as much to a peasant and landowning society as to industrialization, his very unorthodox "ethical" Christianity was to have an enormous impact on American social gospellers.

But the American social gospel was not just a reaction to broader social forces or a consequence of influences from abroad; it was also the extension of earlier and longstanding American Protestant traditions. Thus the puritan desire for theocracy, whatever else it was, was a conviction that the whole social order must come under the subjugation of biblical and hence moral rule. Those committed to a Christianized society became less authoritarian and more willing to use persuasion, as voluntarist evangelicalism had earlier eroded Calvinism; but their goal remained the same—a society that would glorify God. As a unified nation emerged in the aftermath of the American Revolution, many other tributaries joined the stream of New England and colonial Calvinism and energized its sense of social obligation and stewardship: Wesleyan and Finneyite revivalism, with its attendant perfectionism and postmillennial enthusiasm was probably the most important of these. The result, in the mission and reform societies of the so-called benevolent empire, was an effort to form an ideal Christian nation, purged of drunkenness and slavery, and filled with Bibles, churches, and virtuous citizens.

In many ways victory in the war to end slavery and the successes of Reconstruction seemed the fulfillment of reformist dreams, lulling many northern Protestants into a certain complacency about a Christian America, until the acuteness of the surrounding social ills awakened them. Moreover, the convergence of Protestant values and the Protestant populace with the burgeoning middle class was also a powerful sedative.

When American Protestants did awaken to the alarming conditions of life in industrial America, they drew not only on those earlier ideas about a more morally Christian society that had flourished in the benevolent empire but also upon many of the themes of the emergent liberalism of the "new theology." Among the elements of the new theology that were especially stimulating and fruitful for a social Christianity, none was more important than the emphasis on the teaching of Jesus about the "kingdom of God." This gave the strongest authority possible to the ideals of the social gospel, while the theme of the "kingdom" merged with earlier postmillennial hopes to make the social gospel fervently optimistic. Just as liberal theology looked to a more scientific study of scripture for the grounding of its theological ideas in the Bible, so did the social gospellers call for a rigorously scientific study of society, which they did not doubt would abet their efforts.

The wide range of views and approaches that can be encompassed within the limits of the social gospel can be sampled by examining some of its typical proponents. Washington Gladden was not only one of its early spokesmen, but also represented something like the center of the movement. Pastor to several Massachusetts congregations before his long pastorate at the First Congregational Church of Columbus, Ohio (1882–1914), as early as 1875 he called for more just treatment of workers and worried about their absence from Protestant pews. Highly critical of the "bloated fortunes" and unscrupulous methods of the Gilded Age millionaire industrialists, he advocated a more cooperative economic order and a more compassionate economic theory than that represented by the prevailing laissez-faire capitalism. If he sometimes called his position "socialist," it was in the vague sense of the earlier British "Christian socialists" rather than with the meaning of the word as it was used by European theorists.

The major book of another congregationalist social gospeller, Josiah Strong, first appeared in 1885. *Our Country* blended alarm over America's grave urban problems with Christian nationalism and social gospel meliorism. Strong labored indefatigably to shape a cooperative Protestant social movement.

The more cautious end of the social gospel spectrum is represented by a far less important figure, Charles Oliver Brown, congregationalist pastor in Kalamazoo, Dubuque, and San Francisco. In 1886 his *Talks on Labor Troubles* was published in Chicago and in that tumultuous year of the Haymarket riot acknowledged the justice of laborers' grievances at the same time that it warned them away from the poisonous doctrines of Karl Marx. For Brown the solution was to be found in the recapturing of true equality of opportunity based on the kind of hardworking, sober persons idealized by Finneyite evangelicalism. Brown's version of the social gospel was more backward-looking than that of Gladden or Strong, but equally optimistic.

A more radical version of the social gospel movement was represented by William Dwight Porter Bliss and George D. Herron. Bliss was an Episcopalian who founded the Church of the Carpenter in Boston as an experiment in Christian socialism. He was also active in the radical labor organization known as the Knights of Labor. Herron's most influential years were spent as a professor of applied Christianity at Iowa College (Grinnell) from where he set out on many speaking tours, popularizing his version of the social gospel through such inflammatory dicta as "a rich Christian is a contradiction in terms" or "Christianity is the religion of which socialism is the practice." Personal problems eventually drove him from the ministry. Both before and after he left the ministry he was involved in the activities of the American socialist party.

The Baptist Walter Rauschenbusch best represents the kind of theological reflection to which the social gospel movement gave rise. His *A Theology for the Social Gospel*, published in 1917, one year before his death, sought to reformulate Christian theology in the light of the social movement that was having such impact on the Protestant churches. Thus he stressed the importance of the kingdom of God as a category of Christian theology and sought to reformulate such ancient doctrines as original sin and the atonement in the light of their potential meaning for the social gospel.

Not all the leaders of the social gospel movement were clergy. Richard T. Ely was an Episcopal layman active in the movement. A professor of Economics at Johns Hopkins and later the University of Wisconsin, he labored for a scientific economics that would be more ethical and also less favorable to free market capitalism. He joined Strong and Herron in 1893 in founding the American Institute of Christian Sociology that would blend social reform along Christian lines with the best social science.

By the turn of the century the social gospel had gained considerable momentum in the northern Protestant denominations. Many urban parishes were organized as "institutional churches" engaged in numerous social service activities while denominational and interdenominational organizations for the promotion of social gospel values—such as the Brotherhood of the Kingdom, founded by Walter Rauschenbusch and like-minded associates—flourished. Local and regional organizations to promote Christian citizenship or more specific aims multiplied. Religious charitable organizations enlisted the efforts of reform-minded Protestants, although the social gospellers made it clear that their ideal went farther than the mere care of those harmed by bad social arrangements; it involved the criticism and transformation of existing social arrangements.

Social gospel ideals were not only disseminated by these organizations and the innumerable sermons of its exponents, but also through many other means. A number of hymns were redolent of its spirit, including the still widely sung "O Master Let Me Walk with Thee," by Washington Gladden. Books and tracts also spread the message, including many of those works studied by Wright. The large number of tracts, hymns, and novels begotten by the movement suggests something of its popularity—not every religious movement gave rise to such a wealth of song and story.

The influence of the social gospel movement was considerable, though it was not perhaps of the sort that its leaders had desired. It was never truly successful in enlisting the participation of the laboring masses in the Protestant congregations—the great aim of Washington Gladden; but it did win over to the cause of reform a large part of the northern urban middle class that was affiliated with the major Protestant denominations, thereby becoming a significant factor in such success as the progressive movement achieved. Its influence on American political life was also far from negligible: both William Jennings Bryan and Woodrow Wilson can be regarded as deeply imbued with the social gospel outlook, and Norman Thomas illustrates the movement of a social gospeller into politics as he abandoned the Presbyterian ministry for the leadership of the Socialist Party.

In the middle of the twentieth century the social gospel movement suffered reverses. The 1920s witnessed a sharp change in the direction of the reform spirit, and neo-Orthodox theology assaulted the liberalism upon which much of the social gospel was premised. Reinhold Niebuhr's Christian realism was widely regarded as the death knell of the older social gospel. Nonetheless by the late twentieth century the picture looks somewhat different. Not only does Niebuhr's critique appear, with distance, to be more of a family quarrel than a total rejection of the social gospel, but many of the newer theologies of liberation have returned to the theme of divine immanence so central to the new theology and the social gospel. Moreover, various forms of Christian radicalism have flourished since the 1960s that would have seemed extreme to some of those old social gospellers. In any case, the materials examined by Wright can with this distance be seen as a significant aspect of the emergence of a characteristically Gilded Age form of social Christianity.

One way to locate the importance of the social Christian novels is by triangulation: comparing and contrasting them with three well-known novels. Harriet Beecher Stowe's *Uncle Tom's Cabin* represents a kind of precedent; two others, also from the late nineteenth century, show vital connections and contrasts.

Alerted by remarks of several of the authors under study, Robert Wright correctly accepted *Uncle Tom's Cabin* as a prototype for the best of the social Christian novels. This is an apt judgment for several reasons. There are parallels in their literary characteristics. Stowe accepted the conventions of the sentimental fiction on which she had been nurtured. She did not try for originality but used the techniques of characterization, language, plot, and didacticism that had marked the genre with which she was most familiar. Similarly, as Wright points out in detail, the social Christian novelists worked within the traditions of Victorian prose. They used stilted vocabulary, involved sentence structure, and two-dimensional characterization. Without hesitation they infused moral values into the narrative. They were quick to seize satire and allegory as methods of communication.

If Stowe's novel transcended its genre in any single respect, it was in the degree to which her tale was based on careful research into the subject in question. She had, in fact, begun her labors by compiling newspaper clippings covering events in the slave empire that she had intended to publish as a compendium similar to Theodore Dwight Weld's powerfully influential *Slavery As It Is*. Challenged by readers who doubted the representative quality of her story, Stowe later produced her evidence—the carefully preserved newspaper excerpts—as documentation, calling it *A Key to Uncle Tom's Cabin*.

As Wright points out, the best of the social Christian novels shared this trait. Although their presentation was not more "realistic" (in the manner of Stephen Crane) than was *Uncle Tom*, the most persuasive of them based their narratives on a careful inquiry into conditions of labor, problems of management, changes in seminary curriculum, or other social issues. Like Stowe, some of these authors had done their homework. Their descriptions and recommendations were effective in proportion to the amount of investigative labor that underlay the fiction.

Most tellingly, *Uncle Tom's Cabin* served as a model because it attempted to move society through a tale whose principal figure exemplified Christian virtue. Uncle Tom earned his pejorative connotation as a toady to the white man's wishes through the way he was portrayed in tent shows and riverboat melodramas. The character in the novel, however, was explicitly Christlike. He used the power of his faith to repress a violent response to violent mistreatment. He educated his tormentors with a show of superior virtue. In a manner that was painfully Christlike, Tom's martyrdom was to the novel what the crucifixion was to the New Testament. Stowe's book remains one of the most remarkable examples of the way in which imaginative literature can drive social change. The impetus for social justice supplied by *Uncle Tom's Cabin* is what the social Christian novelist saw in his fondest dreams.

If Stowe provided a model and a goal, Edward Bellamy's *Looking Backward* offered the nearest kinship within contemporary social fiction. Published in 1888, *Looking Backward* produced a spate of imitative romances that lasted as a vogue just beyond the turn of the century. Like the more radical among the works studied by Wright, Bellamy offered his readers a form of socialism, but a socialism clearly based on explicitly Christian principles. Furthermore, the format of the utopian romance bears a curious relationship with the most popular of the social Christian novels.

As with their prototype, most utopian novels depicted a model society remote in time and/or place. Typically a guide would shepherd a time/space traveler through a world of justice and convenience, sometimes pausing to explain how the transition was achieved from the flawed present to the perfect future. The Christian social novels, in their most popular form, simply turned this dynamic inside out. Instead of transporting the reader to a remote society, they introduce a force generated in a remote time and place, most often the principles and even the personality of Jesus of Nazareth. The social model is created in the present or the near future and without any shift of geography: earthly or galactic. It is the religious force that transforms Chicago or Des Moines into a morally improved society.

Although the social Christian novel reversed the utopian formula, the message was the same. Contemporary America suffers from intense and wasteful economic competition. The system puts too much stress on material achievements and materialistic values. The system eliminates the chance for economic justice and for the development of the intellectual, moral, and cultural potential of the individual and the society. The solution lies in the application of Christian ethics.

Modeled on Stowe, paralleled by Bellamy, the Christian novelist also defined himself by antithesis. His opposite was the literary naturalist. Also contemporary with the later novelists in Wright's study, the literary naturalists trace their origins to Kate Chopin, Stephen Crane, and Frank Norris. At its height this movement claimed some of the era's most celebrated writers of fiction—Jack London, Theodore Dreiser—and such poets as Edgar Lee Masters and Edwin Arlington Robinson. The shared premise of naturalists was that the rational individual was driven and controlled by forces larger than himself: the forces of nature (Darwin), the forces of economics (Marx), the forces of the irrational (Freud and his forerunners). The plots of their stories depicted the will of the individual dashed against powerful, uncontrollable natural forces. The individual will was crushed. The forces rolled on inexorably.

Social Christian fiction, with very few exceptions, was a direct rebuttal to this premise. The divinely inspired will of the individual was everything. In place of pessimistic predetermination the gospeller offered an almost unbroken optimism.

If one looks for meaningful opposites in American literary and social history, one could hardly find a greater contrast than between Stephen Crane's *Maggie, a Girl of the Streets* and Charles Sheldon's *In His Steps*. Published within a few years of one another, Crane's work was taken by many as the opening statement of literary naturalism while Sheldon's novel was the popular climax of the social Christian novel. As Maggie falls lower and lower, trapped in the brutal realities of slum and factory, the congregation of Henry Maxwell rises through the application of Christian precepts to a level whose moral excellence foretells a worldwide peaceful Christian social revolution. To readers of fiction who were interested in social problems, both novels offered a measure of verisimilitude. Only Sheldon's offered an ascending vision.

The popularity of some social Christian novels is only one—perhaps the least important—reason for remembering them. Robert Glenn Wright has performed the service of reminding us of their presence. He has further demonstrated that they should not be classed in a single category based on a stereotype. These novels were important for what they opposed and for the evils they helped expose. They formed an important part of a theological debate that affected seminaries and led to the establishment of the institutional church. Unlike the works of their literarily exalted contemporaries, who chose to reflect the assumptions of philosophical naturalism, they offered positive options for man and society. The social Christian novels are, in fact, a wonderful exhibit of the signs of their times: social, religious, literary. Their message was as individually varied and vital as it was collectively singular.

Robert H. Walker
Dewey D. Wallace, Jr.

1

The Varieties of Social Christian Novels

The Mission of American democracy to save the world from the oppression of autocrats was a secular version of the destiny of Christianity to save the world from the governance of Satan.

Ralph H. Gabriel,
The Course of American Democratic Thought

Social Christian novels dramatize some social evil and then propose a solution based on one or more aspects of Christian teaching. They range in subject matter from vague humanitarian efforts to regain a hold on the wayward by means of the brotherhood of Christ to specific, proselytizing denominational appeals and from arguments over the impact of Darwinism to literal and figurative uses of Christ's second coming. As a general characteristic they stress an approach to Christ as a social teacher and the Bible as a practical guide for everyday living. Social justice is strongly emphasized, and Christian principles are presented as a medium for bringing a solution to economic, social, and moral conflicts.

There are four basic types of social Christian novel, some of which have subtypes. In the radicalness of their authors' attitudes about the correct role of the church in public affairs, at one end of the spectrum, are those works that express the authors' concerns with the social and economic imbalance of the time but offer little more than a generalized humanitarianism as a solution. *My Friend the Boss* by Edward E. Hale is a good representative of this type.

A second type is written from the viewpoint of the upper class, whose protagonists engage in some sort of direct effort at reform—offering better housing to their tenants or better working conditions to their employees.

The third type is what is generally called the social gospel novel. In these works the authors usually speak through either a middle-class character (often a minister) or an articulate and intelligent working-class character. The works of Charles M. Sheldon, especially *In His Steps*, are good examples of one major form of the social gospel novel.

The fourth and final type presents attitudes toward radical political philosophy in terms of the teachings of Christianity and the place of the church in such political doctrines as socialism, communism, or anarchism. Some novelists espoused political change and based their arguments on the Bible; others fought political change and used the same source.

It is generally accepted that the social gospel novel—specifically as represented in the work of Sheldon—was the only major form of evangelical Protestant fiction written in the Gilded Age. Reading and reviewing the fiction of the age gives rise to serious questions about this assumption. The scope of the social Christian novel is surprisingly broad, as representative works of the four outlined categories illustrate. In the first category, for example, a novel such as *Ai; a Social Vision* was a fictional prototype of generalized vagueness in offering solutions to social problems. The author, Charles S. Daniel, was aware that class lines appeared to be hardening, that there were too many fiscal panics, too many poor, and too many strikes. Daniel considered these events to be undesirable. However, after a long buildup in which he attacked Christianity for not being sufficiently "reasonable" and "scientific" to keep its hold on men, he presented a platform that, if accepted, would cure the ills of the United States. All men should recognize:

1. The Fatherhood of God, who is the most uplifting life of all things.
2. The brotherhood of man, for sympathy and service.
3. The ceaseless development and advance of the human race by struggle and possession, sorrow and joy, death and life.
4. The establishment of the kingdom of heaven everywhere upon earth.
5. The unreserved recognition of the secular world as containing all sacred things.
6. The unceasing inspiration of man by God.
7. The constant communion of kindred spirits in and between the unseen and the seen.

—Let us assimilate what is reasonable, and then climb to other heights.[1]

There is not much here beyond vague Christian humanism. Among other things, Daniel was never specific in defining what he meant by reasonable.

Other authors with the same basic approach offered a series of reasons why affairs were in such a poor state. In *Nadine: A Romance of Two Lives*, a volume "dedicated to the genius of chaste and ennobling fiction," the author, Nina E. Ellison, suggested that the difficulties resulted from unrestricted immigration, limitations on the coining of silver, and the inequality of rights between men and women. Her solution, aside from Christianizing the world, centered on developing perfect "thought" machines.[2]

Samuel P. Leland in his novel *Peculiar People* put the popularity of socialism at the root of the difficulty. After outlining socialist doctrines in a fairly distorted fashion throughout much of the book, he rejected them because they were too gloomy and pessimistic. His alternative was to accept the Bible and its teachings.[3]

Leland agreed with Ellison, who was sure that foreigners were the cause of all economic and social problems in America:

The most prosperous nations have been those of the purest religious belief. What, then, can be said of the political heathen, with their white faces and anarchist doctrines in America . . . more dangerous to the cause of Christ in the world than ten thousand Buddhists in Asia. . . . It is our foreign population that crowd our penitentiaries and insane asylums. True, the Socialist leaders settle in our great cities, but they receive an alarming amount of support from our foreign farming population. In five years these men become voters. "God forgive our fathers that they made our ballot so cheap."[4]

The way to combat this menace was to make sure all settlers in a community were true Christians (i.e., Presbyterians), and failing that, to seek conversion as rapidly as possible through gospel meetings. If any still refused to see the light, they were to be run out of town.

Many authors also noted the lack of stewardship and gospel-of-wealth humanitarianism, and proposed its institution as a solution to social and economic problems. This view was presented in such novels as Edward E. Hale's *My Friend the Boss* and Mary E. Bennett's *Asaph's Ten Thousand*. Hale, in the preface to his book, stated his position: good government takes time and money.[5] The novel outlined the boss' election to the office of mayor of his city and stopped there. Precisely what Christian measures he would thereupon institute were not stated.

Asaph's Ten Thousand provides more detail. Through her spokesman, the Reverend Mr. Paxton, the author presents a sermon on the separate worlds of the rich and poor. The Reverend Mr. Paxton never questions a social structure built on economic security, and offered only the democratic Golden Rule in the abstract as a means of conduct. Moreover, as the sermon continues, the minister falls back on the life-as-a-vale-of-tears argument. One's final reward was to be found only beyond the grave.[6]

The same novel is instructive in presenting a very cautious attitude toward organized labor. The author presents some of labor's arguments, through the mouth of an outsider who organizes the local mills, foments a strike, and then absconds with the union's dues. George Milford, owner of the mills, has the last word:

"He wasn't born in Milfordville, I know. It never occurred to any of our home-bred folks, I guess, to think they were slaves because they work for their living, or to think they had a right to other folks' property because those folks had more than themselves. That's not a New-England-born notion."[7]

This kind of social Christian fiction stresses three points. Social and economic dislocations are disturbing to the general well-being and the status quo. Those responsible for this disruption are usually foreigners, socialists, or the working class. And the rich have some responsibility for seeing to it that stable conditions are reestablished. Specific methods for accomplishing this task are usually unstated. Lip service to the Golden Rule, the brotherhood of man under the fatherhood of God, and a general spirit of *noblesse oblige* are the distinguishing characteristics of this type of fiction. There are a great many more novels of this type than any other, and because many of them are allegories they will be discussed in Chapter 3.

The second type of social Christian novel is more specific both in presenting the problems of the post–Civil War era and in proposing solutions. The typically wealthy protagonist concretely acts to alleviate the suffering of the poor. In basic point of view this type of novel is allied to the works just mentioned. The major difference lies in the fact that the first type seldom offers concrete proposals or suggests plans of action save purely defensive and restrictive measures such as limiting immigration or being wary of labor organizations. This second type, wherein the heroes and heroines show more active concern with social problems, does offer more concrete plans of action, even if the proposals entail nothing more than a hero, or more likely a heroine, instructing her solicitor to see to the construction of a "working men's hall."

There was a clear agreement among these authors why something had to be done:

No scheme of philanthropy will ever succeed which is not founded on the religion of Jesus Christ. If we would benefit the poor, if we would change the degraded into honorable citizens and happy families, we must begin by striving to make the Bible the law of their daily life; we must instruct them in the Sabbath-school, and turn their feet toward the house of God: by these means only can any people be effectually aided and improved.[8]

Without God, Christ, and biblical teaching the poor would lack the motivation to help themselves. And how were they to be instructed? By those who knew God, Christ, and biblical teaching. Moreover, the proof of their knowledge was in their social and economic status. They were rich and powerful because they were good, and part of their goodness was manifest in their charity toward their uninstructed fellows.

A good rationale for upper-class charity is presented in William C. Stiles's *The Master's Mission: or, The Minister Who Dared*. The hero, the Reverend Mr. Terence Virgil, comments that his ideas are unfashionable in reform ideology. This was true of the *ideas* per se; however, as the other works in this section will demonstrate, the majority of the philanthropists in these novels, while giving lip service to self-help, very much enjoy their role as semidivine dispersers of gifts and goods:

It has been so often sounded abroad that the best method of helping is to induce self-help that it has nearly been forgotten that there is a submerged class of men who have no remedies within their own efforts. The . . . illustration of the fallen dray horse is still an effective one with the poor. He is down and he can never get to his feet without a direct pull from above. And when he is up he must be fed, and sometimes fed a great deal, and for a long time, before he can help himself.[9]

A practical example of the Reverend Mr. Virgil's attitude is well illustrated in Susan Parkman's novel, *Two Noble Women*, wherein the heroine, well-to-do wife of Judge Baldwin, decides to help a thief who is going to come to trial before her husband. Her help at this juncture is both spiritual and practical in that Mrs. Baldwin, with great aplomb, influences her husband to reduce the young man's sentence. She is the "I" in the following:

"Well," said I, rising to go, "I will talk to my husband about you, and I will attend to Sallie's wants while you are kept away from her. And I want you to kneel down night and morning and ask God to bless and guide me in whatever I try to do for you and her. . . . You can be getting ready for heaven here as well as anywhere, and the Holy Spirit will abide with you here. It won't be the first time that God and the angels have visited a jail. Have you access to a Bible every day?"[10]

The young man is to pray for what *she* is doing for him; he is *her* prisoner.

There are a large number of novels that repeated the following pattern. A pampered young girl in her teens is suddenly left an orphaned heiress. She is a nice Christian girl with adequate intelligence but knows nothing of the world—specifically the source of her wealth. She asks the family lawyer, or some such figure, about this and is informed that her capital is in property, or mills, or both. When she asks for details, she gets generalities: "she is not to bother her pretty head." But she goes to see the source of her affluence (tenements, factories) and is appalled, her Christian conscience outraged. Then, she either builds model tenements, sets up day nurseries, or gives her workers raises. Sometimes she does all these and more. The point is that the protagonist goes through a Christian transformation once she learns the true economic state of the workers on whose efforts her wealth depends and realizes that she is in a position to alleviate the poverty of a few at least.

The Petrie Estate is a good example of this type of novel. Charlotte Coverdale has unexpectedly inherited a large fortune. Having previously been a school teacher with advanced blue-stocking ideas, living in genteel poverty, she resolves to put her newly gained wealth to the service of Christian regeneration of the poor; but she does not know how to do so and, moreover, runs into stiff opposition from her more conservative relatives and friends. When she questions Mr. Corliss, her solicitor, about the property that makes up the bulk of her wealth, she is met with the following:

"Really, Miss Coverdale, there is nothing to be done. You can't improve those people. They never will live any other way. They don't want anything better." He picked a thread from the carpet, and twirled it between his fingers.

"But if these houses are so wretched, why am I paid such rents for them?"

"They are worth it. You don't regulate the price. It regulates itself. It's according to the demand, according to the crowding. You'd hardly believe it," said Corliss gayly, "how they pack in."

"I have read of such things," said Charlotte earnestly. "I must go and see my houses."

"Oh, I wouldn't advise it. Your houses aren't so bad as that. You wouldn't find it pleasant, though. We look after everything. The owners of all that property leave it alone. They're in Europe, a good many of them; they're innocent enough about what's going on. Some of 'em live out West. The up-town folks don't cross a certain line east and west here in the city once in a lifetime. They've got their agents to act for them. We act for you," he added briskly.[11]

A number of statements in this passage deserve comment as being representative of certain attitudes found in many such novels. First there is the classic conservative rationale that there is nothing to be done for the poor, that they want nothing better and would only make slums out of improved conditions were the latter offered. This point of view, almost always attacked, recurs in novel after novel.[12] Second there is the mention of the absentee landlord followed by the even more significant line: "The up-town folks don't cross a certain line east and west here in the city once in a lifetime." It is obvious from Charlotte's response, "Could I go there tomorrow?" that she herself had not crossed it. She had never been to the section of the city where her newly acquired property was located. In these novels the crusading authors repeatedly point out how ignorant the wealthy are of the lives of the poor, and they consider this ignorance one of the major barriers to reform. This point is strongly emphasized in what is almost surely the prototype of this kind of social gospel novel, Elizabeth Stuart Phelps Ward's *The Silent Partner*. This novel was published in 1871, twenty-two years before *The Petrie Estate* and fourteen years before *Mildred Farroway's Fortune*, the first of the novels that followed Mrs. Ward's plot pattern.[13] *The Silent Partner* begins with young Perley Kelso's inheriting half ownership of the Hayle and Kelso mills. She is an intelligent, bored, and spoiled young woman whose knowledge of the world outside her "set" is only subconscious, a point symbolized by Perley's joy in sleeping through the daily ringing of the factory bells.[14]

Through a chance meeting with one of the workers at the mills, Sip Garth, Perley begins to learn the extent of her ignorance and the bitter helplessness of the workers. Sip Garth tells Perley that she hates those of Perley's class because they are totally ignorant of how the other half lives: "It ain't because they don't care, it's because they don't *know*; nor do they care *to* know."[15] Perley agrees:

"You do not understand," she cried, "you people who work and suffer, how it is with us! We are born in a dream, I tell you! Look at these rooms! Who would think—in such a room as this—except he dreamed it, that the mothers of very little children died for want of a few hundreds and a change of climate? Why, the curtains in this room cost six! See how it is! You touch us—in such a room—but we dream; we shake you off. If you cry out to us, we only dream that you cry. We are not cruel, we are only asleep."[16]

Perley wakes up and devotes her life and wealth to living the social gospel.

The Silent Partner, while providing the pattern for many works to come, is unusual both in its intensity and point of view. Most of the novels with a philanthropist hero or heroine have a saccharine self-satisfied quality about them that is wholly lacking in Mrs. Ward's work.

Both Julia W. Parson's *The Full Stature of a Man* and Julia A. DeWitt's *Life's Battle Won* have philanthropic heroines who embark on building projects of model tenements which they rent at cost plus five percent. The latter has an interesting exchange between the central character, Mrs. Elsie Fleming, and her building manager:

"How much interest do you expect to receive upon the money you have expended?"

"I thought I ought to get five per cent."

"Will you be satisfied with that amount?"

"Certainly, as my houses are not only an experiment, but a charitable one."

"Some of the New York tenement houses pay from fifteen to twenty per cent, and often much higher."

"Fifteen to twenty per cent!" exclaimed Elsie. "Those pest houses, where death holds a never-ending carnival, pay at that rate!"

"And frequently a great deal more. The denser the crowd, the better the harvest."

"And this is called a Christian country!"

"And many of these landlords are considered Christian men."

"I wonder the ghosts of their victims do not haunt them."

"Perhaps they do," said Mrs. Fleming; "for I have seen faces as haggard and woe worn among the very wealthy as among the very poor. The publishers refused my stories that told the truth and simply painted the pictures I had seen, and they were pictures that robbed me of my sleep."[17]

Other of these novels that stressed Christian stewardship have the same tone but propose varying solutions. They run from "*colonization*—not to other lands, but in the vast tracts unimproved in the United States,"[18] to a sudden giving of gifts outright due to Christian conversion. A fine example of this latter is to be found in Austin Miles's *About My Father's Business*, in which a character, after listening to a stirring sermon of strong social gospel fervor, feels that "a terrible judgment awaits men of my class, unless they repent" and live by the Golden Rule. He then proceeds to offer to pay for the rent and food of workers (who are on strike against the local mill) for a whole year—an offer he carries out— and devote the rest of his life and money "to the betterment of mankind and the glory of God."[19]

The chief characteristic of this type of novel is the relatively passive nature of its heroes and heroines. They do give more than mere lip service to the need for active reform, but the protagonists go to the slums and factories only once. The visit is traumatic enough, and new houses and apartments, higher wages, and better working conditions are the result, but the Lord and Lady Bountifuls direct their reforms from afar; they do not think of trying to know and understand the people they are trying to help.

A variation on this theme—upper-class sponsorship of Christian humanitarian reform after learning how the poor live—is the novel that shows the aristocratic individual—again usually a woman—who actually goes to live in the slums, starts a mission school, a day nursery, a boarding house, or employment bureau. There are many such novels.[20] Those of Julia M. Wright represent this subtype of the philanthropic social Christian novel. Mrs. Wright was an early and prolific writer of this genre, and most of her novels followed the same pattern. As a case in point, when well-to-do Miriam Elliott, the protagonist of *The Shoe Binders of New York* . . . , discovers the plight of the poor, she decides to stay in New York City during the summer months and continue her good works rather than going to Saratoga as she has done in the past. After her cousin Rose asks her if she has gone crazy, she replies:

"No, coming fully to my right mind, I hope. . . . I have been looking at these things carefully of late, and I see that we are God's stewards, responsible to Him for money, and time, and all that we have; and I think we have no right to spend on ourselves more than we need. If the Lord has given me a good work to do among his poor in this city, I have no right to withhold my money, or run away from the work to take my pleasure anywhere."[21]

Miriam starts dressmaking classes, takes slum children to a mission school, and reforms drunken Aunt Nab Wool, who eventually helps Miriam with her work.

Mrs. Wright's *A New Samaritan* is in a similar vein. Persis Thrale, who had been leading a dilettante literary life, is converted to social work among the poor and starts a day nursery, converts some of her property into cheap housing, and nurses the sick. When her lawyer asks, "What set you at all this?" Persis responds that she had long felt that her life had been purposeless and without any useful direction for her talents. True, it is hard to work among the filth and squalor of the poor, but it is "the old story of 'wo, go, lo.' 'Wo unto the world because of offenses.' 'Go, teach.' 'Lo, I am with you always.' " She continues, "We cannot stand afar off and throw alms, as one throws bones to a dog; one must dwell among the needy ones, as Christ to save flesh dwelt in flesh."[22]

Persis is still very much in the Lady Bountiful cast, but unlike many in her station she does recognize that living among the people she is trying to help and gaining their trust and friendship is far more effective than merely giving dollars to charity.

Two other novels by Mrs. Wright are similar in theme but follow different patterns. In *The New York Bible-Woman* the heroine, poor needle-woman Mary Ware, is hired by the rich philanthropist Agnes Warren to visit the sick, teach sewing, and generally do good works in Mrs. Warren's name. When asked, Mrs. Warren defines a "Bible-woman":

"A Christian woman who is employed by some able persons to go about a certain part of the city reading the Bible, teaching the poor about religious and family duties in a friendly way, and helping and encouraging them; caring for the sick, making note of destitute cases, and reporting all to a lady who acts as manager, furnishes relief and gives advice."[23]

In this case Mrs. Warren has it both ways: she is involved with the poor and has exact knowledge of their conditions without having to devote her own time and energy to the mechanics of participatory philanthropy. Mrs. Wright seems to find no quarrel with this kind of compromise, though her real praise is saved for the Bible-woman herself, who presses "on and on where Satan reigns."[24]

The last of Mrs. Wright's novels relevant here is *A Plain Woman's Story*, which tells of a humble Christian serving girl who inherits $6,000 after her mistress' death and establishes a Working Woman's Bureau to help her less fortunate sisters. The novel tells in chilling detail exactly how the Bureau operated.[25] Rules of conduct were followed by instructions for feeding four people on ten cents a day.

Monday: Half a pound of barley, three cents; half a pound of corn meal, two cents; dried beans, three cents; scrap meat, two cents. The corn meal, made into mush, was their breakfast; the beans, with half the scrap meat to give them flavor, made out a dinner; half the barley, boiled with a little scrap meat, made the supper. Here, you see, were three very wholesome, nourishing, digestible dishes, capable of going a long way in supporting existence. Of course, these articles were bought, not on Monday, but on Saturday, so that the beans and the barley were well soaked before cooking. But Mary wasted no nutriment: she boiled the beans and barley in the water they were soaked in, not being able to humor her palate by changing the water and wasting the food-stuff held in it.[26]

Not all of the novels of this type present this grim a confrontation between the needy and their helpers. Josephine Baker's *Gee's Trap* . . . , Henry Fauntleroy's *Who's to Blame*, and Mrs. Grace Livingston Hill's *A Daily Rate* illustrate genuine humanitarian concern on the part of their well-to-do heroes and heroines for the poor whom they were trying to help. Others show the real dangers and problems of upper-middle-class reformers. For example, in *God's Rebel* the hero, first a teacher of economics and then a journalist, loses job after job as a reward for his humanitarian pains and finally enlists to fight to his death in the Spanish American War. And a novel like David Morgan's *A Dream of Christ's Return* shows the frustrations encountered by a Christian minister when he actually tries to preach a social interpretation of God's word.

These novels reveal distinct types of social Christian fiction with wealthy, reforming protagonists: those, like *The Full Stature of a Man*, in which the heroine directs her reform work from afar and those, illustrated by the works of Julia M. Wright, wherein the central character goes into the slums and actually does work.

Within the context of the social Christian novel the third subtype, that of the social gospel novel, was undoubtedly the best known and has usually represented the genre as a whole. There are more social gospel novels than any other type;[27] even so, there is a striking variety of approaches, mainly dictated by the protagonists' social classes and points of view.

The social gospel novel is itself defined by point of view. The first two categories of social Christian fiction—those that expressed a generalized and abstract Christian humanitarianism and those dealing with upper-class excursions into charity work—were told from the patrician point of view. Their heroes and heroines were interested in the common man, but they did not really understand him, nor did they trust him much. Their Christian philanthropy was aimed at subverting the dual threats of mob violence and organized labor. Many were willing to alleviate the disheartening conditions of the poor worker, but at the same time they sought to make a conservative Christian of him, often by means of the Christian doctrines that they equated with respectability—frugality, the dignity of hard work, pride in manly virtue—that would eventually lead to the various rewards in life depicted by Horatio Alger.

The social gospel novels, however, were more democratic. The protagonists in these novels spoke in militant terms for the common man. Workers were not treated fairly, either from the standpoint of their promised rights as Americans or as Christians who believed in the Golden Rule, the Ten Commandments, and the Beatitudes. This was neither religiously right nor politically fair, and the whole social gospel movement, including social gospel novels, sought to rectify the situation.

The man most closely identified with the social gospel novel was Charles Monroe Sheldon. Born in 1857 in Wellsville, New York, he attended Brown University and Andover Theological Seminary; in 1886 he was ordained in the Congregational church. After serving his first pastorate in Waterbury, Vermont, he was called to the Central Congregational Church in Topeka, Kansas, with which he was associated in one way or another for the rest of his life. In 1900 he was asked to edit the *Topeka Daily Capital* for one week and created a storm of interest by increasing the paper's circulation from 30,000 to 370,000 through barring all crime news, censoring the advertising, and even deleting stories about the national political conventions. He remained in Topeka until 1919 when he was asked to become editor in chief of the *Christian Herald* in New York City. He held that position until 1925 when he and his family returned to Topeka. He maintained his residence there until his death in 1946.[28]

Sheldon considered himself a Christian socialist, which he defined as one who "applied the teachings of the Sermon on the Mount to everyday life," and his uniqueness lay in the fact that he was the only major national leader within the social gospel movement who also used the novel as a means of presenting his views.[29] *In His Steps*, undoubtedly the best known of the social gospel novels, has been said to be, after the Bible and Shakespeare, the best seller of all time,[30] although the evidence for such a claim, even then, as Frank Luther Mott in *Golden Multitudes* points out, is dubious.[31]

Two of Sheldon's other novels are particularly relevant in the present context. Both *Richard Bruce: or, the Life That Now Is* and *His Brother's Keeper; or, Christian Stewardship* feature a leading character from the working class presenting the wrongs and wants of labor.

In *Richard Bruce*, a young, handsome, and talented Christian gentleman goes penniless to Chicago to make his fortune and win fame. In true Alger fashion he does so, but his means, methods, and motives were somewhat different from those of Alger's heroes. A number of depressing incidents happen first—his novel is universally rejected by publishers as being too full of ideas and ideals, and he skirts starvation for lack of a job. When the hero finally does get a job, he soon quits rather than work on Sunday. At length Richard meets the Christlike evangelist, John King, and follows him as a disciple. Slowly Richard becomes a leader in his own right, publishes his book in serial form with huge success, preaches the fatherhood of God to the multitude, and becomes a leader of the masses for religious and labor-oriented causes. This combination of leadership was one of Sheldon's favorite themes, as well as a hallmark of much social gospel fiction.

In *His Brother's Keeper*, young Stuart Duncan returns from a year abroad after college to find his best boyhood friend, Eric Vassall, preparing to lead a strike against the mines that Stuart is about to inherit. Just after Stuart steps off the train, he comes upon Eric, himself a worker in the mines, addressing the men:

"Lord, we need thy help to-day. We ask for wisdom. Grant us to know thy will. O Lord! keep us from committing any lawless act. Keep every man here from drunkenness and violence to property or life. We want simply our rights as men. We want wages sufficient to live in comfort. Show us what to do. Keep us to-day from evil. Bless all men who work with their hands. Bless our families. We ask it for Jesus' sake. Amen."[32]

Later in the novel Eric argues labor's cause to Stuart and says that he is not arguing that the workers are perfect, that they never make mistakes. But, he goes on, the men who own the mines and have made their wealth from them have not acted like Christians in their dealings with the men who work for them. "How many of the mine owners have got together and prayed for the wisdom to settle this matter right?"[33]

Except Stuart, who had already been converted to both Christianity and the social gospel, the answer in this case is none. The passage quoted illustrates the desperateness of the man's situation—his Christian manhood threatened, his cause entrusted to God who is asked to direct nonviolent protest, and a religious awakening called for in the capitalists.

A number of other works illustrate this device of the common man's speaking his mind. One of the most didactic of them is *Uncle Sam's Bible* . . . by James B. Converse, which is hardly a novel; rather it is a fine example of the Socratic, didactic tract using the mask of fiction as a medium of expression. The author seeks to answer, through farmer-preacher Jacob Jones, pastor of a small unspecified church in the Midwest, practically every social and political problem of the day.[34]

The author, in good systematic fashion, goes so far as to make a list of twenty-eight principles that, if affirmed, would virtually eliminate all manner of evil in the United States. They rest on the Christlike dignity of labor and the evil of ownership.[35]

Many illustrative quotations could be drawn from *Uncle Sam's Bible*, for it is an archetypal example of the social gospel tract; however, more to the point here is that the rural pastor speaks to and for the common laborer, both rural and urban. His arguments, many of which are ingenious and some amusing to the modern reader, are not framed in any patronizing way. The spirit of the book is anything but that of the humanitarian and philanthropic social Christian writer of fiction. Here, instead of any appeal to charity, the irate man of the people expounds on the wrongs in America and proposes solutions in no uncertain terms. Converse's is a real fire-and-brimstone tirade of religious Jacksonian democracy.

In the same vein, but in the context of mining in Colorado, Beveridge Hill worries about the flaunting of "superfluities" in the presence of the truly needy. The answer, his characters decide, is not legislation. That has failed. Instead, "Let's try Christ's rules, not in part, but entire; embody them in our lives and heaven will begin on earth."[36]

In this dialogue a number of viewpoints representative of social gospel fiction are evident: First is a keen respect for money and the leisure it gives its holder to pursue the life of the mind. Second is a restatement of the platonic ideal of the philosopher-king. It is all right for elected officials to do as they see fit—that is their job. But what they do has to benefit the people they represent; selfishness and self-interest, the amassing of immense wealth beyond the needs of a normal life-span is foolish, ignorant, and evil. Third, there is the call for governmental intervention based on Christian ethics.

One counterpoint to these social gospel arguments for the rights of labor is presented in a very interesting novel, *Dr. Marks, Socialist*. In it, the local mill owner, Peter Varian, demonstrates true understanding of the issues between labor and capital but expresses his concern that the inherent power of organized, hierarchical unions would lead to their own excesses and abuses—a fear not unfounded. "It all depends on how much conscience or policy a given [union] czar happens to have. And no man can suffer more at the hands of an employer than a non-union man often suffers at the hands of his 'brethren' of the unions."[37]

Always, in one form or another, debates in social gospel novels center on the basic antagonism between Christian behavior and the abuse of power. In the above quote Varian expresses the very same fear and resentment expressed by labor spokesmen but as directed toward the capitalist class.

Some of the most effective arguments in social gospel fiction stress the understanding that could be gained by both sides if a successful entrepreneur had himself at one time known want and poverty (the Andrew Carnegie–Horatio Alger story) and consequently not only had firsthand knowledge of the workers' conditions, but also some intuitive understanding of how best to equitably alleviate the situation. Jane D. Chaplin's *Mother West's Neighbors* is a good example of this type of argument.[38]

On the role of Christianity in the laissez-faire system of capitalism in late nineteenth-century America, as defined in the works of Sheldon and Hill, a number of authors were very specific about what they thought should be done by the Protestant churches.

Mrs. Nico Bech-Meyer, in her very pro-labor, fictionalized account of the Pullman Strike, for example, praised the church's present role:

A great many [workers] went to church in the afternoon to listen to words of comfort from their beloved minister. And they left church strengthened in the hope that it was not only in a far-away hereafter that life was meant to be beautiful and true and good. It was to become so here on this earth, as sure as life means joy in the realization of our being.

The peaceful words and the light of truth which shone from the face of their minister and friend, followed them home; and even those who had been most misgiving felt a ray of hope arise; the man who had their destiny in his hand, might be better than they thought; there might be a spot in his soul open yet for the voices of his fellow-men, and that spot might be touched to-morrow.[39]

Mrs. Bech-Meyer's attitude was unusual however; seldom in the novels was the church praised in and of itself. Instead, authors relied on the precepts of Christianity, expressing the belief that the principles and teachings of Christianity were valid and necessary for all, particularly when striving for just relations between labor and capital. Charles M. Sheldon had one of his characters express an already familiar theme:

"I believe the next great factor in what is called the labor question will be the religious factor. I see no possible hope for a better condition unless it is brought about by the appeal to and a belief in Christianity as the real source of final adjustment of men's relations with one another in the social compact. In reality the problem consists in getting men on both sides to act like Christians."[40]

This passage depicts not only one of the dilemmas of the Gilded Age, it harks back to assumptions made by the Puritan oligarchy and modified by the framers of the Declaration of Independence and the Bill of Rights. What good was freedom of religion if a whole spectrum of the population began to drift away from any religion at all? How could one follow the tenets of individualism, pragmatic free enterprise, and empirical capitalism and still be his brother's keeper? Politically it was becoming apparent that there was warfare between the holy trinity of liberty, fraternity, and equality; on the religious level the system of laissez-faire capitalism was finding itself in direct opposition to the human-itarian precepts of Christianity.

One of the questions many authors posed was just how, in the context of the American political system and the new economic and social conditions arising as a result of rapid industrialization, belief in the brotherhood of man and a life patterned after the Golden Rule could be possible. To the writers of the social gospel, far too many congregations were socially and economically conservative, at ease with conditions as they were, and heedless of the plight of labor, both as a mass and on the individual level.

One method of seeking change was a direct frontal assault on the blindness or hypocrisy of the clergy, and the novel lent itself to a number of devices for accomplishing this end. In *"Our Best Society"* . . . , a volume whose cover made the unfounded claim of its being "The *Uncle Tom's Cabin* of the Labor Move-ment," L. Jonas Bubblebuster heavy-handedly satirized the Christian clergy. The following scene depicts the marriage between two villains of the story, Mary Annie Bell and Thomas D. AntiLabor:

The pastor of Mary Annie's papa and mama's great church was there. A great man who never mixed temperance with his religion, and consequently was greatly beloved in Milwaukee. And the pastor of the great AntiLabor church of Chicago, who preached a sermon at least once a month, in which he denounced all labor organizations in the strongest terms, and laborers of the time as anarchists generally. He was a great favorite with Our Best Society. His church would no more admit the family of a working man into its pews, than a southern planter would occupy a pew with one of his ex-slaves. The religion taught in his church was for Our Best Society only; and as their members died they were sent to a heaven exclusively their own.[41]

Here the author's two ministers of the gospel are attacked for their drinking, wholesale condemnation of labor organizations, hypocrisy, stereotyped thinking, bigotry, prejudice, and snobbery—a formidable list. The assault, not overly amusing in its sledgehammer approach, was nonetheless justified. The reverend gentlemen from Milwaukee and Chicago were representative of a certain kind of clerical blindness evident during the Gilded Age.

On a more serious level, but lamenting the same religious and clerical bigotry, the hero of Hulbert Fuller's *God's Rebel*, a young professor of economics named Kenneth Moore, after making clear that his views are not utopian but based on hard fact, concludes that it is "the oppression of the rich, propped up by the church, that perpetuates poverty and makes life hideous." He goes on to declare, "there can be no Christianity, no true fraternity, so long as one half of the world is systematically employed in robbing the other half. It is the system that must be changed, not the people."[42]

Later, in the same novel, Kenneth remembers bitterly that a local minister, the Reverend Mr. Griggs,

had frequently expressed surprise that many people were ceasing to attend church, working-men especially; but alas! it seemed quite impossible for Dr. Griggs to understand it, why the many had lost interest in this columned and vaulted sepulchre of so-called religion that had so persistently outraged their holiest convictions of morality and utilitarianism. "I know nothing of art, nothing of literature, of science, of sociology," the preacher had once stoutly protested from his pulpit: "all I know is Jesus Christ, and of him only shall I speak to you fifty-two Sundays in the year." That there was anything essentially immoral in such a declaration of agnosticism had doubtless never occurred to the preacher.[43]

And again, in an outburst of frustrated fury at the whole profit system and Christianity the professor concludes:

"And the poverty that I see, and the suffering! Oh, it is maddening to behold these things and know the cause! Were I so ignorant or vicious as to accept it all as something designed by God, and so calmly repeat, 'The poor ye have always with you,' in harmony with the good people who go to church, then of course I could forget it—could regard poverty as inevitable. Modern Christianity is such a comfortable sop, you know; it has a never-failing excuse for every evil under the sun. Obviously, that's what it is for. The church is no longer at war with conventional evil, but is one with it."[44]

These passages from *God's Rebel* illustrate fury with those unenlightened, anti-intellectual clergy who supported a capitalistic system that had no more place for the common laborer than did their churches. "The poor ye have always with you," quotes Dr. Griggs; the author argues that this need not be so, that it is the American system of economics, reinforced by an outdated social and moral code that takes the name of Christianity, that is at fault. The author's frustration results from his recognizing what the Bible really taught as opposed to what the ministers of Dr. Grigg's ilk were preaching.

A different point of view is expressed in Cortland Myers's novel *Would Christ Belong to a Labor Union?* In it, minister David Dowling in a sermon that gives the book its name, presents as stirring a plea for organized Christian participation in helping the cause of labor as is to be found in any novel of this genre. Midway in the sermon, after Dowling has outlined the range and scope of "the labor question" in some detail, he proclaims "The Gospel of the Carpenter of Nazareth for the labor union is: 'Justice for the worker. Liberty for society. Salvation for the man.' "[45] And, in the answer to the question the novel's title poses,

"Would He belong to a labor union to-day? Let any man who says not stand up and prove his case. I declare unhesitatingly that every principle, every interest, every act of the life He lived, every line of the Book He inspired, is on the side of toiling men.

"The Church which bears His name and the preacher who follows His example to-day must be in sympathy with every righteous effort on the part of organized labor."[46]

Then, near the close of his sermon, the minister gives his central plea for mutual support between labor and the church:

"If Christ would belong to your union, and help your cause, you ought to belong to His Church and help His cause, out of which the union and every other righteous institution grew. If the Church is not just as it should be, help Christ make it after His pattern. You cannot separate Christ and the Church."[47]

God's Rebel and *Would Christ Belong to a Labor Union?* are social gospel fiction at its most militant. As the quoted passages indicate, both novels are examples of demands for revitalized Christianity that would once again put the churches of America in the vanguard of social reform. Fuller is scathing in his condemnation of the tacit alliance between the tithing robber barons and the complacent ministers who refuse to recognize the social teachings of Christ. In *God's Rebel* the author all but renounces Christianity as a means for achieving reform; yet he never goes quite that far. His attack on a Christianity concerned with the spirit only was ultimately aimed at reviving the church's concern for man in the totality of his temporal as well as his spiritual life.

Myers, on the other hand, in *Would Christ Belong to a Labor Union?*, places the responsibility on the workers to revitalize American Christianity. If the church is blind, it is partially because the workers have deserted it. Christ, the foun-tainhead of all American ethics and morals, would belong to a labor union; could labor then do less than seek its aims through the organ of Christ on earth? Not to do so is to insure the defeat of all that labor was asking in the name of Christian brotherhood.

In contrast to these urgent and militant appeals on behalf of Christianity and the labor movement are two works whose plots portray Christian capitalists who strive to practice exactly what Fuller and Myers expounded—but from manage-ment's side. One succeeds while the other fails. In both cases the protagonists are actively involved in putting their theories into practice. They are not phi-lanthropists, and there is little of the grim condescension apparent in such works as Julia M. Wright's *A New Samaritan* or *A Plain Woman's Story*.

In Florence Converse's *The Burden of Christopher*, Christopher Kenyon, a New England factory owner, decides to implement the new and advanced social and economic teachings he has learned in college. He calls a meeting of his workers and announces:

"I have called you together this evening because I want you to help me. I am not satisfied with the way the factory is being run."

Surely no one uttered a sound, no one stirred, and yet—a shiver went through the hall.

"I have been going over the books during the past six months, and I am not satisfied with the profits"—

Again that shiver, this time audible.

"They are too large."

When two hundred and fifty people catch their breath the sound is a strange one; there is a click in it, and afterwards the air trembles.

A woman in the back of the room whispered, "He's gone crazy. Oh, my God! poor thing!" and bit her lip and her handkerchief to keep back the tears.[48]

Christopher had not gone crazy; he went ahead to explain that he sought labor's answer to industrial problems.[49] The workers' answer is an eight-hour work day and cooperative ownership. Kenyon gives the former, but not doing the latter proves to be his downfall.

In the novel *Our Town* . . . , a factory owner who had done both of the above and more said to a friend:

"My dear sir, when you introduce the practical spirit of Christianity, not the sentimental talk about it, but the very honest spirit of the thing into the question, the men look into the employer's face and believe his words. . . . Why, I've picked men in that mill . . . I haven't sent for them. They've come from New York State, from the West, from all over the country, and asked employment. They are skilled workmen in their craft, and though they were suspicious in all their questions and disposed to find out something underhanded in the management before I hired them on trial, one week's experience has brought them to me with the expression of men looking into the face of a brother. They are men . . . and why shouldn't they be treated as such, and given a chance to rise to a better manhood?"[50]

What Pennington Burr, the mill owner in question, had specifically done is outlined below:

1. The wages of employes are to be adjusted to the value of their services, corresponding with the current rate of wages for similar work. Twenty per cent to be reserved from wages until end of year. Then it is optional with employes whether they receive this amount with interest at six per cent, or one third of the profits of the business to be divided among the employes in the proportion of their wages.

2. In good times, the wages shall be increased in proportion to the prosperity of the mill.

3. Any employe working in Wareham Mills one year can become a stockholder.

4. The books of the mill may always be examined by any one appointed by the employes; in this way the feeling of partnership will be brought about.[51]

Both *The Burden of Christopher* and *Our Town* depict the idealistic entrepreneur who tries to answer the question of how an individual could be both a good Christian and a good capitalist. Christopher Kenyon fails because he does not trust his workers enough. Pennington Burr, the hero of *Our Town*, succeeds, but the author merely states his success. We do not see Burr in the mills, nor do we know what problems he faced whether in the mill or from competition. Burr is able to overcome greed; but, in this novel at least, he becomes in the

process a one-dimensional spokesman for a point of view. A reader could em-
pathize with Kenyon's failure, both as a man and as a result of outside competition
bent on ruining him. The reality of Pennington Burr's success by means of an
adaptation of theoretical communist doctrine put into practice never comes
across.

Nevertheless, these two novels represent answers to the social and economic
problems of the Gilded Age based on one aspect of social gospel thought. The
heroes in each are Christian gentlemen who care for their fellow men as best
they can. In neither case is social legislation in any way involved. The heroes
are individuals who do as they see fit. It was presumably the authors' hope that
more men would follow in the steps of Pennington Burr and retain the principles
but avoid the pitfalls of Christopher Kenyon.

Still other varieties of social gospel fiction, though less central to the major
social and economic problems of the time, are nonetheless significant. For example, a whole body of work—over twenty novels—revolves around attacks on
the growing fashionableness and secularization of the various Protestant denominations. The authors fall into two groups: those who saw growing secularization
as representative of the movement away from the true spiritual significance of
Christianity, and those who saw the trend as a manifestation of widening class
differences, particularly between employer and employee.

In both cases the authors related growing secularism to declining belief in
Christianity as a living force. Those who lamented this on primarily spiritual
grounds witnessed the resulting hypocrisy of church members uninterested in
their souls. Instead, so said the authors, these nominal Christians were concerned
only with their physical well-being. This in turn bred a lack of charity, as well
as hardheartedness toward others, and faith only in material goods. Those who
wrote of this process from the viewpoint of the social gospel movement directly
related a decline in the spiritual health of the capitalist class—for it was to them
that a majority of the authors spoke—to the economic and social inequities and
problems in society at large. To these writers, mill owners could not be true
Christians if they spoke the Lord's Prayer on Sunday and then drove their workers
for long hours at starvation wages the other six days of the week. People who
did this, they contended, were spiritually dwarfed, and part of the outgrowth of
this condition was seen in their inhuman treatment of their workers.

The other type of writing novelists used to attack the growing fashionableness
and secular feeling among the churches was much less subtle. These novelists
pointed out that many of the churches with high toned sermons, paid choirs,
and ostentatious architecture were driving away working class members because
many true Christians no longer felt at home in what was supposed to be God's
house. The critics said that by allowing this to happen, the churches were driving
a wedge between the classes and thus hastening a day of reckoning that might
be destructive to Christianity, capitalism, and the political system of the United
States.

The church's movement away from the spiritual toward the secular is satirized in a volume entitled *"Church Amusements." The Church Dramatic and Terpsichorean Association, (Limited,) Promoters of Novity*, by James F. Conover. Two unemployed actors decide that they could earn a very comfortable living by tendering their services to the more "advanced, forward looking" churches in the country. They begin auspiciously by being engaged for an evening's entertainment by St. Dubious Episcopal Church as a part of the church's fund-raising campaign. The advertisement promised:

THE GREAT EVENT OF THE SEASON!
GRAND ENTERTAINMENT
for the
BENEFIT OF ST. DUBIOUS PARISH!!
A Stupendous Aggregation of Novelty and Talent,
Vocal and Instrumental Music, New Dances, Acrobatic
Feats, a Prize Drill, Pantomimes and a
SCREAMING FARCE!!!
"SHOOT FOLLY AS IT FLIES,"

Irradiated by a Coruscating Cluster of the Amateur
Talent of the Great Parish.
Directed and Promoted by
THE CHURCH DRAMATIC AND TERPSICHOREAN ASSOCIATION!!
Thursday, February 12, at Apollo Hall.
Tickets, one Dollar.   On Sale Everywhere.

Patrons and Patronesses:—Rev. Arius Volney Fogg, DD., LLD., DCL. (Oxon), Hon. Horatio Bempkin, Col. V. G. Noodles, Capt. H. Small Frye, Isadore Pellet, Mrs. Hon. Judge Pepper, Mrs. Hon. DeLancey Wiggin, Mrs. Alderman George Boodle, Mrs. Midas Bond, Mrs Gladys Sport, Mrs. L'High Jinks, Miss Estelle Smile, M. D., and Miss Lucy Bullion.[52]

The production is a mild financial success, but its occurrence splits the church completely and the good Reverend Mr. Fogg, after a prolonged stay in Europe for his health, resigns. Dr. Salt, the Reverend Mr. Fogg's antagonist throughout, sums up the author's attack:

"There has always been worldliness in the church, and history shows that it has been a greater peril than paganism or heresy. This worldly spirit in the Church unceasingly seeks to secularize it. The 'Church work' which has become an euphemism for all sorts of play and hilarious frolic in the Church, is not of the Church, but a perversion of it, a perversion of its divine aim and end, the reckless work of worldly men and women who enter it for anything but to 'perfect holiness in the fear of the Lord.' We hear that the Church must 'attract.' 'If I be lifted up,' He said, '*I will draw* all men unto Me.' Christ who founded the Church and furnished its living power, surely knows what people He expects to enter the Church and how to draw them into it. The giddy, frivolous, pleasure-loving will not be drawn by the uplifted Cross, but the penitent sinner, with a sense of his ruin and peril, will follow to the world's end that emblem of his salvation. The church is for him.'"[53]

The author seems to have had more than a slight strain of Jonathan Edwards in him.

What Dr. Salt specifically attacked was the classic rationale for church "amusements" as presented by hypocritical Deacon Cranky in the novel by the same name:

"It is all wrong to suppose we must give up our enjoyments when we become professors of religon. The unwise course which the church has taken in the past with regard to this subject has crippled her influence with the world, and closed her doors against the young people of our land; because they will have their enjoyments, and they will not join those churches that frown upon amusements. Therefore, in order to draw them into the house of God, and interest them in religion, we ought to have theatrical performances, dancing and such things, mingled with the more solemn instruction of the Sabbath-school. This would make the whole thing popular, and it would solve the difficult question—'how can we retain the young people in our Sabbath-schools?' The same principle holds good with regard to our churches. Popularize religion, and you will have no difficulty in supporting the gospel."[54]

George Guirey, the author of *Deacon Cranky*, also lamented the passing of Burning-Lake–style Calvinism, and was especially critical of modern deacons in general, to whom he assigned a prominent place in the decline of true New England Protestantism.

One wonders whether Mr. Guirey had read a novel published three years earlier, entitled simply *Deacons*, by William H. Murray, and whether *Deacon Cranky* was his rebuttal. Murray also virulently attacked the institution of deacons, but his argument—the antithesis of Guirey's—was that the powerful office of the deaconate in many Protestant denominations was usually filled by the most reactionary conservatives of a congregation, those who saw themselves as the watchdogs for heresy and implacably opposed any change in the church's interest in the community at large. The deacons' code, according to the author, was, "What has not been shall not be," and that the humanity of the teachings of the New Testament was their especial enemy. The net result, said Murray, was that those who needed salvation most were "alienated by bigotry and illiberality," symbolized by gatekeeper deacons, and hence bypassed the church altogether.[55]

Paradoxically, if a certain church of the time took a reform stand on social issues, its critics charged it with "worldliness"—often not attacking the social gospel approach per se, but asserting or implying that an interest in, say, the rights of labor, was analogous to "church amusements," dancing in the Sunday school room, and fund-raising by means of church bazaars. Those who supported the existing order, the church's general disengagement from social and economic events, insisted that the church confine itself to the spiritual aspects of men and women. By attacking such manifestations of worldliness as church socials, dancing, and card playing, they often attacked the social gospel movement through implication. Almost no one argued with the attacks leveled in *Church Amuse-*

ments, or in this passage from *Camerton Slope, A Story of Mining Life* by R. F. Bishop:

There is no intention to cast any reflection whatever on the true religion of Jesus Christ, but the idea [of the novel] is to show that the Church is a place to emphasize the spiritual nature of God and to bring men into harmony with Him. In order that the Church may succeed in her mission she must discontinue the great evils which are taking her from her lofty position and are bringing her down to the arena of pleasure. It is the hope of the true followers of Christ that the Clergy will stop all theological controversies, the discussion of higher criticism, and the playing into the hands of the social and soup kitchen element, and tell men and women of the unsearchable riches of Jesus Christ without fear or favor, trusting in God for the results.[56]

But such phrases as "emphasis on the spiritual nature of God," references to the church's "lofty position," and warnings against "social" involvement cut two ways. Stress on the spiritual denigrated "social involvement" in the double meaning of social—in the "amusement" sense and in the "problem" sense.[57]

The second type of novel that attacks growing secularization and worldliness of the churches in America has no such subtle dialectic behind it as those works just discussed. In a novel such as Eduard DeBrosé's *A Modern Pharisee* the author makes ultra clear that the loss of the church's hold on the common man—specifically the urban laborer—is the church's own fault: even the houses of God have been tempted by the indiscriminate "gilding" of almost all phases of American life, and that this veneer of wealth and well-being has lulled the church into a defense of the status quo that slowly alienates it from the new laboring class.

The variety of attacks on the situation was wide; for example, Charles S. Daniel in his novel *Ai* struck up a minor but recurrent theme when he ridiculed the fund-raising institution of pew renting: A man of modest means comes to church for the first time in many years. He finds few in it, and no ushers, and takes possession of a nice pew. As the service is about to begin, "a pompous-looking old man" arrives and stands by the pew in surprise that it is occupied. The young newcomer offers to make room, but the old gentleman hands him a card on which he has scribbled, "I pay for this pew." "How much?" the newcomer writes back. "Two hundred dollars," writes the old gentleman. "Well worth it," writes the newcomer and leaves the building.[58]

More often the writers' attacks were broader and specifically more damning. The analogy between the church and corrupt politics that follows below was typical:

"There is as much Ring rule and Bossism in the church, to-day, as there are in politics, and the whole system needs a complete revolution.

. . . . .

When the church becomes a mere instrument in the hands of the ambitious for the furthering of their own selfish schemes, and for the gratification of its members' vanity, it is no wonder that the moral sentiment of the community becomes corrupted, and the worship of mammon by the church communicates itself throughout society, and makes possible the political debauchery and corruption that we see on every hand. As long as a preacher's popularity is estimated by the number of slippers he receives each year, instead of the number of good, practical sermons he has preached, the number of conversions he has made, and the practical good deeds he has done, and as long as men are demanded in the pulpit on account of their pliability and obsequiousness to power and wealth, will the church be left in the hands of intriguing women and weak men.''[59]

Another work expresses the same shame that bordered on contempt. After castigating a ''Churchianity'' that for greed, power, and popularity ''welcomes to its fold the very men whom Christ drove from the temple with a whip of cords,'' the protagonist rises to a pitch reminiscent of John Brown a few decades earlier:

''The Church to-day is her worst enemy. By her eagerness to secure temporal power and advancement—to erect costly edifices, sustaining the trappings of the devil, she curries favor with the emissaries of that arch-enemy—those robbers of the sewing woman, and other 'white slaves,' and those influential, well-fed gamblers of the bourses who squeeze the very life-blood from the 'toilers and the moilers.' To square their actions in the eyes of men, for leading this life of pilfering and oppression, these legal highwaymen contribute largely toward the support of the Church, not the institution of God, but that so-called Church which makes form its idol.''[60]

The three works cited—*Ai*, *Armour*, and *A Modern Pharisee*, respectively—summarized the indignation of many authors. The church—any church—had become too much like an elite social meeting place. Pomp, ceremony, paid pews had given it more the aura of a private club than a sanctuary open to all for the worship of God. Lip-service moralism had replaced the true moral teachings of Christianity, and unflattering analogies were constantly made between the dog-eat-dog ethics of business and the social/political orientation of the Protestant denominations. Monetary support of the church, the authors maintained, was often blood money, paid to assuage the guilty conscience of the factory owner, or more cynically, as evidence of the amount of money a man could ''spend'' on something impractical like the house of God and the teachings of His Son.

From the general, rhetorical perorations illustrated above, various authors moved on to illustrate specific complaints, problems, and condemnations. In Julia W. Parson's novel *The Full Stature of a Man*, well-to-do Mrs. Ogden tries unsuccessfully to bring a backsliding member of the congregation, Mr. Allen, back into the Episcopal fold. He tells her flatly that he can't afford to go—that he and his wife were both snubbed, made to feel like paupers, and humiliated wherever they went, whether to church or, in the case of his wife, to the sewing society.

Mrs. Ogden allows that there might be some selfish, rich congregations where what he described could occur, and suggests that he throw in his lot with a poorer one. He replies that he and his wife have tried that too, going to a mission church called St. John's in the Wilderness, but it was almost as bad in the repeated, endless calls for money.

"Now something was needed for repairs, again the minister's salary was short, or something was wanted for home or foreign missions. They were all good objects, I've nothing to say against them, but there was the constant theory advanced that if we would only give, if we would only practice a little self denial, we could give more money. . . . Why, good Lord! Madam, . . . families living on the income we are—and there were dozens in the congregation no better off—have no pennies to squander, nothing but the very closest watchfulness keeps us out of debt! And even this don't do it sometimes! It hasn't me. . . . "

Mrs. Ogden finally offers to pay a contribution in their names if the Allens would come to her church; no one would ever know:

He was touched with her offer, and with a quiver in his voice he said:
"Madam, I thank you for your goodness, but I cannot accept it. I have thought this matter well over, and I think there is a principle involved. I am only one of a large class; we are not willing to be paupers in church matters, any more than in other things. All we want is such a distribution of wealth as will make it possible for our hard work to give us a decent living for our families, and let them have the chances of education that they ought to have. No, Madam," and he rose to his feet in his earnestness, "as long as I can't pay for it, I don't believe the Lord wants me to go to church. He don't ask of any man to put himself in a pauper's place, and I won't do it! At the same time, madam, I thank you for your kind offer."[61]

Mrs. Ogden does not succeed in getting Mr. Allen to become a churchgoer again. And the author's point is clear. Mr. Allen did not feel welcome as a worshipper of Christ. Those who paid any attention to him did so for what he could monetarily give to the church, not what the church could spiritually give Mr. Allen. Mrs. Ogden acknowledges defeat in personally dealing with the poor. She is more successful when, later in the novel, she builds a series of apartments and rents them on a completely cooperative basis.

One final example of a work in which the author castigates the Protestant denominations for being unaware or uncaring of the lot of the tired, the homeless, and the poor in flesh and spirit is a pseudonymous work entitled *In Office; A Story of Washington Life and Society* published in 1891.[62] It is a tale of the *Maggie, A Girl of the Streets* variety. Young, innocent Tula Fairleigh has come from a farm to corrupt Washington, D.C., to get a job. She gets considerably more than that, however; early in her career of decline and fall, she seeks solace by going to church.

After describing the opulence of the structure and the eloquent, polished and learned sermon, which focused strongly on man's duties to his Creator, "Tula wondered vaguely why he had dwelt so much on man's sin against God and so little on man's sin against his fellow-man. Why had he not spoken of the wants of humanity, of the wrongs of God's children, of the pitilessness of heart under many a broadcloth coat in that congregation?[63]

In the main, the social gospel novels that attack the church for alienating many of its members illustrate their authors' deep concern over their churches' social role in the everyday lives of their parishioners. Those writers whose main criticism was directed toward the decrease of true spirituality in American Protestantism linked that spiritual purity to humility, unselfishness, and regard for others. To them, the true essence of Christian teaching was manifest not just in the personal relationship of a person to God, but in the social relationships men and women had with their fellows as well. A lack of concern for others—a cynical disregard for the Golden Rule and all it symbolized—was a condemnation of both that person's spiritual and social state. Social gospel writers who dwelt on these principles sought to drive home this point.

Similarly, the writers who attacked the aristocratic practice of gaining revenue through pew rents, made analogies between the administration of churches and corrupt politics, and pointed out that men who were pillars of many a cathedral were the very ones Christ would have driven from His house were attacking the same lack of Christian morality, but doing so by means of criticizing the end products of the moral decline rather than the causes. Tula Fairleigh's speculations about why Dr. Parnell did not speak of man's duty to his fellow man ultimately questioned the validity of the minister's understanding of Christianity. The same was apparent in Mr. Allen's reasons for not going to church. The corruption of the teachings of Christ into a worship that smacked of Mammon and that disregarded the poor widow in favor of pleading for her mite was what the writers of these social gospel novels condemned. They called for a return of the church's interest in the moral conduct of the lives of men, and for Christian leadership in seeing that that conduct was based on the Biblical concepts of justice and humanity.

One more variety of social gospel fiction—a group of eleven novels—depicted the role of such special charity and self-help lay institutions as the Modern Order of Deaconesses, the King's Daughters Association, and the Young People's Society for Christian Endeavor (Y.P.S.C.E.). The lay Christian institutions all had the common goal of helping the poor, either in the tightly organized manner of the Deaconesses or in the much more fluid manner of the King's Daughters. The Y.P.S.C.E. societies were midway between the two in formal organization, almost always being affiliated with a local Protestant church, though the organization itself was interdenominational.

There are two Deaconess novels, or, to be more precise, one novel and a group of stories that are tied together by recurring characters in the Deaconess organization. The most interesting portion of the latter, *Deaconess Stories*, by Mrs. Lucy J. Meyer, is a foreword by the author outlining the history and purpose of the organization.[64] In it, Mrs. Meyer explained the history of the Order—its origin in the second century A.D., its eclipse during the Middle Ages, and its revival in Germany in the 1830s by a Lutheran minister and in America by the work of the same Mrs. Meyer and her husband Josiah. She also went into some detail outlining the nature of Deaconess work. All in the Order were volunteers, wore a distinctive costume for recognition, and by and large did their work in the slums of large cities. The Deaconesses specialized in hospital work, which is the subject matter of the second novel of this type, Elizabeth E. Holding's *Joy the Deaconess*.[65]

Both authors made clear their conviction that the Deaconess Association was a part of the social gospel movement. All members of the organization taught the Bible and endeavored to live by its principles as a part of their social work among the poor.

Four novels deal with the much more personalized King's Daughters Association.[66] According to Alice E. Curtiss's *The Silver Cross* and Ellen E. Dickinson's *The King's Daughters*, this association originated when the Reverend Mr. Edward E. Hale and nine of his parishioners were delayed in a railway station en route to the funeral of a mutual friend. They were discussing the loss of the deceased, his many virtues and good works, when the Reverend Mr. Hale proposed that the ten of them form a fraternity as a memorial to their dead friend, the idea being to imitate and continue the Christian charities he had started. They called themselves the "Ten Society" and took for their motto lines from one of Mr. Hale's short stories:

> Look up and not down,
> Look out and not in;
> Look forward and not back,
> And Lend a Hand.[67]

They also agreed that each of the ten should also form other tens, ad infinitum. This, apparently, was about 1878. The society, which took for its motto the last line of Hale's poem, grew and ultimately boasted a predominantly female membership, taking the name of The King's Daughters. As a symbol of membership the women chose a small, silver Maltese Cross with the initials I. H. N., standing for "In His Name," inscribed on it. The Cross was fastened to a small piece of purple ribbon.

A description of the organization and the charitable works accomplished by its members is provided by one of the characters in *The Silver Cross*:

"Everybody tries to get ten more, and anybody can start a Ten anywhere and choose what special thing to do. Some of them visit sick people, and some start mission schools, and some do cooking for poor people, and some just try to make things pleasant around them, and some do special things for the churches they belong to. We had one at school for being polite and making things comfortable for the teachers in the classroom, and it was so pleasant! . . . And I know of one lady that built a whole beautiful cottage for sick people, and ever so many are working in hospitals. Oh, there are so many ways! But whatever else they do, everyone is pledged to be . . . on the lookout for chances to help; and whenever you see a purple ribbon like this, with the little cross, you can be sure that the one who wears it will do anything in the world to help you out of any trouble, if you ask her In His Name.''[68]

The King's Daughters novels depict the organization as being primarily interested in the problems of the poor, with their protagonists coming from all walks of life. In Miss Dickinson's *The King's Daughters*, the heroines, an aristocratic mature woman and her granddaughter, are definitely upper class, whereas in *The Silver Cross* the heroine is a hunchback from the lower working class. These novels dramatizing the work of lay Christian organizations have heroines who are unanimously oriented toward the various social problems of the day and use Christian ethics as a basis for their good works. The viewpoint of the authors is not always that of the middle or working class, but neither is it generally that of condescending upper-class philanthropists.

The Y.P.S.C.E. volumes are unusual in that they are politically oriented. *The City of Endeavor*, *The Endeavorers of Maple Grove*, and *Elijah Tone, Citizen* are all concerned to a greater or lesser degree with the reformation of local politics as a part of the Endeavorers' Christian commitment.[69] In Harold M. Davis's *The City of Endeavor*, for example, the city is no other than Brooklyn, New York. The novel tells the story of reconverted Carl Berg's efforts to make Brooklyn into a New Jerusalem. He was almost successful.

In Hattie Gardner's novel the Y.P.S.C.E. succeeds in stopping the trolley service of Maple Grove on Sundays, in closing all the saloons, in shutting down the Sunday theater, Sunday newspapers, the baseball game, ''and kindred devices of His Satanic Majesty. . . . ''[70]

Perhaps the chief interest in this subcategory of social gospel fiction is that there is a subcategory at all. Eleven novels praising three different organizations of Christian laity are not very many of course, but it is interesting that all but two of the novels were published in the 1890s, the apex of the social gospel movement. Considering their nature, nine such novels published over a span of eight years (from 1891 through 1898, with four copyrighted in 1893) give added testimony to the impact of the social gospel movement at an organized, grassroots level.

The chapter to this point has largely dealt with types and varieties of social gospel novels as a major subtype of what has been labeled social Christian fiction. These works have been placed under four general headings: First, novels rendered from the point of view of the working man in which the poor and oppressed state their cause in general terms; second, works dealing specifically with the issues between capital and labor, these primarily from a labor point of view; third, works attacking the secularization of American Protestantism in the last quarter of the nineteenth century, in which authors documented the alienation of large sections of the working class from the church; and finally, novels explaining the involvement of three Protestant lay groups in the service of the social gospel movement.

In the larger context of social Christian novels, one final category of works deserves separate attention. These can be called novels espousing Christian radicalism. Again, the point of view of the authors is helpful in defining this category.

The first two varieties of social Christian novels are distinguished, as we have seen, by attitudes of stewardship and philanthropy based on variations of the doctrine of the gospel of wealth. The four basic varieties of social gospel fiction are identified by their author's criticism of a lack of Christian behavior on the part of the capitalists and churches, and are generally presented from the point of view of the laboring man. The final category of Christian radical fiction, using the combined ethics of Christian humanitarianism and eighteenth-century political rationalism, is presented from labor's standpoint. In these works the authors see the system of laissez-faire capitalism as being at war with both the ethics of Christianity and America's political heritage. They use the principles of Christianity as the basis for arguing against the capitalistic system as it was organized in late nineteenth-century America. Unlike the social gospel novels that deal with the relations between capital and labor—those that seek reform within the framework of the then existing political and economic system—these novels are unified by lengthy sections wherein a character or an author demands a basic socialist, communist, or, in a few cases, anarchist change in that system.

These novels fall into four general types: those whose basic point is that Christ Himself was a socialist; those that argue socialism from other biblical and Christian tenets; straight socialist arguments from a humanitarian standpoint without much reliance on Christian dogma; and novels that, after presenting Christian socialist views, attempt to refute them.

Of those in the first category, the most obvious is a work by Archibald McCowan entitled simply *Christ, the Socialist*.[71] Verging on being plotless, the story deals with a running argument between the Presbyterian Reverend Mr. David Burkley and his friend and antagonist, school teacher Robert Stewart. Stewart argues that Christ was a socialist and therefore the best and only correct form of government should be socialism. The Reverend Mr. Burkley is originally very much unconvinced but little by little is won over, and when near the end of the novel Stewart dies, Burkley takes up the Christian socialist cause in his stead. There are other incidents in the plot, but their only use is to serve as methods of showing the correctness of Stewart's stand.

McCowan begins his ideological conflict early in the novel with the following:

It was in the heat of an argument, in which Burkley was getting worsted, that he exclaimed rather angrily, ''Why, Stewart, you are a rank socialist!''

''So was Jesus Christ,'' was the quiet rejoinder.

''What!'' cried Burkley, aghast at such an assertion, ''Where in all the Bible do you find proof for that?''

''In the very first sermon Christ preached—the sermon on the mount.''[72]

The discussion between the two men is lengthy and finally ends in a draw. On another day when they renew the argument, but when he is already weakening,

Burkley uses the classic conservative argument that is quoted again and again in the novels—Christ's "The poor ye have always with you." Stewart responds:

"Yes, but Christ does not say it is right, neither does he say that we *will* always have the poor with us. It was not contempt for the poor that made Christ utter these words. It was to rebuke the hypocrisy of Judas Iscariot. Jesus was one of the poor himself; he suffered in his own person all the privations incident to poverty. His great heart beat for the poor, but his mission on earth was to redeem the souls of men, not to abolish poverty. Nevertheless, his sermons and parables teem with advice, which, if men would only follow, would soon revolutionize the world."[73]

In *About My Father's Business*, another minister, this time Episcopalian, argues the same concept, though in the context of a sermon:

"Socialism is Christianity applied to social reforms in that it allows or causes to allow a more equal distribution of the products of labor, by the elevation of the working classes by a just and generous appreciation of their rights, and of the essential brotherhood of humanity; which Christ ever recognized. Jesus Christ was a socialist of the highest and most noble type."[74]

And in Edgar Bross's *A Modern Pharisee*, the stalwart hero, Willard Millard, succinctly sums up his thinking on the subject:

Jesus taught the doctrine of common sense and a true socialism—an ideal democracy. His chief aim was to destroy moral rottenness in high places and low. He instilled charity, benevolence and humility.[75]

The position of these three authors is clear: they equate socialism with political equality and buttress their arguments with a literal interpretation of Christ's teachings that emphasize the brotherhood of man. Moreover, the idealism and optimism commented on earlier is stated clearly and without apology. To many liberal theologians who supported the social gospel and presented their beliefs in political terms, European socialism was the next logical step in the fulfillment of Enlightenment political theory *and* the social tenets of the New Testament. The form of government represented in the republic of America was a fine step toward ideal democracy, but it was obviously subject to abuses. Jefferson had substituted as a self-evident truth the right of all men to the "pursuit of happiness" for John Locke's "property" in the famous trilogy in the Declaration of Independence. That happiness was made up of equal parts of man's physical and spiritual well-being. Protestant Christianity should see to the spirit; to many, the doctrines of socialism could see to the physical.

Metzerott, Shoemaker, by Katherine Woods, got to the heart of the matter by taking as its theme the confrontation between Christian socialism and atheist socialism—this, twenty-eight years before the Russian Revolution. This work is considerably more sophisticated than those of its type previously cited.[76] Karl

Metzerott is a militant atheist who raises his son to be the same. Two clerics, the Catholic Father McClosky and the Protestant Reverend Ernest Clare—both Christian socialists—come to their city, and slowly Louis, Karl's son, comes to accept the preachers' values instead of his father's. The elder Metzerott, in his rage and jealousy, is accidentally responsible for his son's death at the novel's end. Earlier in the story, however, when Karl and the Catholic priest are on good terms, the following scene takes place:

Father McClosky: "Do you suppose I should not hail the advent of *true* Socialism as the dawn of new light and life for the world?"

"Eh? a new convert! But stop! there was a qualifying word. *True* Socialism; that is, with all its distinctive features omitted."

"Not at all. Socialism with all its vital organs strengthened and purified; in short— Christianity."

"I thought so! Christianity! Why, Christianity has had her fling for eighteen centuries, and what has she done!"

"The first thing she did was to establish a commune," replied the Irishman. "You can read a full account of it in the Book of Acts, including the history of some weak disciples, who, having perhaps been trained in tiger-hunting, were not fully equal to the occasion during a reign of peace. As the first recorded experiment in Socialism, it ought to interest you."

"But the experiment failed."

"Failed? In the reign of Tiberius, with Nero and Caligula and all those fellows to come after? Well, rather! The world wasn't quite ready for it, not by some eighteen centuries, so Christianity fell back on her intrenchments, as you might say, and, while she reserved the spirit of socialism, let go the letter."[77]

Father McClosky and the Reverend Mr. Clare are both convinced that the time is now ripe for the rebirth of the "letter." Finally, after the tragedy of his son's death, Karl, a broken man, also becomes a Christian socialist.

There are six works that best present Christian socialism on biblical and theological grounds other than through metaphorical presentations of Christ himself.[78] Of these, two, *The King's Highway* and *Murvale Eastman, Christian Socialist*, are of special interest. In Mrs. Barr's *The King's Highway*, one of the major characters, a newspaper man by the name of John McAslin, has been sickened by the conditions of the working poor and at a labor meeting takes the floor and says that "Socialism . . . is the essential spirit of Christianity . . . , the socialism of the New Testament." It is recognizing "the Gospel of the first century. But this socialism the Church does not practise; she does not even preach it. . . . If Christ should suddenly stand upon Broadway," he continues, "and if the poor and homeless round him flocked, Where would he lead them? To the churches? Nay! At those shut doors no Christ would 'stand and knock.' "[79]

In another portion of the book, the author presents an ominous song called "The Battle Hymn of Christian Socialism":

The day of the Lord is at hand, at hand:
Its storms roll up the sky;
The nations sleep starving on heaps of gold,
The dreamers all toss and sigh.
The night is darkest before the morn,
When the pain is sorest the child is born:
And the day of the Lord is at hand!
Gather you, gather you, angels of God.
Freedom, mercy, and truth!
Come, for the earth is grown coward and old,
Come down and renew us her youth.
Wisdom, self-sacrifice, daring, and love!
Haste to the battle-field, stoop from above,
To the day of the Lord at hand![80]

It was clear that the true highway of the King followed a literal interpretation of biblical social idealism. Creeds, dogmas, and traditions had, in Mrs. Barr's view, obscured the true teaching of Christ. What He said demanded a true democratic revolution based not on Locke's or Jefferson's famous trio, but one more recent, the French Revolution's liberty, fraternity, and equality. The American and European revolutions were steps toward the King's highway; what remained was the next and final step, socialism based on New Testament Christianity, and the author was convinced that in 1897, "the day of the Lord was at hand."

In Tourgée's *Murvale Eastman, Christian Socialist*, clergyman Murvale Eastman, organizes a League of Christian Socialists in his wealthy church. Even though a number of the beliefs of the league—summarized below—sound familiar to us, they offend many in Eastman's Church of the Golden Lilies and eventually the minister resigns to devote himself fully to the principles of Christian socialism.

This complex novel includes various love stories, problems of mistaken identity, and lost heirs. In the process Christian socialism as the propaganda message of Tourgée is sometimes overshadowed by other elements of the plot; nonetheless *Murvale Eastman* presents the most detailed statement of the doctrines of Christian socialism to be found in any social Christian fiction. The "Declaration of Principles of the League of Christian Socialists" numbered nine points that can be summarized as stressing: (1) that the true function of Christian civilization is the economic and social improvement of all people individually and collectively; (2) that the strong and powerful should lead the fight in helping to bring about this improvement; (3) that a concerted effort to eliminate poverty as the chief cause of crime and vice should take precedence over punishing individuals who break society's laws; (4) that social and political reform should take place within the structure of law, not by revolution; (5) that everyone should strive to effect all of the above principles; and (6) "that, believing the positive purpose to 'do unto others as you would that they should do to you' is a far more efficient force in the improvement of human conditions than any restraining power, this League will seek to promote its objects (1) By endeavoring to shape and direct public sentiment; (2) By seeking to obtain desirable legislation; (3) By securing the enforcement of just laws and the modification or repeal of bad ones.''[81]

In each of the other four novels that advocate Christian socialism as a solution to the social and economic problems of the time, parallel arguments can be found. The town that was redeemed in Sheldon's short novel *The Redemption of Freetown* was a black ghetto in the city of Merton. A group of leading citizens, led by their minister, builds a large settlement house—complete with kindergarten, kitchen, reading and sewing rooms, and a dispensary—that is permanently endowed and is to be used as a meeting place for the underprivileged of Freetown. Not only that, but as the minister says in summing up the scheme,

"The question now is, Can we get *people*, the best and best-known, and most able to go over there and live with the people? That, to my mind, is the heart of the problem. . . . When Christian Merton is willing to give itself for unchristian Freetown, it will be redeemed. The question really is, How many of the best men and women are ready to go and live for a while in that house?''[82]

The people are willing, and Freetown—like so many cities of today in its problems—is redeemed.

In *The Social Crime* Minnie L. Armstrong, the co-author of the novel, presented both her theme and proposed solution to the "crime" of the title in the introduction, "As a writer of books and newspaper articles, and a student of the Labor question, I feel that the need of mankind is, to know how to co-operate with, instead of co-operate against each other."

In concert with her co-author, George N. Sceets, a labor leader and former editor of *The Knights of Labor*, she then proposes an entire cooperative town based on principles of Chirstian socialism.[83]

In the other two relevant volumes, *Speaking of Ellen* and *Would Christ Belong to a Labor Union?*, the solution to the plight of the working man is the same as that outlined in *The Social Crime*, some sort of cooperative socialistic endeavor sanctioned by the capitalists and government alike.

In the group of works commented upon thus far, the authors based their positions on the dual principles of Christianity, especially that of the New Testament, and the political doctrines expressed during the early days of our republic. It is significant that the institution appealed to, and criticized most resoundingly, was not the state but the church. These novels espousing Christian socialism present the accepted role of the Protestant church as a sponsoring agency of social reform. That the churches were not fully meeting this responsibility would seem to be the primary reason the novels were written—to convince the ministers and the laity of the country that a nation that announced itself to be "under God" must see to it that it conducted itself in keeping with God's precepts. If statesmen were remiss in this because they were seduced by power, it was the church's responsibility to remind them and the voters who gave them office that the nation must follow the words of God or suffer the fate of other lands that refused to listen: destruction.

In keeping with this idea, it is noteworthy that there are only three novels that argue socialism without any significant religious background to make the cause more palatable. The most elaborate is George Farnell's *Rev. Josiah Hilton, The Apostle of a New Age.*[84] The title is misleading. By novel's end Mr. Hilton does give up the ministry and leave for the far west to preach socialism, but the true advocate of the system, and the one who is instrumental in the minister's choosing this course of action, is a layman named Charles Trevor.

Trevor's arguments—and the novel is little more than a series of monologues given by him to an interested group of friends—say very little about Christianity and a great deal about Marxian economics, though Marx's name is never used. The volume is unique in this respect. Even though the book is short, it is concentrated, and the author knew his Marx well. Both of the other volumes are much more novelistic, less didactic, and less well informed, and when the respective authors propose their socialistic solutions, they do so in a more casual way than Mr. Farnell.

In Katherine Woods's *A Web of Gold*, published the year after *Metzerott, Shoemaker*, the hero is a young and handsome anarchist who has been sent to destroy the Hillborough Flour Factory run by Philip Godfrey. Mr. Godfrey is a very good man, however—the ideal Christian capitalist—and Victor Maurice St. Andre, the anarchist, falls in love with Godfrey's daughter, Agatha. After considerable soul-searching, St. Andre does not destroy the flour mill and, at his trial before his anarchist superiors, he presents his case. After explaining his training and upbringing, he says:

"I went to Hillhope in the first flush of the zeal which followed my full initiation. I found there the world, the society, the laws and customs I had been taught to hate, to overthrow by any methods; and I found them under their best aspects, I admit, and without their possible corruptions; but, comrades, I found something else; I found truth and freedom, the very truth, the same freedom, I had been taught to love and long for; embryonic perhaps, only half recognized, yet perfect in all their beautiful parts.... As I studied them, I asked myself, 'Can truth grow by means of fraud and falsehood, or freedom—*mon pardon*—by tyranny?' and I could find but one answer. Our methods may have been needful to awaken the people, but the people are now awake.... Freedom, brotherhood, are in the air; everywhere men are consciously or unconsciously breathing them in; secrecy, fraud, violence, are weapons of which the truth has no need."[85]

The chief inquisitor of the trial surprisingly agreed and freed Victor from the anarchist pledge.[86] The novel ends happily with Agatha and Victor's marriage and their setting up the flour factory on socialist lines.

In Julia Parson's *The Full Stature of a Man*, working-class heroine Milly Burton, when talking to Sidney Ogden, the rich young man whom she ultimately marries, denies any knowledge of "communism" and denies being a communist.

Yet her analysis of the economic problems of the time is repeated again and again in period novels. She begins,

"It does not seem to me that the problem to-day is how to make money, but how to distribute it."

"You are not a communist," he exclaimed with energy and amazement.

Then, after demurely saying she is very young, knows nothing of political economy, has no grasp of the trouble between labor and capital, she launches into an involved metaphor concerning the latter that left her husband utterly speechless:

"It seems to me that money represents the life or blood of the body politic, and that the circulation of it is wrong. As we say when we are sick, the head or heart, or whatever it is, is congested, and we do not look for health until the proper circulation is restored. Nor can the head be indifferent as long as the hands or feet are not drawing their share of the vital fluid. The so-called superior portions of the body suffer as much or more, even, than the extremities. If this state of things is not relieved, we look for disease and death; and they surely come. I am saying all this very crudely, but do you catch my idea?"

"Yes, I think I do; the upper or moneyed class cannot be indifferent to the poor. But are you not something of a communist?"

"Not if I know what communism is. I don't carry even a very small red flag," she said smilingly. "They insist upon a violent division of the wealth of the land, while I— well, let me go back to the illustration again; I would regard each community as a man, and I would have this life blood, this money which represents the labor of the world, so distributed that each portion of the body should receive what was its own, what it could use—that is, all that would keep it in its highest health."[87]

George Farnell, Katherine Woods, and Julia Parsons all suggested socialism or communism as the solution to economic and social dislocations without basing their appeals upon Christian doctrine. Of the three, however, only Farnell was truly militant and knew exactly what he was advocating. Both Mrs. Woods and Mrs. Parsons saw their solutions through the sentimental coloring of doing good by means of dogmas they probably did not fully understand.

The last set of novels that deals with political radicalism in Christian terms does so in isolated cases. The authors set up socialist, or in two cases, anarchist, straw men in order to attack the philosophy presented as being far too radical, un-American, and un-Christian.

The socialist solution to society's ills was treated lightly by Harriette A. Keyser in her novel *Thorns in Your Sides*.[88] At one point in the story a character labeled "The Advanced Thinker," a socialist, is in rather dire physical straits because of his views. The hero of the novel, an Anglican churchman, ministers to him in his distress and the hungry socialist eventually abandons his principles for a cup of broth.[89]

Such levity was unusual; most of the authors treated the threat of socialism with what they thought to be dead seriousness. In *Uncle Sam's Bible*, for example, the all-knowing Reverend Mr. Jacob Jones offered such quaint summaries as that the main purpose of socialism is to "own all the capital and do all the work, farming, manufacturing, etc.; in other words . . . to make us all rich.'' Socialism is not a matter of earthly justice, but ''a beautiful dream. It will be realized in the New Jerusalem. . . . It will be a communistic city, too; for there will be no rich and no poor.'' It will also be anarchist because there will be no policemen in it. However, Boston is not yet Jerusalem, nor Tennessee or Massachusetts, Eden. ''When justice is introduced it will be time enough to think of these airy mansions of the fancy.''[90]

Henry Fauntleroy, while sharing some of the Reverend Jones's views, expresses himself this way in *Who's to Blame?*:

''As the great mass of the people are poor, and know only hard struggle, privation, and want, it is not surprising that there is a growing effort on the part of poverty to organize a protest, in the form of the Commune and Socialism, against the abnormal condition of the wealthy class. These associations are right in their great fundamental idea of equality and brotherhood, and it is not strange they fight Christianity and the Churches, which they find so imbued with the spirit of caste and the pretension of money. They are turned to infidelity by the false and wrong aspect religion is made to present. But they commit a great mistake that while antagonizing the *false* they do not embrace the *true* and found their movement on the genuine teachings of Christ. . . . They will never achieve any success while the ideas they advance are wholly selfish and materialistic, and unassociated with any spiritual and religious sentiment.''[91]

Both authors stressed pragmatic idealism, and their attack was not so much on the ideals of communism and socialism as on the corrupt practices of American capitalist economics that had taken the Christ out of Christianity and replaced Him with the dollar sign.

In his novel *Dr. Marks, Socialist*, Marion C. Smith was extremely liberal in discussing everything from Christianity to socialism, save for one area—anarchism. With the sole exception of Katherine P. Woods's *A Web of Gold*, none of the authors had anything good, or even neutral, to say about anarchy. Dr. Marks is quite explicit on the subject. Talking to one of his helpers in the slums he says, ''Remember that Anarchism is the curse of our cause; that law and order, crystallized into a rational and beneficent government, must ever be the bulwark of reform.''[92] And arguing with two German anarchists, one of whom is to become his murderer at the novel's end, the doctor passionately defends socialism while condemning anarchism.[93]

The other attack on anarchism, and in this case socialism as well, is in a lengthy sequence in Alice Bartlett's *A New Aristocracy*.[94] The heroine, Margaret Murchison, is disturbed over the conduct of her younger brother Gilbert and has followed him to a labor meeting. While there she hears two inflammatory anarchist speeches.

In the first, presented by a woman who waves ''her long arms like a windmill,'' the speaker preaches the gospel of discontent and the abolition of all law save natural law. ''But you say . . . that anarchy is disreputable. That is just what we want it to be. . . . We don't want to be reputable, and I thank God that I am utterly disreputable. We leave respectablity for the Christian capitalist, the slave-driver, the monopolist. Why, a man cannot be a Christian anarchist, because anarchy is only of the earth.'' She ends her harangue by attacking the state as an entity: ''If we want liberty, there is no other way to get it but to do as the state does and resort to armed force.''[95]

After the second speech Margaret can stand no more. When her brother gives a similar speech (she has been spying on him out of fear for his peculiar conduct), she springs to the speaker's platform and, after telling of her own hard toil and admitting the many grave wrongs inflicted on the working class, she warns that violence and destruction will get them nowhere, that they will find themselves only ''still deeper in the mire of dissatisfaction and wrong.'' But what was the alternative she asked rhetorically? Not the force of the brute, but the reason of the human. ''But you are no doubt asking where that reason must begin. Back of all sophistries, back of all calculation, on that primitive plane of the newly awakened—the conscience!''

It is but a short step for her from man's conscience to Christianity, and in fulsome tones she speaks of Christ as a working man. She makes clear that she is ''not talking . . . of the religion that the occupants of velvet pulpits preach to the occupants of velvet pews, nor of the Christianity, so called, that is reserved for the rich man who builds churches where he and his class may worship in unsullied seclusion,'' but of the Christ as carpenter and the author of the parable of the good Samaritan. Then after a flurry of really quite wonderful mixed metaphors in which she emphasizes that reason would soon show capital that its interests were ultimately identical to those of labor, she closes with, ''But before we mend the steps of those who oppress us, let us as individuals sweep the inner chambers of the heart, and garnish them anew for the long-waited guest of universal justice.''[96]

By now it is no doubt abundantly clear that solutions of radical political action were not popular among social Christian novelists. The reasons were various. The narrator of *Uncle Sam's Bible* found the ideas good, true and beautiful, but utopian. After lumping the doctrines of communism, socialism, and anarchism all together, the Reverend Mr. Jones condemned them for being impractical and uncommitted to his definition of justice. Henry Fauntleroy, author of *Who's to Blame?*, likewise found the ideas worthy but criticized them from the standpoint of the radical's antipathy toward the church. To him believers in socialism and anarchy were misled because they saw only the ''false aspect of religion,'' instead of the true and ''genuine teachings of Christ.'' Dr. Marks called himself a socialist, but in trying to formulate just what he meant by the term, we come up with an anarchist Christian humanism. His approach to anarchy was theo-retical, completely devoid of and antagonistic to the violence attending the East European interpretation of the term. Finally Margaret Murchison, heroine of *A New Aristocracy*, expanded the attitude expressed in *Who's to Blame?* But before the author, speaking through the heroine, attacked the radical doctrines of an-archism for being self-defeating, unmanly, and unchristian, she dutifully presented the dangers, threats, and reasons for the radical position. Her rebuttal, phrased in the same melodramatic rhetoric as the radical's proposals, led right back to the classic social gospel stance. She stated that the cause of labor, of right, of progress, must be hinged to the teachings of Christ. "It was not . . . until the gentle Nazarene walked the earth that its toilers began to grope upward toward the light of reason and conscience." He was the working man incarnate, and only His true teachings could lead the worker and the capitalist to realize that their interests were identical, that one could not prevail without the other, and that Christian justice was the only true way for men to deal with each other.

This opening analysis has outlined the major types of social Christian fiction predominant between 1865 and 1900. The only large and distinct area not touched upon has been the type of novel that uses allegory as its chief means of expression, which will be discussed in Chapter 3.

To recapitulate, there are four basic types of social Christian fiction: (1) those novels that present a picture of broad social discontent and suggest general Christian remedies as a solution; (2) those that advocate social improvement by means of upper-class leadership; (3) the traditional social gospel novels that argue various forms of middle- and working-class self-help based on the Christian ethics of the New Testament; and (4) works that advocate or oppose some form of Christianity based on political radicalism as the solution to the economic and social ills of late nineteenth-century America. The scope of the novels is thus much broader than one might have been led to believe. For example, the interpretation presented by Professor Wallace E. Davies in his article entitled "Religious Issues in Late Nineteenth-Century American Novels,"[97] as summed up in the following quotation, is still quite commonly accepted:

Nothing could document better the extent of strong guilt feelings over the growth of poverty, economic inequality, class distinctions, and the churches' neglect of the working class, than Social Christian novels, yet in them . . . the problems are always viewed through the eyes of the middle class. Hence there is a rejection not only of revolutionary violence but also of any drastic changes in the social system. Instead, it is hoped that drawing people's attention to their Christian obligations will be sufficient to improve conditions.[98]

Davies makes three major points: the novels were always written from a middle-class point of view; the middle class rejected violence as a solution to the problems of the time, and the novelists did not advocate any drastic changes in the social system. The first point is not sustained by the facts. It is true that the diction of the novels was often labored—what we have come to think of as the stereotypical Victorian American prose; but once one gets beyond these stylistic conventions, the attitudes and ideas expressed in many of the social gospel novels and the Christian radical works were not middle class but working class.[99]

As to Davies's second point—the rejection of violence as a means of political reform—the only two exceptions I found, which will be discussed in a later chapter, only point up the validity of his interpretation. As we have seen in the majority of the Christian radical works discussed at the end of this chapter, revolution as such is consistently decried.

His third point—that the novelists rejected drastic changes in the social system—is debatable and perhaps hinges on the sense of the word "drastic." It is clear from many of the selections quoted that the novelists did indeed advocate changes in the social system. Most works lack concrete suggestions for nationwide change, but often the attitudes expressed followed those presented in *The Story of a Cañon*—that the troubles of the working class were caused by the capitalist system and the greedy men who controlled it to their advantage without regard for their fellow men. Most social Christian novelists advocated a change in the people—a return to the true teachings of Jesus Christ—*and* at least some change in the social system. Many recognized, without saying so, that it was far easier to change political and economic systems than to change human nature.

My questioning of Davies's conclusions is in no way meant to single them out as being especially in error. His comments represent the general identification of all social Christian fiction solely in terms of the social gospel category of the genre and assume that the works are generally tracts of middle-class piety that present moral lessons in the pattern of *In His Steps*.[100] As the discussion and analysis of the novels in this chapter has shown, there are at least two internal contradictions to this kind of stereotyping. First, most social gospel novels do not demonstrate a middle- or upper-class bias, even though the authors themselves may well have been of the higher classes. Instead, in line with the social gospel movement (itself coming from the middle class), they tended to sympathize with labor's point of view and were generally concerned with alleviating the *causes*—political, economic, and social—of the antagonism between the urban laboring class and the capitalists. The appeal of these works is primarily religious, a kind of spiritual muckraking that anticipated later secular forms of protest and demands for reform.

Second, those social Christian works that do predominantly present an upper- or middle-class attitude approach the problems between capital and labor from the standpoint of stewardship, or trying to mitigate the *effects* of a brutalized laissez-faire system through the traditional avenues of organized and individual charity and philanthropy. Thus the problems described in the social gospel novels are by no means "always viewed through the eyes of the middle class." Only one category of social Christian fiction, that which advocates stewardship and Andrew Carnegie's gospel of wealth, is essentially middle class in orientation.[101]

A final summarizing point should be stressed at this juncture. In the novels just categorized the religious element was, by definition, predominant; but, as was especially apparent in such works as Tourgée's *Murvale Eastman* and Sheldon's *The Redemption of Freetown*, what was then a radical interpretation of Christian ethics in the social realm has since become the accepted dogma of liberal political thought.

2

The Effect of Social Change on Theology as Represented in the Social Christian Novel

The first chapter of this study outlined basic types of social Christian fiction and illustrated some of the more important methods by which the Protestant churches of America came to grips with the social and economic problems of the Gilded Age. As was apparent, one of the difficulties within the social gospel movement as a whole was in the Protestant leaders' reaching an agreement on how involved the church should become in temporal rather than spiritual matters, and, assuming direct social participation was in order, what form it should take. How involved should the church become, what means should it use, what would be the effects of this involvement?

In this chapter I will explore the views of social Christian novelists on four prominent problems of the time: church involvement in social reform; dissension within sects over dogma, ritual, and denominationalism; the Roman Catholic church; and the impact of science as seen in "higher criticism," the social and theological implications of Darwinism, and the industrial and scientific revolution in general.

It is clear that many of the novelists were critical of organized charity as demeaning to an individual's pride, that it often made class distinctions even more apparent than before the offers of help, and that charity itself, while in some cases alleviating the effects of severe poverty, did little or nothing to attack the economic causes that led to poverty. What the majority of social Christian novelists requested was social justice based on Christian ethics and democratic principles rather than alms giving.

Yet, was it the province of organized Christianity to embroil itself in questions of social justice and practical politics? Many sincerely believed that the church, an institution dedicated to the spiritual welfare of man, should not become engaged in social, economic, and political problems; such matters were the province of local, state, and national government only. There were other reasons for noninvolvement: a hypocritical use of Christianity that might salve a man's conscience when he went to church every Sunday morning and tithed but that otherwise kept Christ's teachings carefully separate from anything as mundane and meaningful as wages and hours; and just plain ignorance—of the conditions of the working class in tenement or factory, of what it meant to work twelve to sixteen hours a day six days a week, of what it felt like to go to bed hungry. This problem of social ignorance—which was often accompanied within the same individual by fervent aesthetic spiritualism—has been touched on previously and is a major theme in many of the novels. One aspect of it was well summed up in the description of Dr. Bland in *Dwellers in Gotham*. The author was fair in pointing out Dr. Bland's commitments, strengths, and learning. He was a good Christian in every sense, "Utterly unworldly, gentle hearted, pureminded, his was more the life of a mediaeval saint than of a man of his generation. He was far more familiar with the life of Corinth or Antioch or Ephesus than with the city in which he lived." In his spirituality, "never once had it occurred to him that the Church, like leaven entering the meal, like salt arresting the process of decay, like light in the midst of darkness, was to take part in the common affairs of life." And that St. Ezekiel's, Dr. Bland's church, should be a refuge for the tried and tempted, the downtrodden and poor, and a defender of the oppressed—such an idea, let alone its actualization, had never occurred and would never occur. "How could it?" asked the author. Dr. Bland "had never met with poverty, nor with crime, nor with coarse, brutal sin in any form."[1]

Dr. Bland's character is set; if brought to his attention, the sufferings of the poor would always remain an abstraction to him. There are, of course, many characters, exemplified by Perley Kelso in Elizabeth S. Ward's *The Silent Partner*, who finally do see and feel the problems and devote their lives to combatting the economic system that bred such suffering. Other characters, however, fully understand the economic system, the plight of the poor, the arguments of the reformers, but answer with a paraphrase of Herbert Spencer's interpretation of social Darwinism. The following, one speaker in a conversation between two factory owners, is a good example:

"My dear fellow, do you disapprove of a tangent to a circle because it touches the circumference only at one point? or of the perpetual equidistance of two parallel lines? It might be more in accordance with the precepts of the gospel for the lines to become one; but they can't do it, and remain parallel; and that's just what's the matter with religion and business; you can't bring 'em together without spoiling both. I keep my religion in one pigeon-hole and my business affairs in another, and never allow them to interfere. You may say what you like of the plan, but it is on a scientific basis, and it *succeeds*. If I were to try a sort of siphon connection between the two, I should empty my business only to spoil my religion."

"Look at it this way, Godfrey. What do we find succeeds in the world of nature? is it religion? No, sir; it wasn't religion, but skill and science that invented the steamboat and the telephone; though, mind you, neither of them is irreligious *per se*, they simply stand apart from religion, on different ground altogether. Well, then, if we ask what succeeds in the business world, we get the same answer,—skill and science. Skill and science invented the trust, my dear fellow; and, by thunder, I don't see the shadow of a reason why it should be expected to be any more religious than a locomotive."[2]

The factory owner's argument is interesting. His analogy between geometry and religion and business and religion is obviously false—neither geometry nor religion would be "spoiled" if parallel lines ceased being parallel. But his pragmatic pigeon-holing of ideas and concepts is what has made his life a success: skill and science operating in a moral vacuum proved success in terms of dollars, and that is all that interests him. He has as much feeling as a locomotive and about as much religion.

A similar but more personalized conversation takes place in *Christ, the Socialist* when the Reverend Mr. Burkley visits Mr. Simmons, the local factory owner, on behalf of one of the minister's parishioners:

"You are a Christian man, I hope, a believer in Jesus Christ, and he tells us to do unto others as we would be done by. Now, Mr. Simmons, would you like to be in Jennings's place?"

"No, I would not; but that has nothing to do with it. This factory belongs to me, and surely a man may do what he likes with his own."

"Certainly, certainly, Mr. Simmons, and yet it seems to me that Jennings had also some interest in the mill. He had so much faith in the permanency of his position that he invested all his savings in a home for himself.... You surely might be able to give him something to do, so that he need not be obliged to sell his home and go among strangers? He has been a faithful servant, and is surely entitled to some consideration. Sixteen years is a long time to serve the same master."

"I have paid Jennings well for his services," said Simmons; "I owe him nothing. The man I have turns out more work for less money, and I would be a fool to do otherwise than I have done."

"Well, perhaps, looking at it in a business light, you may be right; but it is hard on the poor, that they have so much competition to meet."

"No more than I have," broke in Mr. Simmons, sharply. "Business is competition all through. The strong win, the weak go to the wall."[3]

Mr. Simmons admits that he would not want to be in the place of the man he has discharged, a victim of competition. Jennings was fired because another man could turn out more work for less pay. If Mr. Simmons kept Jennings for Christian humanitarian reasons, he would lose money and would thus be less able to compete with other manufacturers. His humanitarianism would be a sign of economic weakness, and only "the strong win, the weak go to the wall." Thus according to Mr. Simmons Jennings had to be fired.

These two extremes—blind spiritualism as represented by Dr. Bland on the one hand, and pragmatic economics that led only to profit on the other—were the basic reasons given for preventing the church from meaningfully involving itself in social affairs. Slowly, however, through the sting of dwindling church attendance, charges of fashionable worldliness, and outright hypocrisy, many ministers and laymen started to reevaluate the church's social role. Problems were everywhere. When the physician hero of *Dr. Marks, Socialist* complained to a minister that "my quarrel with the Church is that she is willing to take the world as she finds it, without altering the conditions," the priest replied:

"It is what our Lord did. . . . He planted His principles only in the hearts of men. From their fruition comes the change of conditions, and from that only."
  "The process is too slow," exclaimed the other, fiercely.
  "You have said that you believe in God," continued the priest. "Can you not let Him manage His kingdom?"[4]

The question was a good one. Dr. Marks did not have an answer ready in words, but in action he said no, that mankind through free will and the ability to choose— the gifts of rationality and conscience given by God—must act to better itself.
  Once one was willing to accept this view—which was by no means the preponderant one—the next question was: How does one act for the betterment of his kind? Or, put another way, how far dared man go in acting for and through his Maker, and above all, how did a man know that what he did was right?
  For example, the Reverend John Henry from the novel by the same name, just graduated from a seminary and innocent, was made the pastor of a large and wealthy metropolitan church. It did not take long for him to see the squalor and hardship all around him. He felt, knew, that something had to be done and that his church should be involved. After organizing his thoughts and questions, he laid them before a senior minister of the same city, and this was what he was told:

"My dear sir . . . the emergency which you have encountered is not new. We older ministers have all encountered it. We have found it best to accept conditions as we find them, and not to quarrel with unalterable facts. There is no use in offending your congregation if you do not thereby reach the evils you seek to remedy. There is no use in driving the evils from the Church if they are still to be in the world. You impoverish your church to no advantage. You will be astonished, if you proceed upon the determination to keep peace in your church at whatever cost, how very little you have to compromise the most rigid principles. We must trust to the individual conscience. It is for the shepherd to lead, and for the flock to follow or not, as it chooses.[5]

The elder minister was asking Henry to see and understand the way of the world and compromise accordingly. The novel ends ambiguously. Henry does compromise, but just how much the reader is not sure.
  The question of involvement is treated in another fashion in a scene from

Cortland Myers's *Would Christ Belong to a Labor Union?* Henry Fielding, the minister, is speaking at a Union meeting:

"I sat a few hours ago by the side of a young man—he is now dead. . . . He was a member of one of the labor unions. He was perfectly conscious until his death, and died while I was there. What was my first business in his presence and the presence of death? Every man of you will answer at once, 'To do all in my power to make that poor fellow ready to meet God. To help him in the final preparation for the next world.'

"It would be folly and criminal to talk to him about this world, and trades, and work, and the wrongs of society. Eternity was just ahead of him, and was the only reality now.

"That is only an incident which illustrates the character of my whole life. I stand on the edge of the grave between immortal souls and their destiny.

"My first business must necessarily be their salvation hereafter. You say I am too other-worldly. How can I be otherwise? Yes, how can any thinking man put the next world secondary to this. If the preacher is 'too other-worldly', most men are too much 'this-worldly.' "[6]

This passage is an excellent example of many of the ministers' dilemmas. Their first allegiance is, of course, to the spirit (though many of the novelists carefully avoided putting it in those terms), and yet, is it to the spirit only? Dr. Bland and Mr. Simmons would answer yes, but for quite different reasons. Henry Fielding answers no, that the spirit is his first concern but the body his second and that the health of the latter has a bearing—and he had pointed out that Christ well knew—on the strength of the former. (As already discussed, the minister answers unequivocally that Christ would belong to a labor union, and therefore working men should be a part of Christ's union—the church.)[7]

So far the novels described have dealt with the role of the church in social reform in the abstract. Once it is established (in a given novel) that the church should actively participate, the question is how. Ordinarily the answer is fairly clear-cut, as most of the discussion and citations in Chapter 1 indicated. In two works various answers are discussed at some length. When Murvale Eastman first proposes the formation of a League of Christian Socialists as a part of the Church of the Golden Lilies, the laity breaks into factions of dispute, primarily over "the relation which such an organization should sustain to the Church." The crux of the argument was whether over time more people would be brought to accept Christ as their redeemer if the rule "Do unto others as you would that they should do to you" were applied than by any other means. In other words, would bettering human conditions be not only the highest duty of the believer, but the most efficient method of redeeming mankind?[8]

The answer to this fundamental question is that because the Golden Rule is the heart of Christ's social teachings no one can be a member of Christ's church without pledging allegiance to it. The Church of the Golden Lilies votes to completely support the League of Christian Socialists, and Murvale Eastman accepts the League's presidency. Tourgée's thesis, however, is that the church's ultimate function is "not to prescribe methods, not to devise remedies; that is the function of government, the duty of society. The function of the Church is only to inspire action, to provide impulse, to exalt and purify motive, to incline men to apply the Christ-spirit to collective human relations."[9] Thus action relevant to particular social crises is not outlined in the novel in any detail.

It was this problem of direct action that was the hardest to resolve. In a long chapter of Robert Cowdrey's *A Tramp in Society* entitled "Starving in the Streets of Chicago," the clergy of that city meet to discuss what could and should be done to alleviate the wretched state of the poor as documented by a series of editorials in the Chicago press.[10] The Reverend Mr. Hercher speaks first and advocates once again that the poor

"be taught to believe that it is God's will that they should bear the heat and burden of the day, and we will hear no more of their complaining. Then the peace that passeth all understanding will take possession of them, and they will gladly accept the law of Christ that says, 'Servants, obey your masters.' We must teach them to believe that if they do this they will receive their full reward in the hereafter."[11]

Rabbi Chaska agrees with Reverend Hercher, saying that in spite of all, the world is getting better all the time.

The next speaker, the Reverend Mr. Brush, points out that 117,000 of the people in Chicago are living in wretched and abject poverty and proposes that the wealthy of the city organize a charity fund that would provide free baths, concert halls, libraries, and proper places for those suffering from diphtheria.[12]

The man who speaks next maintains that all the present problems are due to a lack of enforcement of compulsory education. The speaker who follows is not so sure. He points to the huge rate of unemployment and suggests that if a man's labor is made more productive by education, he is depriving others of a job.[13]

A number of individuals suggest various forms of charity while others warn of its dangers in contemporary terms—warning, for example, of the man who feels the world owes him a living. Others point out that "the poor ye have always with you." But finally the last speaker and hero of the novel, Edgar Bartlett, says that there would be no need for charity if true justice prevailed. He goes on to say that charity is only a stopgap measure, and then asks:

"Can you look upon these wretched dying men and then believe that an All-wise Being created them with every necessary power to produce the food by which they might live, and then failed to provide them with the opportunity to labor? Such a creator would be a brute beneath the notice of self-respecting men! Call this power God or nature, as you choose; I cannot but believe that the same power that created them also gave them the right to use the opportunity by which they can produce their daily bread. And, believing this, I am forced to declare to you . . . that no man has the right to deprive them of the chance to freely use those opportunities."[14]

What is of note in the novel is the extended discussion of the church's role in relation to economic maladjustment. Most of the solutions proposed are standard: This life is full of woe by Adam's act. Nothing can be done but look toward an afterlife and stoically, righteously endure the inequalities of temporal existence. Make available to the people examples of what is best in humankind—an imaginative faculty as expressed in art. This would at least make the hardships of living a little more bearable. Educate the masses; if they truly understood their world, then they would be more able to cope with it and perhaps even better it. No, don't educate them. Who would be willing to hoe the garden when everyone was "educated"? And the solution of organized charity, the pragmatic finger in the dike. The author's own proposal—the abolishing of all rent on land—is unique in the fiction read.

The Social Revolution by Henry Martel and *God's Rebel* by Hulbert Fuller are unique in another sense. Only these two authors of all those works dealt with in this review examined organized Christianity and not only found it wanting but actually considered it a barrier to social progress. Both authors believed that the Christian church was worthless, plagued with reactionary capitalism, and should be destroyed as an institution inhibiting mankind's potential. Thus, at the opposite extreme from, say, Mary Bennett, the author of *Asaph's Ten Thousand*, and the Reverend Mr. Hercher in *A Tramp in Society*, who suggested resignation and acceptance of the individual's allotted station in the great chain of being, Martel and Fuller suggested the opposite.

For example, in *God's Rebel*, the protagonist says, "To be told in this age and generation that God had cursed the earth, and to allege it as an excuse for famine and starvation . . . was enough to make a man's blood boil. Quite as much, even, as to be told by a Roman Catholic cardinal that we must continue to have poor people in order to *stimulate* the benevolent faculties of the rich!"[15] His anger and disillusion finally lead him to the conclusion

that organized Christianity and Democracy are absolutely incompatible—dead arms around a vital being's neck. Every law of growth and development is in direct opposition to any institutional thing like the church; we behold the proof of it in noting that wherever the human race has made an advance it has had first to get rid of some stupid tenet of alleged Christianity. Oh, yes; it is all right for a monarchy; part and parcel of it, in fact. But for a republic such as ours, I believe it to be the most dangerous and blinding superstition that threatens our progress.[16]

The author ends the novel on a bleak note. Hero Kenneth Moore, who has a doctorate in economics, loses job after job because of his radical beliefs and eventually seeks his death in the Spanish American War.

The vision of Henry Martel in *The Social Revolution* is more violent, though no more optimistic. The central character, Mark Richardson, having nothing but scorn for the church, advocates social revolution. Before this could be effected, however, one of Richardson's converts is accidentally responsible for the hero's death. The tone and content of the novel become clear as the protagonist exhorts the church to care for the poor:

"Do you know how much hell there is within a stone's throw of us here? And the Church doesn't lift its hand to relieve one jot of the suffering.

"It only quotes the Bible, 'The poor always ye have with you,' as if it was God's high purpose that poverty should exist, that its millionaire members might have the luxury of intensifying this poverty by an occasional dole of charity. I tell you . . . the Church is the most powerful instrument of oppression which the poor have to contend against, and unless the robbers, and cheats, and debauchees whom it invests with the garb of respectability, are spewed out of its mouth, and it begins to do something for the landless, and the homeless, and the harlot, and the waifs of society, it is doomed."[17]

There is no doubt about the hero's convictions, and he preaches his revolution against the church throughout the novel. Toward its end, in one of his most bitter tirades, he says:

"The Church claims that it alone can found social regeneration. The masses have deserted it. It has become lonely in its isolation and respectability, and yet it still claims the power to heal the ills of our times. Now what remedy does it propose to apply. Charity. What do you think of it, gentlemen? It has millionaire devotees, . . . men who have monopolized the natural resources of the earth, and wielded the enormous power thus acquired to crush our competition; men who wreck railroads and ruin thousands of confiding shareholders, and cut down to the lowest point at which life can be sustained and reproduced, the wages of their operatives; men who entice operatives to work in the mines and then lock them out in order to starve them to accept lower wages; men who speculate in bread stuffs and raise the cost of those who receive beggarly wages. . . . And now we hear of the 'associated charities,' which is explained to mean scientific charity, to which these rich men are expected to contribute. There would be no need of 'charity' in this sense, if the Church and society would insist upon justice instead of charity."[18]

It is noteworthy that even in these two novels—*God's Rebel* and *The Social Revolution*—in which the questions of why and how the church should lead in social reform are dismissed as hopeless, that neither author attacked the true doctrines of Christianity as he understood them. The scorn of both authors was reserved for the church as a tempted and fallen institution. Charged with preserving and expounding the doctrines of Christianity, the church had instead, to these authors, become Christianity's vital enemy.

These novels demonstrate the basic attitudes of the authors on several questions: Should the churches of America become involved in the economic and social problems of the day? If so, why? If the duty is clear, then what methods are fitting? The answer is that the church had to become an active participant in fostering not only spiritual but economic and social reform. Why? Because the Golden Rule and our historical sense of justice said so. When pressed, some of the authors allowed, though not in so many words, that a measure of the authority of both the Golden Rule and our sense of justice was the degree to which they were flouted and disobeyed.

How was the church to lead? To this question there was no consistent answer. Methods ranged from charity to self-help to the single tax to no taxation, and more. The one constant to which almost all appealed was justice, by which they meant the justice promulgated in Christian ethics and the justice of the civil lawmakers and courts. As to the last question, could the church really help if it so desired, the question was ordinarily rhetorical. The obvious answer—to which the whole genre of social Christian fiction gave testimony—was yes, of course. Only in *God's Rebel* and *The Social Revolution* were the authors so disillusioned and bitter that the answer was no.

In another area of theological concern prominent in the novels—arguments over dogma, ritual, and denominationalism itself—authors who argued for a liberalization of approaches to social problems predominated, though conservative resistance was by no means lacking. The liberals, those who wanted their churches directly involved in social reform on the side of the working man, generally argued for a relaxation of rigid dogmatism in two fundamental ways: First, in order for Christianity to remain a vital force, it had to keep up with the changing social and economic developments of the nation; such vitality was impossible within a strictly denominational framework. Fratricidal sectarianism—various interpretations of the Bible and ways to be baptized, saved, damned—was like so many leeches on the body of a socially active Christianity. Before living faith could be once again a powerful social and spiritual force within the nation, it had to be more united, and denominational differences and disputes had to be severely constrained or eliminated altogether.

The demand for a change in the churches' attitude was most graphically demonstrated by writers who depicted the growing estrangement between the urban workers and the churches. This point has been demonstrated repeatedly, but in one sense it cannot be emphasized too strongly. To end this estrangement was a primary goal of the organized social gospel movement. A Salvation Army worker speaking to a conservative clergyman in *About My Father's Business* summed up the demands of this movement:

"What we need to-day . . . [is] for the clergy of the larger churches to come down to a level with the common people, assuring them that they are their best friends; for the people in general cannot understand the church of to-day in its position towards them; but when men in your station come to join them in common, and to help them in their struggle, things will take a different turn."[19]

Before this estrangement could be ended, a change in theological point of view had to take place, but this was difficult to accomplish. A sudden "conversion" in the attitude of some clergymen about the church's social role was clearly an oversimplification of the problem and its solution. The clergy in America were intelligent men with years of education and training. Their views on questions of dogma and social responsibility were not acquired at random or without thought. It was not surprising that during the 1870s and 1880s American Protestantism was predominantly conservative on social issues preoccupied with the spiritual side of man as a means of combatting, or coming to terms with, the impact of science—specifically Darwinism.

The church, all of Christianity, was under attack from many sides, and it took considerable force to wrench American Protestantism away from the battle fields of intellectual rebellion and make it pay attention to what was causing a sudden dwindling of congregations. American urban workers were not concerned with Darwinism, and they had probably never heard of Ernest Renan. They *were* concerned with increasing social inequality, about which the churches seemed disinterested. As Jonas Underwood, the salty old New England worker in *Murvale Eastman*, said to his wife:

"I haven't any quarrel with religion, except as it tends to make the strong stronger and the weak weaker, or palliates the failure of the strong to do right, and magnifies the tendency of the weak to do wrong. . . . It honors achievement and despises failure. It esteems the strong and pities the weak. It builds churches for the rich and chapels for the poor. It gives alms to the helpless and advice to the struggling. But one that is worth saving will die before he will accept alms, and he who is struggling is only made weaker by empty-handed advice.

"In a sense I will admit, Hannah, that religion is a good thing; it enables men and women to endure what they would not otherwise submit to. That is the way it guards the peace of society. . . . It often induces the wrong-doer to adopt more tolerable methods, and always compels the oppressed to take more civilized means of righting their wrongs. In other words, it makes men endure wrong more cheerfully and seek to right it more peaceably. Without its influence the poor would kill the rich who create poverty and grow fat upon want."[20]

Jonas hit on three things at once: the church's tacit acceptance of a Spencerian interpretation of social Darwinism; the lack of social justice; and a definition of the role of religion that sounded very much like Marx's "opium of the people" dictum. The indictments were all relevant, and stinging. Protestantism was going to have to pay attention to the Jonas Underwoods. But before it could do so, there had to be changes in what was emphasized in the whole of Christian dogma. As John McAslin, one of the heroes of *The King's Highway*, said to his rich father-in-law and mother-in-law to be:

"We must feel with others, be touched by their suffering, and busy for their happiness. We must do as Christ did, lay our hands upon the poor, and even the leper, and not stand afar off and throw them a piece of gold."

"But that is the business of the church."

"Mrs. Lloyd, the church of the past is dying now of its own respectability; the church of the future must make the divine secular, and the secular divine."

"But how?"

"It must cover the whole ground of ordinary life, with its multitude of interests and requirements. It is a miserably selfish religion which busies itself about what will happen when we die, which goes to church and repeats creeds, and totally ignores the great law of human brotherhood set forth by Christ as the very rule of his Kingdom."

"The world has got to be carried on, sir," said Mr. Lloyd, with a little temper, "and pray tell me, how is the law of human brotherhood to be brought into business? It is pure nonsense! Who cares for this 'brotherhood' question, when it is a matter of push, or the chance of making a corner, or of cutting prices, or of buying in the cheapest market? You may rant about equality, human brotherhood and liberty, but what does it amount to? There are no such things in the market-places of the world.''[21]

That there was no Christian brotherhood evident in the marketplaces of the world was precisely what the majority of social Christian fiction sought to rectify. The pragmatic laissez-faire world of business had made undeclared war on at least half the principles of Christianity. But the point to be emphasized in the passage is the radical demand that the church change its dogmatic orientation from life after death to seeing to it that death did not hold sway over vast numbers of the living.

One method, one of the best, for changing doctrine was through the theological schools. If changes could be brought about there—as was increasingly the case, according to many of the novels—then there was hope.[22] Commenting on only one new discipline of the social sciences, the young minister in a novel entitled *Postmarked "Colima,"* after telling the heroine that he was leaving his small church at Land's End, Maine, for a more challenging assignment, and praising the noble and rewarding nature of the Christian ministry, predicted that the study of sociology would soon become a part of the prescribed course of study in theological seminaries across the land, and how enlightening this would be for clergy and laity alike.[23]

Two works are pertinent in respect to the effect of education on religious beliefs in general. In Helen H. C. Gardener's *Is This Your Son, My Lord?*, an interesting work that will come up again in the chapter, one of the major characters, Harvey Ball, has a discussion with his parents about religion, the basic outlines of which might sound familiar to many. His parents express hurt and surprise over the fact that Harvey does not believe in the Bible as the direct word of God. "Aren't our beliefs good enough for you, son?" they reproach him. Harvey replies:

"I have read and studied and thought in new lines and channels that were not open to you. I have tried to make good use of the opportunities you gave me, and, father, it really seems to me that this is a far higher compliment to you and to mother, than for me to have stopped where you did,—where you were forced to stop,—because you had no further opportunities to go on."[24]

Mr. and Mrs. Ball accept their son's argument, and Harvey goes ahead to be spokesman for the author's point of view—a thorough belief in the ethics of Christianity while disregarding what he considered its outworn and illogical creeds, dogmas, and rituals.

The other work that treated with education, in this case a young man's education for the ministry, was *From Heaven to New York*. In it the hero, Melville Goodheart, was not only unsuccessful in meeting the requirements for a modern church, but his failure led ultimately to his death. The author of the novel, Isaac

G. Reed, Jr., devotes a rather lengthy chapter to Melville's education for the ministry, and then recounts the reasons for the young man's failure. A mixture of satire and indignation express the author's feelings about what constituted an acceptable clergyman in the second half of the nineteenth century in America:

Now it was one of Melville's misfortunes from the start that neither his exterior nor his manner were what is commonly called "clerical." The world believes in trade-marks of all kinds: the doctor must have his gig, the judge must have his wig, the king must have his crown, the soldier must have his uniform. . . . Consequently, the priest must have his trade-mark too: he must have "clerical" looks and habits, which were precisely what Melville Goodheart did not have. He was thin, but he was not sour; he was genial, not severe; he was addicted to laughing, not sighing. True, he eschewed jewelry, and wore black; but then he wore the ordinary black necktie, not the "regulation" ministerial white cravat, and besides—horribile dictu—he was fond of a quiet game of cards and a post-prandial cigar.

He found that in theology, as in law, words are substituted for things, and that the letter of the Bible is too often adhered to, and its spirit too often and too utterly forgotten; that the Text of Scripture is worshipped, while the God of Scripture is degraded; that the word of God is forced to read like the word of a fool, and to be so interpreted as to present a mass of obscenity and absurdity—a bundle of contradictions to history, to reason, to science, to the human heart and to itself."[25]

Melville, a real person, not a stereotyped social object, did not fit the clerical "trade-mark" described. He did not fit because he was himself, not a fabricated clergyman. Then, when he went to seminary, he saw the discrepancy between what should be—the living religion of Christianity—and theology, dogma that emphasized human pettiness, vanity, and foolhardiness. Melville persevered, however, and got his degree, thinking that all would be well once he began to preach, that "the theology of life [would] atone for the theology of letters."[26]

But Melville was not a popular minister. He was honest; he did not flatter wealthy men or silly women. "He was neither a fop, a fool, nor a child, but a full-grown man as well as a clergyman." And Melville lost one ministerial post after another.

Without satire and in less impassioned prose, the hero of James W. Coulter's *The Larger Faith*, a Colorado cowboy, explains in a letter to a friend his views on the differences between real religion and orthodox forms of worship:

"You have confused religion with orthodoxy. Religion and orthodoxy are not only different things—they are opposite things and antagonistic the one to the other. They act from entirely different motives, so to speak. They spring from entirely different sources. . . . Orthodoxy recognizes no truth outside its own teachings, no road to heaven but the one fenced in by its creed. . . .

"Religion never incited a war, conducted a crusade, fought a battle or held an inquisition on the faith of any person. Orthodoxy has done all these things in the name of religion. Religion never put a human being to death. Orthodoxy has killed untold thousands."[27]

Later in the novel a Reverend Mr. Winter visits the hero's Colorado ranch as a part of a physical and mental rest cure. After listening to and talking with Bill Young, the philosophical cowboy, the minister begins to understand the "larger faith" of the title, and after some harrowing scenes with the orthodox elders and ministers of the Presbyterian Church, Winter abandons the Calvinistic faith, goes to New England, and establishes a church dedicated to the New Testament principles of Christ alone. At the close of a sermon in the new church, Mr. Winter explains that he has taken this action because, despite upbringing, habits, and assumptions of twenty-five years, and wholeheartedly believing that the members of the Presbyterian church were good people and true believers according to their personal views, "I felt impelled to withdraw . . . because the creed of the church, the dogmas, the articles of faith, were in my judgment hampering and hindering and overshadowing the cause of religion."[28]

The authors of *From Heaven to New York* and *The Larger Faith* thus make the same point: orthodox, established Protestantism had become but the shell of real Christianity. This was bad enough, but the churches, to these authors, were not just neutral and harmless. The stance of the ministers and many of the parishioners was doing real harm by approving a stereotyped hypocrisy of Christian form without content, of lip service to Christ rather than service itself.

In another novel that deals with the problems of liberalizing sectarian dogma, Elmore E. Peake's *The Darlingtons*, the approach and plot are more sophisticated than usual. Stephen Kaltenborn, a wellborn and rich Methodist minister in his thirties, comes to his profession fairly late, driven by a need to be more than a wealthy man of society and business, and he is essentially satisfied with his choice. The first church to which he is assigned is conservative, small, and midwestern, in a railroad town dominated by Charles Darlington and his family. Kaltenborn meets and falls in love with Carol Darlington, a beautiful, intelligent, and efficient young woman, a forerunner of many heroines of contemporary American fiction.

The Darlingtons belong to an unspecified "aristocratic" church, and the main conflict in the novel has to do with Stephen's attempt to win Carol and gain her acceptance, not of the Methodist church as it was, but as it could be. He expresses his motivation for working to bring about changes in Methodism when he says to Carol: "I wish I could make you understand just how I feel toward these people in my church, . . . I am not laboring to save them for heaven. I want to make them fit to live."[29]

Stephen Kaltenborn is one of the best examples of a particular faith in reason and education that is uniquely American in quality. He also well illustrates some aspects of the dilemma of Protestantism in the United States. Could the church, whose fundamental acknowledged aim is the spiritual salvation of man through enforcing dogma on the one hand and ethics on the other, give primary allegiance to the ethics in terms of social, economic, and political reform? This, in essence, was what the social gospel movement tried to bring about, and its partial success was paradoxically at the expense of its spiritual power.

In a later part of the same novel Kaltenborn asks Carol to give up a theater party because his church has hired an evangelist who plans to give a ringing sermon on the evils of the theater.

"My people are poor," he says, "and belong to a democratic church. Many of your pleasures are hopelessly beyond their reach, and others of them cross their consciences. For me, their pastor, to associate with you, is a thorn in their flesh at best. I have seen it all along, and it has troubled me. More than once I have thought it my duty to give up your friendship, for the sake of the work I have already given up so much for. But you have helped me in more ways than one, and I am doubtful even now as to what my duty is. Yet those doubts will be removed if you persist in giving your party; for, take my word for it, I see a crisis at hand."[30]

Carol gives up the party and marries Kaltenborn, but the author leaves unresolved the tangled questions of how to cope with class differences, narrow church dogma, and the social role of the church.

What the novel really illustrates is a much larger problem—the tension between the theory of pure democracy predicated on a static unchanging equality of men and the idea of social progress, which meant change led by an undemocratic elite. The key sentence in the passage cited above is the first one. One of the logical extensions of commentary critical of dogmatic denominationalism as a block to social Christian reform was an offensive against denominationalism per se. In novels that argue this position, the authors, instead of asking for spiritual and social reform within a particular Protestant denomination, reason that organization by denomination is itself an enemy of true Christian action; since all worship the same God as presented in the Bible, what is needed is unified Protestant action, regardless of differing dogma.

The best example of an elaboration of this attitude is Washington Gladden's *The Christian League of Connecticut*, a work wholly dedicated to the principles of nondenominational Christian cooperation in reform, relief, and home missionary work.[31] The Christian League of the book is the idea of Walter Franklin, banker, and Theodore Strong, minister of the Second Congregational Church of New Albion, Connecticut. Little by little the two men convince virtually all of the Protestant denominations of the town to become members of the league whose ideals and work are expressed in its constitution.[32] Gladden overcomes the problem of theology and dogma versus social action in the most obvious way—by utterly dividing the two. The league is to be concerned solely with secular problems; "doctrinal and theological discussions of any kind" are never to be allowed at its meetings.

There were a number of other writers who, while they did not present anti-sectarian appeals, did espouse as the major theme of their books nondenominationalism as one part of their attempt to involve the church in reform. Such works as *The Burden of Christopher*, *The Larger Faith*, and *Salome Shepard, Reformer* all take this position.[33] *The King's Highway* and *Souls in Pawn* devote lengthy sections to arguing the necessity of reducing denominational influence. In the former, for example, the hero of the novel argues for unity regardless of denomination:

"The Church of the future will . . . not teach men Methodism, or Presbyterianism, or Catholicism; she will teach them justice, truth, tolerance, humanity to the whole animal world, and a boundless loving-kindness and pity for the sick, the morally and mentally deficient, the poor and the suffering. She will not pass by any wrong that may spring from the circumstances of the day; she will be justly angry at it, and with unrelenting perseverance get that wrong definitely stamped and transfixed."[34]

In *Souls in Pawn* the heroine, trying to reclaim Richard, a renegade Catholic, maintains that "there is only one church and Christ is the door to it." She allows that "some people try to get in through the rungs of Saint Peter's chair." But Christ is the only door, and "if any man enter in he shall be saved." Richard asks whether her church had no creed. She replies, "None whatever, except belief in Christ." We stand "for an undenominational Gospel."[35]

Sixty pages later, Richard is still unconvinced, and brings up the matter to her again. Katherine replies,

"It matters not what church you go to, but it matters a great deal what you are. I am not trying to make a Protestant of you. I care not what creed you subscribe your name to, as long as Christ is the founder of it, and the One in which it lives and moves and has its being."

"That is very broad; you are indeed liberal," said Richard, looking at her in amazement.

"The Gospel is liberal; therefore I am," said Katherine. "Faith in Christ and forgiveness through His atoning blood is the sum and substance of it. Roman Catholics, Baptists, Episcopalians, Methodists, Presbyterians, and all the other members of the evangelical faith believe the same thing. They only differ in the non-essentials. The only thing that I demand is that the non-essentials be according to the Word of God. It is only in the matter of church government that many of the sects differ at all."[36]

Stalwart denominational resistance to such attitudes and approaches encompassed much more than "church government," and Katherine had very different conceptions of what constituted "non-essentials" than those writers who fought any change in matters of dogma. For those individuals it was their interpretation of the Bible, sincerely believed in, that was the reason for their denomination; to attack their interpretation was for them tantamount to attacking Christianity.

A number of the novels well illustrate this attitude. As might be anticipated, the Reverend Mr. Jones of *Uncle Sam's Bible*, speaking from his own righteously dogmatic point of view, had an easy solution:

"If those who cannot receive all the teachings of the Bible on all subjects, without any reserve or any qualifications whatever, would profess themselves infidels and leave the church, the Gospel, religion, would be a great gainer. It is the traitors within, and not the skeptics without, who injure religion and hinder the establishment of Christ's kingdom in the world.''[37]

From a more oblique angle, in his sustained, bitter attack on the evil AntiLabor family, the author of *"Our Best Society"* put it:

The great AntiLabor church of Boomtown was a scientific church, a great broadminded liberal church. In this church everybody was allowed to profess just what he or she chose to profess, as long as he or she worshiped the great AntiLabors, and professed just what they did. The great AntiLabor church was a progressive church, it submitted every subject to the test of reason, and professed what best suited their moral and business interests and tastes.

They weighed Christ in the balance and gave Him credit of having been a very good man, of simple habits, for his day and age; and after thoroughly investigating the history of the Creator kindly permitted Him to be worshiped in their church. Such was the piety of Our Best Society in Boomtown.[38]

The passage is representative of the ambivalence that many of the novels show. While *"Our Best Society"* often argues the humanity of Christianity on reasonable, commonsense grounds, the author could turn around and scorn the evil AntiLabors for "submit[ting] every subject to the test of reason," thus equating reason with pragmatic, business-minded injustice and opposing it to the ideal reasonable humanism of the New Testament.

Again obliquely from a completely different vantage, the author of *John and I and The Church* in a chapter called "The Church has a Boom" records what happens when the heroine's husband's simple evangelical preaching rather suddenly becomes too provincial for the nouveaux riches of their prospering city.

After a while we came to understand. The church wanted a preacher with a "record" behind him like a trotting-horse or a fast-time engine. One who had shone in New York or London or Chicago, as pastor of some "tony" Church; one who would "cover a multitude of sins," especially such trifling sins as beset our church. They wanted a minister whose discourses would be flowery and sparkling with imagination; who would choose a text occasionally from somewhere outside of the Bible, and also indulge in "lovely quotations from the poets."[39]

This situation could almost be projected into the setting of Elmore Peake's *The Darlingtons*. The problem: how did one raise the level of intellectual sophistication of a denomination or congregation and sharpen its sense of moral responsibility toward social and economic problems without sacrificing spiritual content and fundamental dogma? The answers were varied, but few were entirely satisfactory.

Many other novels deal in one way or another with a conservative defense of separate denominationalism.[40] Of them, one especially militant example deserves special comment—*Mr. World and Miss Church-Member; or, The Secret Service of Satan. An Allegory*, by the Reverend William S. Harrris.[41]

The tone of the novel is set in the Introduction by Bishop Rudolph Dubbs. After lavish praise of the work both as literature and as showing the "various efforts of Satan and his agents to lead Christians away from God and day," he ends by saying that he hopes that in the second edition of Mr. Harris's work he will attack the evils of the theater more fully but "not unmask Satan so early in his intercourse with the worldly church."[42] To my knowledge there was no second edition.

In one section of the allegory Miss Church-Member, who through misguided charitable efforts to save Mr. World was on the path to hell herself, is fitted with a special pair of evil glasses that "illuminate" the Bible for her in very questionable terms. The narrator of the novel, watching the panorama of Miss Church-Member's gradual fall from grace, had with him one Blackana, an agent of the Devil who interpreted his master's various schemes for trapping the unwary. When the narrator asked Blackana what he thought of Miss Church-Member, he replied:

"Satan estimates such a one as a valuable aid to his cause, for she is now working against Jesus Christ on her imaginary road to Heaven. Nothing is more helpful to Satan than when members of the church believe that parts of the Bible are untrue. It is indeed gratifying to us," continued Blackana with a fiendish smile, "to see the twentieth century of the so-called Christian era opening with the church wrangling over her Bible more desperately than ever, and some of the learned leaders, and those of lesser light, laying the lash on him who believes that the regularly revised version of Scripture is of sufficient authority and approved of God."[43]

It is seldom, and only in situations of the utmost importance, that God Himself speaks in the novel, and when He does He makes clear His attitude on the "higher criticism" and "learned leaders" tampering with the Word. Scripture is to be accepted as it is.

Later in the journey of the unfortunate couple, in a chapter labeled "The Rival Churches," Mr. World and Miss Church-Member go to a church where there is much pomp and ritual that she finds very satisfying. During the sermon the minister suggests that the theater, music and the dance could be helpful to man's spiritual and natural life, and that, as a student, a man would do well to know of "some milder types of indulgence" so that he could then "be better qualified to defend the right and resist the wrong."[44]

Miss Church-Member finds the arguments very appealing and enjoys the service thoroughly—she is well on the way to damnation by now—and when Mr. World suggests she formally change her sectarian alliance, she readily agrees that this might be wise. Mr. World takes her to the home of the minister who gave the sermon. The minister, after listening to her previous religious views, which she now sees as bigoted, invites her to join his church, explaining, however, that anyone wishing to join his church had to agree, among other things, to seek social respectability, always "manifest a liberal spirit so as to keep in touch with the progress of the world," know all phases of life possible, cultivate grace and culture, and go to church faithfully, "except in cases of sickness or disinclination."

When finally asked whether she would like to become a member of the church described, Miss Church-Member declines, giving for her reason that she believed she could do more good by staying in her own church and seeking quietly to change it from within by "trying to get some of its members to be more like I am." She adds, "I always had a missionary spirit."

Mr. World and the minister agree and the minister adds, "And may you succeed in your plans, . . . There are millions who belong to my church in spirit, but who hold visible connection with some radical church of the King's Highway."[45]

Mr. Harris makes quite clear that any deviation from orthodoxy—a specific denomination is not mentioned in the novel, but the tone is unremittingly Calvinistic—leads swiftly and surely to hell. This reactionary stance combined with strong anti-intellectualism is an extreme one but represents one measure of resistance to theological scholarship, the social gospel, and change in general.

Interestingly, there are no novels whose theme was a specific attack on the tenets of the social gospel movement itself. It at least seems plausible that someone, in the late 1890s, for example, might have written a novel that openly condemned the social gospel movement as detrimental to what he or she considered the true spirit of Christianity—concern for the soul of man both on earth and after death. This person might have maintained that the social gospel, by involving the church in political and economic disputes, would ultimately weaken the power and prestige of Christianity by involving it in the marketplace, thereby making it just one more tool to be manipulated.

One possible reason why no such work, at least to my knowledge, was written is that the conservatives either ignored the social gospel or they avoided it by using the diversionary tactics of evangelicalism, especially "radical adventism," of which the Jehovah's Witnesses and Plymouth Brethren are the most famous. Dispensational premillennialism and sanctification had interdenominational appeal, and the seeds of Fundamentalism as we know it today were sown during the period. The Fundamentalists did not care about social gospel tenets, except to condemn the "worldliness" of the churches and leaders who espoused its values.[46]

The question of evaluating the social Christian novel as an agent of social action or as an instrument of evangelism is pertinent here. Grier Nicholl has pointed out that Henry F. May, William D. McLaughlin, Jr., and H. Richard Niebuhr believed that evangelical revivalism became "increasingly divorced from the Protestant movement of social and economic reform known as the 'social gospel.' "[47] Nicholl disagrees. He supports Timothy L. Smith's position, expressed in *Revivalism and Social Reform*, that evangelical revivalism in the North stimulated Protestant missions in the northern slums. Specifically, Nicholl contends that "contrary to the assumption that evangelism and the social gospel were incompatible, many Christian social novels demonstrate the positive impact of evangelism upon the social gospel.''[48]

It can be argued that the two differing interpretations of evangelism—sectarian soul saving versus social action—were to a large extent either clarified or resolved in these novels. Evangelism can have two different meanings: first, a movement that seeks to gain individual commitment to Christ; second, in its more general sense, militant or crusading zeal. Both senses are well illustrated in social Christian fiction.

As we saw in Chapter 1, the first type of social Christian fiction was written by men and women who were abstractly concerned with social discontent but who suggested only the most vague humanitarian clichés as solutions. The authors actually spoke as evangelical capitalists whose primary aim was to maintain a social system wherein their methods of gaining wealth would be secure. Evangelism in the sense of bringing souls to Christ was almost nonexistent in these novels. Selected biblical principles (mostly from the Old Testament) were used only as a device for keeping the laborers subservient.

The second type of social Christian fiction advocated social improvement by means of upper-class leadership and the stewardship of wealth. The authors of this kind of novel generally had the same goals as the authors of the first type, except that the action proposed is more specifically softened by a humanitarianism whose appeal is based both on the pride of being a philanthropist and abstract New Testament Christianity. This category of social gospel fiction, substantial in size, was probably written by liberal clergy and church members who were in the forefront of the intellectual/theological battles of the day, especially those controversies involving modern science, philosophy, and scholarship. But these same men and women in the mainstream of Protestant liberalism were often complacent and conservative when it came to contemporary social and political issues. Ahlstrom importantly points out that ''Social Gospelers were usually theological liberals; but the statement cannot be reversed.''[49]

In the category of the social gospel novel, the situation is very different. Most of these workers are evangelical in both senses. Their authors saw that the Christian denominations were losing their hold on the new urban industrial class. They saw that this new working class was oppressed and downtrodden in a way inimical to New Testament Christian doctrine and the tenets of American democracy. And they saw that the Protestant churches of America were unwilling to seek to rectify or change either of the above situations.

In these novels it would appear that the controversy over evangelism for Christ versus evangelism as a stimulator of social action would be dramatized, but I do not believe that it is. Virtually all writers of social gospel fiction were evangelical in both senses, and logically so because of the problems they saw. *Would Christ Belong to a Labor Union?* is an archetypal example of the social gospel novel, and its author, Cortland Myers, argues that the foundation of the belief in the social and economic principles of free enterprise under a republican system of government is to be found, finally, not in dedication to a particular political and economic theory, but in the teachings of Christ as expounded in the New Testament. He maintains that the poverty and oppression experienced by the new industrial working class resulted from the practices of men of wealth and power who used the political and economic freedoms available to them while turning their backs on the moral responsibilities and teachings of Christ. He further argues that it is the responsibility of the Christian churches of America as institutions dedicated to expounding and explicating the word of God, and as keepers of the collective conscience of the people of the United States, to see that the injustices and wrongs attendant upon industrialization are rectified.

Thus Myers, as representative of the social gospel novelist, crusades for Christ *and* for social reform. Both the employer and employee must first of all be brought back to belief in, and a practical regard for, the New Testament principles of Christianity. Once this has been done, the majority of the disputes between capital and labor will be resolved because those on both sides will live their lives according to the doctrines of Christ. (The relevance of *In His Steps* is obvious here.) Finally, it is then the role of the institutionalized churches of America to pass judgment on how far men conduct their lives according to Christian ethics. So the two strands of evangelism become one, though the active belief in Christ and a life patterned on His teachings are the binding force.

This brings us back to the point that no novels directly attack the principles of the social gospel movement. This does not mean that there is no fiction that opposes what liberal Christian reformers were seeking to accomplish, only that there is no fictional frontal assault. As already illustrated, the authors of the first two types of social Christian fiction were not motivated by any desire to change either the political or economic climate of the Gilded Age. They sought to soften the effects of economic privation and social injustice only enough to secure the system from open rebellion and class warfare. And the authors of the novels were often very clever. Like those of their more secular counterparts, their answers to social and economic unrest came from very carefully selected biblical tenets: "servants obey your masters"; "the poor ye have always with you"; this life is only a vale of tears to be endured until judgment after death, and organized charity. When attacked for not truly being Christian, these men, righteously indignant, vehemently denied the charge. It all depended on what principles of the Bible one supported.

It is also clear that in some cases the question of denominationalism was relevant to the issue of a conservative defense of the status quo, and the medium was old-fashioned evangelical sectarianism itself. *The Darlingtons*, *John and I and the Church*, and *Mr. World and Miss Church-Member* are all instructive on this point. The protagonist of *The Darlingtons*, Stephen Kaltenborn, was trying to educate the congregation of his small midwestern church away from narrow Methodist doctrines that led to fundamental distrust of the arts and humanities. The narrator of *John and I and the Church* revealed in some respects a congregation's change in perhaps the very way that Kaltenborn sought—an interest and response to the humanities and the intellectual life. But John, the minister, was not trained in these things, did not see their relevance to the Christian life, and was eventually dismissed from his pastorate because the people wanted a more "tony" minister. In *Mr. World and Miss Church-Member* denominational doctrines are again closely related to militant anti-intellectualism.

It can be argued that most sectarian disputes were presented in terms of a liberalization of dogma that had strong secular/reform overtones versus a conservative resistance to change both theologically and in the realm of social and economic issues—or, put another way, *The Darlingtons* versus *Mr. World and Miss Church-Member*.

This interpretation gains further strength from a series of works whose themes are strictly denominational in nature: *Alice McDonald; or, the Heroine of Principle*; *A Story of the Early Cumberland Church*; *Westbrook Parsonage*; *Is This Your Son, My Lord?*; *Bryan Maurice*, and *Philip MacGregor*.[50] *Alice McDonald* tells the story of the conversion of the McDonald family and their neighbors from old-time orthodox Presbyterianism to the marginally more liberal doctrines of the Cumberland Presbyterians. *Westbrook Parsonage* is the story of a low churchman's battle against High Anglicanism on the road to Rome. *Is This Your Son, My Lord?* satirizes both transcendental Unitarianism and High Anglicanism, commenting that the two are not really religions at all but bizarre mixtures of Judaism, Paulinism, Buddhism, ethical culture, and nineteenth-century platonism.[51] The last two novels both tell of young men seeking faith that would satisfy the spirit as well as the mind. Bryan Maurice eventually becomes a High Anglican. Philip MacGregor comes to his redemption and death through a combination of Catholicism, Anglicanism, and Unitarianism, though the essential substance of his faith is Roman Catholic.

Social issues as such are not argued in any of these five novels; however, this kind of novel displays two elements of importance to the social gospel movement. First, the theologically conservative protagonists in the works are pictured as socially conservative. Second, by engaging in denominational quarrels, and writing novels about them, the authors show the concerns of their respective faiths, and these concerns are not social and economic but metaphysical and doctrinal. None of the five novels speaks to political or economic issues; their characters are inwardly motivated, not outwardly. The social realities that led to the social gospel to begin with were irrelevant to the author's concerns.

Another interesting characteristic of these—*Westbrook Parsonage*, *Is This Your Son, My Lord?*, *Bryan Maurice*, *Philip MacGregor*—is that each points in two directions: the logic of Catholicism as the stronghold of a firm emotional commitment to Christianity undiluted by demands of reason, history, and science, and the direct opposite—the pull of rationalized agnosticism and atheism strengthened by too many compromises between faith and an increasingly materialistic, scientific, and pragmatic age.

Of more immediate interest is the attitude of writers of social Christian fiction to the Roman Catholic church. Out of the 145 works considered in this survey, only twenty mention Catholicism, and of these, some do so only in the most casual manner. In very few cases is there a direct attack on the church. One can only speculate why this is true. Although national attitudes were by no means as extreme as during the attacks of Lyman Beecher in 1834 and the Maria Monk scandal of 1836, the general feeling against Catholicism was still strong. Aaron Abell quoted James E. Yeatman, a reform leader in St. Louis, as saying that the Catholic church was fastening upon American cities in order "that she may take possession of the nation."[52] In 1885 Richard T. Ely noted that the "Catholic revealed an acquaintance with the movements of the masses—the Protestant ignorance."[53] At a Cincinnati Conference of the Methodist Episcopal Church in 1889 the minutes of the meetings contained the statement: "Too long has Rome been allowed a practical monopoly of the humanitarian agencies of religion."[54]

Considering the fact that the "New Immigration" from Catholic eastern and southern Europe began in the middle and late 1880s, and that concern was voiced about these events well before the turn of the century, it is genuinely surprising that the novels do not have more to say about Catholicism than they do. Of the novels that do express an attitude toward the church, seven of the twenty were either neutral or praised the church. Even in the remaining thirteen works, the authors of only four, including the already noted *Westbrook Parsonage* with its strong low church bias, devote any sizeable portion of their novels to attacking Catholicism.

As examples of praise, Katherine Woods's *Metzerott, Shoemaker* is perhaps the most striking. One of the major characters is not only a Roman Catholic priest but a dedicated and outspoken Christian socialist as well. Quotations from the novel in the last part of Chapter 1 illustrate the priest's stand as well as the author's approving attitude.

Another work that praises Catholicism is *Camerton Slope* by R. F. Bishop.[55] The story deals with events in a coal mining town in Pennsylvania, specifically various battles between the heroes—Scotch miners—and the villains—Irish miners, especially those who were in league with the Molly Maguires. As a counterbalance to the bad Catholic Irish, the hero of the novel is Roman Catholic Father Rafferty. It is through Father Rafferty that Methodists, Baptists, Presbyterians, and Catholics get along very well with each other in the novel. He, moreover, is one of the main characters responsible for the defeat of the Mollies.

Is This Your Son, My Lord? has some interesting passages on the Catholic Church. The heroine's father, John Stone, praises the church's consistency.[56] Mr. Stone takes an absolute stand. His contempt for extended metaphorical and symbolic interpretations of Christianity as a means of dismissing historical and scientific evidence is sharp and to the point.

From another vantage, even an extremely conservative allegory somewhat similar to *Mr. World and Miss Church-Member*, the Reverend Albert B. King's *Memorable Voyages of Rebel and Victory*, has qualified praise for *true* Christians within the Catholic faith. How "true Roman Catholic Christians" are to be separated from other Catholics the author does not explain.[57]

In the fiction that attacks Catholicism, it is interesting to note the authors' grounds. In *Annie Cooper's Friends* the author attacks the church for having burned Joan of Arc. In Mattie Boteler's *The Conversion of Brian O'Dillon* the hero is not a Christian initially, for his mother was Catholic, a drunkard, and "under the malevolent influence of a priest." Without going into specific detail, Boteler sees obvious cause-and-effect relationships between the priest's "malevolent influence" and the hero's infidelity. When O'Dillon is converted, it is, of course, to Protestantism.

Julia M. Wright's *A Plain Woman's Story*, the only one of Mrs. Wright's many works that mentions Catholicism, does so in a curious context. At one point in the novel the heroine, Joan Hazzard, is explaining the mechanics of her relief work to a friend, and in the process complains that

"the priest, who has never contributed a dime to the support of my house or any one in it, undertakes to interfere with my administration by giving orders to my inmates about their conduct here, and presumes to set aside my rules. It is the prejudice of the priest, not the conscience of the girl, which speaks. If I begin to administer my house to suit the notions of those who have nothing to do with it, I shall soon have disorder and ruin."[58]

Wright voices an attitude that was commonly expressed—that Catholics had a prejudice against the Bible and were not allowed to read it without ecclesiastical supervision and interpretation. In this particular case the author never explains how the priest interferes with the mechanics of the heroine's Working Woman's Bureau or what becomes of the girl involved.

When the subject of Roman Catholicism comes up in *About My Father's Business*, it does so in a manner similar to that of Harriet McKeever's *Westbrook Parsonage*—as fear of pomp and "sensuous display" that corrupts the faithful. In *About My Father's Business*, it is the very Methodist Mr. Bushwick, operator of a mission that the new minister of Bushwick's church opposes, who explains:

"The Methodist Church is taking on the ideas of the Romish Church as fast as is possible, and I really believe that the time has come in the church's history, that a good revival must break out in order to save the reputation which she bears. The next thing you will see will be the burning of incense, and I don't doubt that there are preachers to-day that would try it, if they did not fear church censure."[59]

And in Milton Scott's *Henry Elwood*, the hero, who is at this time a Presbyterian minister suspected of heresy, says to one of his interrogators:

"If our business is to quicken the spiritual life of our people, we need to be ourselves quickened by the Spirit of the Lord; and where the Spirit of the Lord is, there is LIBERTY! I do not object to the infallibility of the Pope because he is a bad man, or to the infallibility of the Catholic church because it is a bad institution; but because to recognize the infallibility of either would do violence to my reason, and deprive me of many individual functions which it is both my privilege and duty to exercise. Our Confession of Faith, when first framed, was very largely an assertion of individual liberty and a protest against authority; and to make it a means of binding men's consciences and restricting their thought—which we are apt to do when we interpret it too literally—is not only to misunderstand it, but to pervert its meaning and object."[60]

Here is explicitly stated what has been commented on earlier—the American synthesis of eighteenth-century principles of reason and political liberty with the spirit of Protestantism in terms of "individual liberty and a protest against authority." As Elwood says, his rejection of Catholicism is on the grounds of the church's presumption of infallibility. In like terms, he eventually repudiates Presbyterianism for reasons similar to Alice McDonald's, because its dogmas and articles of the Confession of Faith have become absolutes that restrict the use of his questing reason.

In the novels thus far, the reasons for anti-Catholic remarks have been varied though specific—from unhappiness over the martyrdom of Joan of Arc to a distrust of the aesthetic appeal of portions of the Catholic service as a satanic snare; from a correlation between female alcoholism and being a Catholic to the more rational complaint about restrictions placed on personal liberty by faith in the infallibility of the Pope. Only in *A Plain Woman's Story* is the complaint directly related to reform and mission work, although Mr. Bushwick in *About My Father's Business* strongly implies that the Methodist minister of his church wants to close the church-supported mission because the minister is leaning toward Catholicism.

Only three novels (excluding *Westbrook Parsonage*) contain what might be considered sustained attacks on Catholicism—Mary Ellen Bamford's *Jessie's Three Resolutions*, Harriette A. Keyser's *Thorns in Your Sides*, and the Reverend Henry Morgan's *Boston Inside Out!* In the first of these, the author is concerned with missionary work, both at home and abroad, and her dislike of Catholicism centers on Catholic influence in South America and Portugal. Without ever being concrete, Mary Ellen Bamford expresses her conviction that the teachings of Catholicism are quite simply wrong, and she laments the effectual Catholic domination of various parts of the world.

Her Jessie reads an encyclopedia article about Ecuador and laments that Roman Catholicism is the only Western religion sanctioned in that nation, "and the Catholic Church not modified . . . as in America by contact daily with protestantism, but the Catholic Church in all the blackness of its ignorance, and wickedness, and superstition, in a land where protestantism is forbidden."[61]

Throughout the novel the heroine is given to such statements as, "O Church of Rome! How strong you are! What can I do against your strength?"[62] Such comments are interspersed with praise for her own church: "I am proud of my denomination. . . . The Baptists do aspire to the best things—accuracy and clearness in translation."[63]

The situation in Harriette A. Keyser's *Thorns in Your Sides* is quite different in that the author's anti-Catholicism shows itself in the intricacies of the plot.

The novel, set in New York City, concerns the combat between an Anglican priest, the Reverend Dan Guardian, and his archenemy, Catholic Terence O'Farrell. Guardian, the hero, is considered the general enemy of Catholics for they regard him, along with the whole Anglican church, as renegades from the true church. O'Farrell, portrayed as an illiterate Irish hod carrier, alderman, and dynamiter, vehemently hates Guardian because O'Farrell has found that the medieval ancestors of the two men had fought in Britain and that the Angles had beaten the Irish. O'Farrell is determined to avenge this ancient insult. To this end he teams up with a Russian anarchist demolition expert and the two of them destroy St. Agnes's, the Reverend Guardian's church. The minister and his daughter are fortunately spared by means of a premonition; but O'Farrell escapes to Europe just before he is to be arrested, and eventually he manages to achieve his vengeance when Guardian and his daughter visit Ireland.

Catholic political domination is one of the major themes of a book written by the Reverend Henry Morgan called *Boston Inside Out! Sins of a Great City! A Story of Real Life*.[64] In its impassioned bigotry against the Church, the novel is unique among the works studied. The portrayal of Father Titus as a greedy libertine who rapes a young girl who has come for confession and drives another into madness is melodramatically repulsive. The Reverend Morgan, narrator of the novel and a composite of William Lloyd Garrison and Anthony Comstock, relishes battling, not slavery, but the evil trinity of "Drink, Transcendental Unitarianism, and Roman Catholicism."

In the course of the novel Father Titus explains how the Church had traditionally worked to gain political control of a nation:

"The policy of our church in every country is to side with the minority party; to gain their gratitude by substantial help, so that when the day of prosperity arrives we may ride with them into power. In America the Democratic party best subserves our ends and aims,—through that party, which is strong in great cities, our influence is felt in every department of municipal government. The bulk of our strength lies in the cities. Yes, Brother Poindexter, our church is a powerful organization. To sum up, the poor believe in us. The Democrats swear by us. Politicians are afraid of us. Convicts cling to us as to an ark of refuge. Gamblers who reverence nothing else, reverence our religion. Before the priests they take their hats off and humbly say, '*Your Reverence*.' In short, wherever sin, poverty, and crime exist in large masses, there is our harvest-field, and there we reap a prolific harvest; for Holy Mother Church alone supplies the great want of nature,— shifting upon herself, the burden of moral and spiritual responsibility, and taking away the fear, the dread, the very sting of death. The true test of religion is the death-bed. It is only the child of the true church whose pathway to heaven is made smooth and placid, and devoid of every source of terror."[65]

This novel, full of bigoted emotional appeals of all kinds, is the only one of its kind found during my research.

These novels, then—*Westbrook Parsonage*, *Jessie's Three Resolutions*, *Thorns in Your Sides*, and *Boston Inside Out*—illustrate the range of attitudes and approaches toward Catholicism apparent in the social Christian novels that deal with the subject at any length. Generalizations about the four are hard to make. One common characteristic is a hatred and fear of Catholicism, and in the last two at least, these feelings are based on an inability to estimate the full power of the Church, especially on a political basis. Even on this subject however, it is noteworthy that the authors' arguments are either vague and general or based on emotional rhetoric. In no case is the church systematically attacked as a force aligned against social reform or as a power antithetical to American democracy. And it is significant how little comment, pro or con, the Roman church receives in the novels. The majority of social Christian novelists apparently recognized that the Catholic church was not the villain responsible for the social and economic problems of the time, nor did they evidently feel that it was a fundamental cause in the decline of Protestantism as a social force. It should be pointed out that the Catholic church in the United States was generally conservative during the last half of the nineteenth century and explicitly attempted to avoid criticism. Both Pope Leo XIII and Pope Pius X were conservative in doctrinal and social affairs.[66]

I have noted earlier that in a few novels, such as *Is This Your Son, My Lord?* and *Philip MacGregor*, their authors' positions toward Catholicism and the question of faith in general are the result of a confrontation between reason and emotional religious commitment. In them and others the dualism between faith and reason takes on the aspect of an either/or choice. If some form of religious dogmatism, as an absolute standard, is a logical position to take with regard to the relentless demands of reason, science, and history, its antithesis—agnosticism or atheism—is the other. Five works deal with this theme in some detail.[67] In *Doubting Castle, Henry Elwood*, and *The Only Way Out* the authors show their protagonists' internal struggles between religious faith and the dictates of reason founded on scientific investigations, which apparently conflict with various statements in the Bible. In each work the central characters either maintain their faith or are finally converted. In *Mr. World and Miss Church-Member* the author is content to make a wholesale anti-intellectual attack on any of the branches of science that cast doubt on a literal interpretation of biblical truth. Only in *Is This Your Son, My Lord?* does the author argue the cause of intellectual knowledge at the expense of spiritual comfort.

Since *Mr. World and Miss Church-Member* will be discussed in Chapter 3, some comment on Helen H. C. Gardener's *Is This Your Son, My Lord?* and Milton R. Scott's *Henry Elwood* will represent the positions taken in all five novels. Scott argues against agnosticism while presenting the agnostic's case in detail. The novel is cast in the form of a series of arguments between Elwood, a liberal Presbyterian minister, and his friend, Professor Humboldt, a teacher of natural science at the state university in the town where Henry is established. The professor uses empirical arguments in a lengthy debate against "flexible" theology.[68] A climax is reached in the following exchange:

"Are you claiming, then, that Christianity is a subject of evolution, instead of a direct and absolute revelation from heaven?" asked the Professor, with some assurance.

"Rather do I claim that it is a revelation from heaven *and* a subject of evolution. If evolution is the universal law or principle of the universe, why should not Christianity be brought within its scope and operation? Why should it not adapt itself to the advances of science and the development of the human intellect? Why should it not have leave to GROW, as well as the trees and the grass that are before our eyes?"[69]

Finally, at the end of the debate, after Professor Humboldt asks how Elwood knows that his religious conceptions are true if they are ever changing and evolving, Henry braces himself in the Cartesian corner and answers with his proof of God's existence: "I believe—I know—that he is, because I am; and I know that I am, because he is!"[70] Thus, since God is, and could do anything, including increase human knowledge on all fronts, Elwood, and other theologians, could, indeed should, from time to time change their outlook on the nature and manifestation of divine truth.

Passages already commented upon from Mrs. Gardener's *Is This Your Son, My Lord?* pertain to the same question. The author sums up her position when she has John Stone say to his friend Edward Ball:

"If you believe without a doubt, the story of the creation, the Garden of Eden legend, the snake tale,—which is necessary to the fall of man,—and the 'In Adam all men died' theory; if you accept the possibility of vicarious atonement, and can think it not a vicious idea; if you believe Christ was a God and had no human father, and that his death could in any way relieve you of your own responsibility, or make an All-Wise God change his mind about damning you; if you are sure of such a God, such a creation, such a temptation, such a fall, such a Christ, such an atonement, and that it could have the results claimed,—then you are able to argue with some show of consistency. But drop one single link, admit one single doubt or question, and you are gone. Your whole system is worthless."[71]

Mr. Ball is convinced by Mr. Stone's dramatic either/or presentation and, with some reluctance, accepts an agnostic position.

The same kind of discussion takes place early in Scott's novel when Henry Elwood and his good friend Homer Vernon are in Union Theological Seminary. Vernon is assailed with doubts about the absolute validity of miracles and the Bible itself and announces his intention to leave the seminary for medical school. Henry, who has had some of the same doubts, argues with his friend, but Vernon cannot accept any arguments that prove that the writers of the Bible were above all error or any possibility of error and leaves the seminary.

Years later, when Vernon is a medical doctor and Elwood has finished his religious training, the two men meet and again discuss the subject of faith. At the end of the conversation Vernon says:

"I was taught that the message of the preacher was given to him in the Bible, in plain and distinct terms, and that all he had to do was to declare it to men, whether they would receive it or not—such at least was my understanding of the teaching I received. Still I believe some preachers are taking a wider range now, and are trying to reconcile Christianity with Reason and Science and Philosophy, instead of proving its divine origin by miracles and prophecies. I even read in a paper the other day that the influence of German Rationalism is beginning to be felt in Union Seminary, and that some of its professors are denying the infallibility or the 'inerrancy' of the Bible. Preaching has become a very different thing from what I supposed it was when I quit the Seminary. Doctors of Divinity lose faith in their specific remedies and their formulated prescriptions as well as Doctors of Medicine—and both of them continue to practice their professions because the people need their services and call for them. I guess there is some analogy between their cases after all.''[72]

While Vernon is aware of changes in theological thinking, he is not really happy with them. He still believes, or wants to believe, that Christianity should not attempt to reconcile reason and science, that faith in the divine nature of Christianity is the cornerstone of religious belief, and that to try to demonstrate the validity of that faith in terms of the scientific method is useless and destructive.

A number of the novels comment on the breaches, apparent or real, between religious belief and scientific truth, but none of the works deals with the consequences of the "Higher Criticism" in the depth that both *Henry Elwood* and *Is This Your Son, My Lord?* do. Instead there are asides, either in praise of religion against science or vice versa; proof of the power of scientific development to change men's lives; comments on eugenics; and forays into pseudoscience.[73]

In Margaret Robinson's *Souls in Pawn*, for example, the heroine expresses a familiar sentiment when she declares Science to be a "holy field . . . sure to become one of the strongest secular agencies of righteousness" and in the long run a buttress of religious faith.[74] Robinson's idea, expressed by numerous writers, was that the more man learned through his God-given intellect of the intricacies and complexities of the world around him, the greater would be his praise and awe of God for His creation, and for allowing humble man to learn some of what was endless possible knowledge.

In Harold M. Davis's *The City of Endeavor* there is a section of the sermon in which the minister uses an extended analogy between the power of Christian work and fellowship and generated electricity. The analogy has the tone of a plea. God can speak through science as well as through the spirit of man; man should not be deceived by the tangible manifestations of engineering feats, but should be an engineer of the spiritual world as well. It is for man to turn on the current of God and make other men feel it, make the American city holy, the city of God. In context, there is something depressingly plaintive about the appeal.[75]

A passage found in Elizabeth Grinnell's *For the Sake of a Name* describes a similar approach. Paul Silver, the minister of a slum named Deep Gutter, explains that one way to evict devilish ideas from an idle mind is to fill the mind with thoughts of Christ. "As a means to this end we lead them by the way of natural science,'' says the minister and proceeds to explain that the approach has had remarkable results.[76]

In both cases the ministers seek to use the findings of scientific method in stimulating men and women to greater faith. Science is seen not as a danger to belief but as a means of furthering it.

Some of the novels praise science and its methods as something to hold onto in a world changing a little too fast for some of the characters' comfort. For example, in trying to allay the unhappiness of the hero of Daniel C. Beard's *Moonblight*, his mentor, a professor of geology, says: "Apply this test to everything—can it be demonstrated? If so, adopt it without fear, for it is the truth, and truth is divine.''[77] The hero does so and is comforted; all he has to remember is that truth is by definition divine.

A similar attitude is expressed by a character in Ellen E. Dickinson's *The King's Daughters*, though in this case there is a note of pessimism—of retreating to the objective world of science as a last resort against the chaos of men and society, "That evening the Professor solaced himself with a protracted observation of 'his friends, the stars.' 'They shine for me,' he soliloquized, 'as they shone for David of old, matchless, pure, and unchangeable. They, at least, are never disappointing.' ''[78]

In the same stoic tone, but more specifically, the professor of economics says to the heroine of Florence Converse's *The Burden of Christopher*, "School yourself in the scientific attitude, my daughter; it is your only salvation. . . . If we cannot be hopeful, we can be scientific; though we lose all faith, we may still preserve that receptivity of mind which is the open door to science. Be receptive, my dear, and be patient.''[79] It is probably nothing more than coincidence that in the last three instances cited the statement of reliance upon science is presented by a college professor.

In Henry Fauntleroy's *Who's to Blame?* the author takes a position toward science that is unique in the novels. Toward the end of the work the great Chicago fire figures in the plot, and Fauntleroy interprets this event as an example of the direct interference of God in the lives of men. God has destroyed Chicago because it was a wicked city, as he had destroyed Sodom and Gomorrah. The author then uses this interpretation to attack the

many people who think [that] it sounds smart, and that they make an impression upon those they talk with that they are learned and scientific, by ignoring all interposition of Providence in the affairs of the world, and by ascribing all the tragedies and calamities of life to natural causes, and accounting for every event on natural principles of cause and effect.

After elaborating his point of view further, he goes on sarcastically:

How strange it is to hear men, who ought to pause in abject humility before the simple blade of grass that presents mysteries of production baffling to all science and all human comprehension, attempting, with a conceit quite equal to the immensity of the subject in size, the easiest solution of all the wonders crowding a space that has no limits, and filling a time which has neither beginning nor end—with condescending complacency dethroning God from the government of his own mighty works, and making him even unnecessary to his creation! Of course, these superior minds, whose apprehensions far surpass the sublimest plans and administration of the God who made them—the most insignificant of his works—feel the most amiable compassion for the credulity that receives as true the accounts all along through the Scriptures of physical punishment by the intervention of God for moral guilt.[80]

Among other illustrations that the author presents as evidence for his general position is the belief "that in Eastern countries where there is the most vice and wickedness, there prevail the most deadly epidemics." Because the inhabitants of those areas are not Christian, they are more wicked and their wickedness is punished by God in the form of a high death rate. After further commentary of a similar sort Fauntleroy returns to the Chicago fire and iterates his position that Chicago's destruction is justified, using the circular argument of divine intervention as a part of his proof.[81]

On another level entirely, four of the novels comment on Herbert Spencer's interpretation of social Darwinism, though in only one case is Spencer mentioned by name. The author of *John and I and the Church*, Elizabeth Grinnell, is the least critical of Spencer's position, though even she is ambivalent[82]; the other three forcefully disagree with him.

In Hulbert Fuller's *God's Rebel* the hero at one point lashed out at "the senile vagaries of Herbert Spencer to the effect that 'the necessities which Nature imposes upon us are not to be evaded, even by the joint efforts of university graduates and working-men delegates.' "[83]

Fuller's book as a whole was potent for 1899, the year in which it was published. The author, a medical doctor, was as radical in his beliefs as any of the authors discussed. In effect, he believed that the scientific method used by Darwin could liberate humanity from all sorts of restrictions—physical, mental, and spiritual.[84]

Archibald McCowan in his *Christ, the Socialist* is almost as forceful. In discussing the capitalist system, protagonist Robert Stewart attacks Spencer:

"Our present system has had every opportunity to prove itself, but its most ardent admirer can not truthfully say that it even approaches Christ's standard. Judged by the Word of God our civilization is a gigantic failure. It is the strong against the weak, the cunning and unscrupulous against the honest and unsophisticated. People talk glibly about 'the survival of the fittest,' without recognizing the irony conveyed in the expression. A late writer, commenting on this, said that society, as at present constituted, might be compared to a jungle, where the 'fittest' comprise the lions, tigers, and such other animals as, by superior strength or cunning, are enabled to prey upon the weaker denizens of the forest. Translated, I take this to mean that the fittest to survive in our nineteenth century civilization are those who, if justice were done, would probably be in the penitentiary."[85]

McCowan was sure that rationalizing laissez-faire capitalism using the law of the jungle was ultimately self-defeating. If the strong became invincible and their position impregnable enough, a social and intellectual plateau would be reached that would eventually lead to either revolution or socioeconomic suicide. The theory of unrestricted competition assumed a state of fluid economic mobility. When that mobility was lacking, as was becoming the case by the 1890s, both the theory and practice of laissez-faire broke down.[86]

Another passage, one from Percival R. Benson's *The Rev. John Henry*, helps to demonstrate the novelists' attitudes toward Darwinism. It is milder in tone than either of the preceding and emphasizes the possible role of society in striving to control the environment, rather than attacking the existing economic system, which inhibited some efforts to make that control a reality. Benson's question has a very contemporary ring.

Conduct must be a matter of the relationship between virtue and temptation. Society concerns itself with conduct. It strives to compel good conduct by punishing bad conduct. Why might it not concern itself with the environment of the individual, since upon the environment of the individual depends the measure of his virtue and his temptation, whereby conduct is largely determined?[87]

These passages are the only ones that deal with social Darwinism as such, and it is interesting to note that despite Herbert Spencer's popularity in the United States, none of these writers adopted and defended his views. Instead all, with the possible exception of Elizabeth Grinnell, emphasized humanity's ability to direct evolutionary change to some extent rather than the necessity of accepting the more brutalizing elements of survival of the fittest—which was Spencer's phrase, not Darwin's—as a given fact of life.

Unique among the novels is Charles S. Daniel's *Ai*, an example of a work that touches upon another outgrowth of Darwinism—eugenics. In a passage that was probably intended to shock the reader, Impey, the representative of radicalism in the work, says:

"We must lay it down as a hard and fast rule that humanity as we find it in the slums can only be improved on principles of Natural Selection."

"By that you mean what?"

"That men can be improved only by aiding and cultivating the fittest; the farmer would say, by killing off bad stock, and carefully crossing the best stock, and giving them scientific attention with regard to housing and feeding. The gardener would say, by rooting out and burning up the weeds, and giving plenty of room thereby to the good plants, that need nourishment and careful scientific attention."[88]

Impey's implied plans for the scientific breeding of humanity are not developed in the novel nor are they discussed again.

Still on the subject of science, or in this case pseudoscience, in *Ruth and Marie* by Emma P. Bauder, Ruth, the all-knowing servant explains to her mistress

Marie that the lameness of her mistress's small son was caused by a confrontation with her drunken husband before the baby was born.[89]

Ruth's account of emotional trauma physically affecting a yet unborn child brings to mind the theories of Oliver W. Holmes in *Elsie Venner; a Romance of Destiny* and *The Guardian Angel*. In both works the major characters are the victims of prenatal influence which during their long lives they could not overcome. The theory of such influence was obviously still being propounded in 1895, the year that *Ruth and Marie* was published.

In sum, the novelists' attitudes toward science in the abstract and on the biological level, exclusive of the impact of the "higher criticism," were generally positive. Their praise takes varied forms—from seeing the scientist as a tool of God in explicating His handiwork to approving scientific method as the only way to achieve absolute truth. The authors underscored their faith in progress through the use of inductive reasoning. There were exceptions, however—the ambivalent fatalism seen in *The Burden of Christopher*, the despair voiced in *Doubting Castle*, and the prophetic anti-intellectualism based on the book of Revelation expressed in Fauntleroy's interpretation of the Chicago fire of 1871— but most of the novelists who commented on the scientific revolution saw it as an aid to both man and religion.

What is surprising is that not more of the authors of social Christian fiction deal with this subject. As shown, only two works deal to any extent with the "scientific" approach to history that led to the rationalizing process known as the "higher criticism," and, while twenty-seven works (listed in footnote 73) touch on other aspects of scientific advances, they do so casually. In only one of the twenty-seven, *Who's to Blame?*, does the author use the incipient conflict between spiritual faith and faith in science as a fundamental theme.

At the outset of this chapter, four areas were designated for comment: specific arguments found within the novels relative to church-led social reform; discussions centering on denominationalism, including an interpretation of works whose themes are sectarian in nature; attitudes expressed toward the Roman Catholic church; and lastly, the authors' reactions to the growth and influence of phases of scientific thought that related to the principles of Christianity.

In the first case, the arguments against the church becoming an active participant in secular reform measures were that the spiritual strength of Christianity would be compromised if the churches became involved in secular debate and that the doctrines of Christianity had no true relevance to the affairs of this world—that Christian ethics were abstract, symbolic. To take them literally would be to throw the social and economic structure of the nation into chaos. Opposed to these positions, those who fought for a social gospel said that a large portion of the real spirit of Christianity was found in the social teachings of the New Testament and summed up in the Golden Rule. Arguing that the church must evolve and change as society changed, they pleaded that the rapid industrialization of the United States, attended by a vast realignment of the social and economic status of its people, demanded that the churches shift their emphasis from concern primarily for the spiritual welfare of men and women to equal consideration for their temporal well-being as defined by the precepts of Christian justice. To them, the employer who paid lip service to these principles of Christian conduct on Sunday and then proceeded to pay his employees starvation wages for inhuman hours of toil the other six days of the week was nothing but a hypocrite of the lowest order. Those who preached the social gospel seldom negated the free enterprise system of capitalism or sought to circumscribe the liberty of the individual; rather they argued that capitalism versus Christianity was a false dichotomy. The two systems of behavior could function well together without recourse to either anarchy or industrial autocracy, provided that laws enacted by Christian men dedicated to republican institutions of government were enforced.

The questions raised about the truths or falsehoods underlying Protestant denominationalism and individual dogmas and rituals were, it was argued, outgrowths of the positions taken above. Most authors who presented a case for liberalizing dogmatic stands did so to illustrate one avenue for bringing their churches into greater intellectual and social awareness. If ministers and congregations would spend less time arguing biblical interpretations that separated them from other denominations, then they might all have more time, and perhaps inclination, to involve themselves with the pressing problems of the late nineteenth-century world. The conservative defense of existing norms is also found in the novels. Ritual itself was seldom a point of dispute except in works dealing with the Episcopal church. There are surprisingly few comments on the Roman Catholic church in the novels, and even more surprising, almost half (seven out of twenty) either laud the church itself or have heroes who were Catholic. Consistency, absoluteness, and awe for such a venerable, historical institution were the qualities of the church most often praised. Unlike Calvinism of old, the church had not bent to encompass changing fashions of scholarship, and new modes of government and economics. Nor had she particularly resisted; she had just remained.

Serious attacks on Catholicism exploited the anti-Irish feeling of the time, identified the church with the Old World and all its corruption, and raised the spectre of unseen Catholic plots to take over the government of the United States. There are only four novels in which anti-Catholicism can be said to be a primary theme.

The novelists' attitudes on the "higher criticism" and social Darwinism—although the expressions of these are few—are among the most interesting positions expressed in the novels. The historical approach toward understanding and validating events described in the Bible was generally frowned upon, either because such methods were sacrilegious or irrelevant, or because they tended to simplify faith by making it consistent with logical deduction. As to transposing Darwin's biological findings to a social setting, no novelist subscribed to Spencer's antihumanistic interpretation of socioeconomic jungle warfare; instead, the authors all supported the view that Darwin's discoveries made it infinitely more possible for man to shape his world for the better. While some authors expressed doubts about where science was ultimately leading humanity, most of them were optimistic about the oncoming scientific age and saw little conflict with their religious faith.

3

The Social Christian Novel as Literature

Social Christian novels, as a species of late nineteenth-century American fiction, are moralistic and didactic in their approach, Victorian in style and content, and generally poorly written. Their characteristics could be summed up as follows: They tend to be relatively long, usually between three and four hundred pages. Their plot lines are uncomplicated and the same is ordinarily true of the characters, who are seldom three dimensional. The reader sees them as the writer intended—the embodiments of an attitude or idea either applauded or deplored. Most of the works were "thesis novels." The authors' themes and arguments take precedence over other elements of the craft of fiction, and seldom if ever is there any ambiguity in the point of view.

Stylistically, the authors tend to use long complex sentences, carefully balanced parallel constructions, and polysyllabic diction. Such words as conundrum, comatose, lacrymose, quixotic, and juggernaut turn up in novel after novel. Last, the setting in the majority of works is urban, or moves from a rural to an urban locale. Since most of the novels are protests against the social and economic inequalities suffered by the new industrial working class, the city—which most of the authors saw as an evil in itself—was the logical background against which to voice such protests.[1]

An outstanding quality of the novels is their sincerity. They are unquestionably thinly disguised tracts in which their authors dramatized and sentimentalized the problems of the time as they saw them. As such they were successful. Although the total impact of the works on ecclesiastical and social reform is difficult to estimate, from the volume of them—145 social Christian novels published between the end of the Civil War and the turn of the century—one can assume that publishers would not have printed so many of them if they had not been in demand.

On the negative side, as literature none of the novels is great, excellent, or even first-rate by modern critical standards. Many of the characteristics just listed help diminish any chance for a truly powerful work. The authors' greatest limitations were in characterization and presentation of theme.

What some of the authors themselves have to say about their work—what they sought to accomplish and why they used the medium of fiction—is instructive. Some of the prefaces and introductions reveal the author's intentions, and in a few cases characters within various works also express their creators' attitudes on the moral and philosophical role of fiction. One of the most interesting statements directly made by an author, partially because of the work's popularity, is Charles M. Sheldon's 1935 preface to *In His Steps*. In it he briefly recounted the history of the novel and revealed his reason for writing it—to give his views on how to live the ideal religious life in the imitation of Christ:

The story *In His Steps* was written in 1896, and it was read a chapter at a time to my young people, Sunday evenings in the Central Congregational Church, Topeka, Kansas. While it was being read it was being published in the *Chicago Advance*, a religious weekly, as a serial. The publisher did not know the conditions of the copyright law, and he filed only one copy of the *Advance* each week with the department, instead of two, which the law required. On that account the copyright was defective, and the story was thrown into the "public domain" when the Advance Company put it out in a ten cent paper edition. Owing to the fact that no one had any legal ownership in the book, sixteen different publishers in America and fifty in Europe and Australia put out the book in various editions from an English penny to eight shillings. Mr. Bowden, the London publisher, sold over 3,000,000 copies of the penny edition on the streets of London.

. . . . .

While conditions have changed in the years since the story was written, the principal of human conduct remains the same. I do not need to say that I am thankful that owing to the defective copyright the book has had a larger reading on account of the great number of publishers. . . . I am informed by the *Publisher's Weekly* that the book has had more circulation than any other book except the Bible. If this is true, no one is more grateful than I am, as it confirms the faith I have always held that no subject is more interesting and vital to the human race than religion.

CHARLES M. SHELDON

Topeka, Kansas, 1935[2]

In His Steps itself I will discuss later in this chapter, but the foreword expressed Sheldon's consistent philosophy during a long life that held that Christ's life, in the most literal sense, should be the basis for judging men's and women's actions. Sheldon wrote a great many novels, all of which argued the same thesis. And, judging from what is known of the man, he was completely sincere when he expressed his thanks for the defective copyright that enabled thousands to read his novel who would otherwise have never had the chance.

Explaining the rationale behind a work in more detail, Elizabeth S. P. Ward wrote an introductory "note" to *The Silent Partner* in which she explained exactly why she wrote the novel and the sources from which she gained her information:

Had Christian ingenuity been generally synonymous with the conduct of manufacturing corporations, I should have found no occasion for the writing of this book.

I believe that a wide-spread ignorance exists among us regarding the abuses of our factory system, more especially, but not exclusively, as exhibited in many of the country mills.

I desire it to be understood that every alarming sign and every painful statement which I have given in these pages concerning the condition of the manufacturing districts could be matched with far less cheerful reading, and with far more pungent perplexities, from the pages of the Reports of the Massachusetts Bureau of Statistics of Labor, to which, with other documents of a kindred nature, and to the personal assistance of friends who have "testified that they have seen," I am deeply in debt for the ribs of my story.

E. S. P.

Andover, December, 1870.[3]

Mrs. Ward's indictment in this early prototype of social gospel fiction set the pattern for the many works that followed. She attacked manufacturing corporations that had not used "Christian ingenuity" in their relations with their employees, and in the process sought to educate and rouse the complacent majority of the public to protest the abuses of the factory system. In unusual fashion, Mrs. Ward buttressed her argument by documenting the sources of information she used in the plot and subplots of her novel.

The Reverend Henry Morgan, author of *Boston Inside Out!*, wrote a long introduction to the novel that is both amusing and appalling. Entitled "Why This Exposé," he recounts his determination to explore America following a Paris sojourn:

I started for home, and on arriving I hired over fifty agents to probe Boston's sins; and many copyists to write up the facts embodied in this book.

Not half my facts have I used. The most startling have been suppressed. Some of the characters have been veiled to cover reputations that suffer, heads that ache, and hearts that bleed. If no awakening is produced, no action taken to suppress the evils I expose, no warning note sounded by pulpit, press, or people, then I shall be heard again. Then I shall publish a key of these facts, also facts withheld, giving names, dates, places, and particulars.[4]

The Reverend Mr. Morgan did at least as good a job of decrying the evils of his city as could be wished. His ministry-of-fear technique of reform was fortunately not espoused by many of the authors read—perhaps because Morgan achieved his purpose (although he did write a sequel, which is unobtainable).

Morgan's melodramatic tone is not representative of the authors' introductions and prefaces. Most expressed their reasons for writing in conventional pietistic terms, such as the last sentence of the "prelude" to *Dr. Wallsten's Way* by the Reverend Thomas L. Bailey: "If a single thought can be gained, by any honest worker for the cause of truth and the welfare of humanity, from these pages, the writer's object will have been gained, and may the blessing of God go with and rest upon them."[5]

Mrs. Ellen E. Dickinson hoped that *The King's Daughters* would "find approval with all those who wear 'the silver cross and purple ribbon,' " and that the novel would be the "means of very many others joining the organization." She also assured her readers that while the characters are fictitious, "many of the incidents are true, a web of romance holding them together as the tapestry weaver ties the cords on which his pictures are designed, so as to harmonize the coloring and combination of materials with the best effects."[6]

Sometimes there are editorial notes, introductions, publisher's prefaces, and the like written by others in praise of the authors' efforts. Often these introductions are frankly denominational in orientation and explain one reason for the book's publication. Considering the number of works that were published by denominational presses, it is quite possible that many were intended to be didactically propagandistic, though that intent is not expressed.[7]

J. Thompson Gill, the author of *Within and Without*, wrote in his preface that his novel is "properly a philosophical, lego-ethical and religious work" and that he used the medium of "romance" to present his views "merely [as] a convenient form for impressing popular understanding." He also stresses, however, that his novel is "a work of art" and should be treated accordingly.

Other prefaces focus on various vices, such as the evils of strong drink in Julia M. Wright's *The New York Bible-Woman*. William H. Murray explained in his *Deacons* how the novel began as a lecture delivered on the New England lyceum circuit to 250,000 people, and how its great success in drawing attention to the abuse of that office had led to the lecture's publication. George Farnell, the author of *Rev. Josiah Hilton*, dedicated his treatise on theoretical communism to Edward Bellamy and made it clear that the novel was an explication of *Looking Backward* and an extension of *Equality*. Frank B. Cowgill in the introduction to *A Dream of Christ's Return* by David Morgan tells how when the author came to him after dreaming of how things should be instead of how they were, Mr. Cowgill urged Morgan to chronicle his experience for the public.

While Milton R. Scott's *Ernest Marble, the Labor Agitator*, does not have a preface, it does have a thirty-page appendix made up of quotations from Henry George's *Progress and Poverty*, Andrew Carnegie's defense of arbitration and unions, portions of Washington Gladden's *Tools and the Man*, Benjamin Kidd's *Social Evolution*, Edward Bellamy's *Looking Backward*, Thomas Carlyle's *Past and Present*, and Carroll D. Wright's article in the *Forum*, "May a Man Conduct His Business as He Pleases?" The appendix ends with reprints of the preface to Albion W. Tourgée's *Murvale Eastman* and Elizabeth Barrett Browning's "Cry of the Children." Had there been any doubt before, the author's orientation toward social problems and their solution becomes clear.

The prefaces and introductions are far more explicit on the social and intellectual aims of their authors than they are on why they chose to express their ideas in fictional form. In only four instances did authors comment on why they used the novel rather than nonfiction: as mentioned, J. Thompson Gill in *Within and Without* used the form of the romance "merely [as] a convenient form for impressing popular understanding"; Ellen E. Dickinson in *The King's Daughters* used a tapestry simile to the effect that the use of fiction drew together her examples of Christian service for the best-patterned effect. In the preface to *Westbrook Parsonage* Harriet B. McKeever says that one reason she wrote her novel was that there were many "tracts, stories, and hymns" arguing on the side of high church ritual, but that she had "met with nothing in the shape of a story, touching these subjects, on the other." She goes on, "It is not likely that young persons will read controversial articles; but it may be that a story embodying Protestant truth will interest many youthful readers, and lead them to read more deeply works that will enlighten the understanding and strengthen their faith, in the great religious issues of the day."[8] And J. B. Logan, the author of *Alice McDonald*, in his original introduction to the novel says that

> the object of the writer in preparing these letters was to present, in the form of a story, to all who might read them, and especially to the *young*, some of the thrilling characters, difficulties and incidents connected with the early days of the Cumberland Presbyterian Church—the persecutions, trials and buffetings which our fathers passed through.
>   . . . . .
> The debates and arguments introduced in connection with . . . [the] history, as well as the authors quoted, are not fiction. The discussions have occurred, in substance, over and over again, within the author's own hearing, and are, therefore, perfectly reliable. They are placed in the form of a narrative, in the hope that they will be the more readily read and weighed than, perhaps, they would be if presented in a mere abstract form.[9]

These four works make up the only direct evidence given by the authors about why they chose to use the novel form for presenting their arguments. Mrs. Dickinson's reason was aesthetic; Mrs. McKeever and the Reverend Mr. Logan both stressed their desire to appeal to the young people of their respective sects, and Mr. Gill and the Reverend Mr. Logan used narrative because they thought it would thereby reach a wider audience than if they presented their ideas "in a mere abstract form."

The reasons were all well justified and could have been anticipated. Mrs. Dickinson's *The King's Daughters*, like a number of the novels, is made up of a series of relatively unintegrated vignettes, this one telling of the good works of rich Marion Fay and her grandmother. The two took up philanthropy and established a day nursery, and organized visits to "shut-ins," a "truth-telling" group, an "anti-gossip" group, a charity Thanksgiving Dinner for New York newsboys, as well as other good works. It was the author's purpose to show how ladies of wealth and fashion could profitably make use of their time by helping others. Rather than give a drab listing of good works in an essay in some religious periodical, Mrs. Dickinson made her points in a novel that had the added advantage of including a romanticized love story about Marion and a debauched sculptor whom she reformed and married. One can safely assume that *The King's Daughters* reached a wider audience in novelistic form than it might have done as an essay. The same would hold true for a number of social Christian works.

The thesis novels *Westbrook Parsonage* and *Alice McDonald* are directed at "young people." Mrs. McKeever is clear in stating that she hoped to reach, through a novel, the youth of the Episcopal church that might not otherwise come in contact with her point of view. Logan, more obliquely, tried to have it both ways by claiming that *Alice McDonald* was not a novel, at least in the ordinary sense, yet cast his "letters" in narrative form "in the hope that they might be more readily read and weighed."

By unfortunate happenstance, none of the works of nonsectarian social gospel fiction has a preface or introduction that explains the author's decision to frame his or her argument in fictional form. But perhaps one is questioning the obvious. It was probably true that a novel would reach many readers who would not see, or who would be bored by, an essay in the *Forum* on the same subject. Besides, there was certainly no lack of social gospel tracts and solidly serious essays. Moreover, the novel had the license of *not* having to be truthful. Particularly in Victorian America before the realists' revolution it could "harmonize" and romanticize events so that virtually every ending was a happy one. Very few social Christian novels end in tragedy. Thus the reader—and the author—did not have to face the everyday realities of failure or stalemate. And, of course, the elemental lure of the novel for the author of being able, logically and emotionally, to control and conclude all events was present in the social Christian genre as well as in other forms of fiction.

The characters in the various novels also speak for their authors about what fiction should and should not do. The good Reverend Jacob Jones, the protagonist of James B. Converse's *Uncle Sam's Bible*, expresses a peculiar combination of reactionary and progressive opinions on almost every subject, delivering all with great authority. In regard to literature he is staunchly against censorship and is quite sure that "literature also increases the material and moral welfare of the people."[10] He does not specify how he believes either is accomplished.

The heroine of *A Modern Pharisee*, in keeping with the attitude expressed by Bross in his preface, comments:

"Well, I must confess I have no desire for reading, save occasionally, merely for the sake of amusement. If I can gather facts from a novel, or be led to see the truth of some proposition to which I have been blind, I feel amply repaid. What you deem essentials in *Looking Backward* [the love story], I look upon as mere framework, the skeleton to which clings the warm flesh through the arteries of which circulates and throbs the rich crimson blood of intellectuality. Plot simply holds the reader's attention, while the creator hammers away, driving relentlessly with each heavy blow, sentiment and argument into the heart and mind of the reader.''[11]

According to Bross the novel should be a mode of instruction. If it did not do so it was suspect. Mere entertainment was certainly not sufficient justification for spending time with a book.

In the novels, by far the most interesting and unexpected comments having to do with literature are those that argue for or against the new trend of realism. There are not many that express a position—four or five—and most of these briefly and by implication; still, that in popular, religious fiction of the time any of the authors should have presented their stand was unlooked for, and one might project from this that some of the authors were not as parochial as they might at first have appeared.

The novels touching on the merits of realism are Leander S. Keyser's *The Only Way Out*, *Murvale Eastman*, *The Petrie Estate*, *John and I and the Church*, and *Mr. World and Miss Church-Member*. Mrs. Helen D. Brown, author of *The Petrie Estate*, welcomed more realistic writing, both psychologically and externally. At one point in the novel her heroine says:

"The good novel often seems to me more real than life itself. . . . It is so much the record of the inner life, of what the naked eye can never see. It is the real, inner world that the novelist sees. He is the mind-reader. The novelist has a great task to reveal us to each other, to interpret us, to educate our sympathies.''[12]

A few pages earlier the same speaker showed that she equated realism with the depiction of poverty:[13]

The day on which she first saw lower New York was one never to be erased from her imagination. Cheerful and determined, she had started upon her trip of exploration; she returned haggard, with eyes absent and haunted. What she saw she had many times read of, as all the world has read in these latter days. Scenes shifted before her eyes with troubling familiarity; for she had been an imaginative reader, and had seen while she read. The general outlines of tenement-house life she had by heart: the foul neglect of the city street; the tall building teeming with dirty children; the dark, cluttered, and squalid rooms. But now literary description translated itself into details. A neglected street was a street which had accumulated a rich soil of filth, in which vile rags and papers flew about, stinking garbage lay along the gutter, and a dead cat in the middle of the way had been run over more than once. A journey up four flights of tenement stairs through dirt and darkness, Charlotte found more instructive than a course in reading.[14]

The novel from which the quotation is taken combines ironic detachment with astute observation that makes the work better than the ordinary.

In a less self-conscious and sophisticated manner a section of Elizabeth Grinnell's *John and I and the Church* expressed the author's attitude toward fiction:

It is only a story conceived by the author to induce all little boys to be good. There is not a particle of truth in it. The result is, if a boy is good and obedient and the reward is not forthcoming he pouts and grows sullen. A bit of Sunday-school fiction has spoiled many a boy. Better to have taught the lesson that visible reward is as scarce as humming birds at Christmas time when the snow is three feet deep in the garden. Reward is not more sure to the boy than is success to the man.[15]

The last portion of the quotation reminds one of Mark Twain and shows again the connection between reality in fiction and reality in life. Mrs. Grinnell was a strong believer in presenting aspects of life as they are, not as she wished them to be. She did not like much of what she saw, but she aimed at fidelity to experience in her fiction.

In Leander Keyser's *The Only Way Out* there is a scene in which the agnostic hero, courting Miss West, his Christian love, asks her the following:

"By what criterion . . . would you judge a work of fiction?"

"By its moral effect upon the reader. If it fills his mind with morbid imaginations or makes him dissatisfied with his lot, or disheartens him in his efforts to help his fellow-men, and puts misanthropic notions into his head, I certainly think it unhealthful. Stories that are written in a cynical or pessimistic tone are calculated to cut the nerve of all moral effort, and are baleful in their effects. On the other hand, if a story enlarges the reader's sympathies, makes him less selfish, inspires him to the attainment of higher moral excellence, and at the same time relaxes his over-strained energies, then it is an evangel, a blessing to those who read it."[16]

Keyser believed that the novel should be morally elevating, hold the reader's attention, and describe the "brighter phases of human life" that William Dean Howells advocated. And if there was any conflict between art and ethics, which Keyser thought unlikely, the presentation of sound ethics should obviously take precedence.

Both the style and content of the above passage are interesting. Miss West is forthright and direct in her ideas. The second sentence in the second paragraph contains three well-balanced and parallel qualifying phrases followed by the speaker's judgment on the question. The last sentence in the paragraph parallels the construction and concludes by answering the hero's question. Sentences so constructed are typical of the novels. The diction used is also similar to that found in many. In the same paragraph, "morbid," "baleful," "misanthropic," "unhealthful," "moral excellence," and "moral effort" are used—all words common in American religious prose of the period. Formality, stateliness, and didacticism are generally typical of social Christian works.

Albion W. Tourgée did not like the realists, and his dislike was quite specific. In a section that fused criticism of the scientist with criticism of literary realism, he took both to task for analyzing the nature of man solely on a biological and environmental level without recognizing the due power of man's soul, sentiments, and emotions. One can hear the echoes of Hawthorne clearly:

The soul does not measure time by seconds, nor yet by heart-beats, but by modifications in its own quality and character. The watches of the world may stop; the planets may cease to measure the flight of time; the body may retain its pristine vigor—but in an hour, a moment almost, the heart may grow old, the man be transformed.

It is this fact that the mere scientist is sure to neglect in his estimate of humanity. He says of man, of a people, or a race, given good climate, physical conditions of a specific character, [that] certain results will follow [for that people]. Presently the conditions are all fulfilled and the results do *not* follow. Why? Simply because the mightiest part of the human being was left out of account in the scientist's estimate. So, too, that pessimistic philosophy which calls itself "realism" in art and literature, always is, and always will be, at fault when it tries to solve the riddle of humanity. It says human nature, human character, is a result of the operation of natural laws. So it is; but those laws are not all physical, nor purely mental. . . . Impulse, affections, sentiments, convictions, emotions—these are more potent than all other forces in shaping the man and, if general in their application, the multitude. Every man's knowledge, almost every man's experience, is full of transformation scenes. It is a literal fact that "love works miracles"; so do hate and fear and the continuing power of cumulative ill. . . . It is in these soul-forces, even more than in physical laws and conditions, that the secret of progress and the highest truth of human life lie hid.[17]

At another point in the novel Tourgée has a character equate realism with meanness.[18] And again, in the same vein but striking at a different facet of European naturalism:

It is the fashion of the time. Innocence is no longer deemed a desirable quality; and there are many good people who declare that familiarity with vice is not detrimental to manly worth or womanly purity. It is only romantic notions of love and virtue that we fear to-day; and these we seek to forestall by prescribing for the young soul the carefully elaborated daily record of the world's infamies, and substituting "realistic" impurity as a motive for "healthy fiction," instead of the silly sentimentalism of old-fashioned love. No matter; a generation to whose lips the pessimistic foulness of Tolstoi and his imitators has been commended as an inspiring cordial, not only by the high-priests of literature, but by ministers of God, is perhaps beyond fear of peril from the highly-spiced narratives of social peccadillos which abound in the daily press. News is the most important element of knowledge; and naughtiness the most important feature of news. Such is the verdict of to-day.[19]

Murvale Eastman was published in 1890, five years after Howells's *The Rise of Silas Latham* but a year before his collected *Criticism and Fiction*. Stephen Crane's *Maggie* came out in 1893, Hamlin Garland's credo *Crumbling Idols* the following year, and *Sister Carrie* at the turn of the century. Thus Tourgée, even before the American realists turned toward Emile Zola's doctrines, anticipated much of the serious criticism of naturalism.

The last novel that deals with the social function of literature has the most to say on the subject. The Reverend Mr. William S. Harris in his allegory *Mr. World and Miss Church-Member* devotes almost thirty pages to attacking the potentially evil influence of various types of literature on men and women who are on their way to either heaven or hell. The two principal characters of the book's title are metaphorically traveling the Broad Highway to hell, though not as yet irrevocably damned, when they come to the "Devil's Schools of Literature." There the couple are beguiled by all sorts of subtle snares of Satan. After Mr. World and Miss Church-Member have heard a "Jesuitical" lecture on "The License of Pure Fiction" for example, the author presents his interpretation of the devil's suggestions for successful authorship that stress sacrificing everything to fads and popularity.[20]

The same work also complains of novels that dilute spirituality with elements that are physical, social, or theologically liberal.[21] The evil is any liberalization of a Calvinistic view of the world. Strait the gate and narrow the way: Mr. Harris never doubts his perspective nor questions the geography that leads him toward the City of God.

In the works under consideration, virtually all of the authors sought to reflect in their fiction the principles they espoused either in the preface or through a character's statements in the novel itself. Helen D. Brown wanted to make her fiction mirror the horrible conditions found in the slums of New York, and she partially succeeded in doing so. Elizabeth Grinnell was more interested in airing her unhappiness with Protestant churches that had become "high toned" than she was with any theory of literature per se. However, because she wanted, as she said, to tell a truthful story, she too was in some respects successful, although her theological views in praise of old-fashioned puritan values were so repetitiously presented that the novel as a novel was considerably weakened.

The position of Leander S. Keyser in *The Only Way Out*, that there was no antagonism between true art and true Christian ethics, was presumably what he tried to demonstrate in the form and content of his novel. The work centers on the problem of how an intellectual can believe in reason, science, the Bible, and an anthropomorphic God all at the same time. The "only way out" is by means of an act of faith. The agnostic hero in his anxious doubt finally receives his spiritual conversion by means of prayer. The novel is tract-like and its characters underdeveloped, but its theme is well presented. Leroy Ransom, the hero, is unhappy because he is not a Christian; he becomes happier when he falls in love with Christian Carrie West and she turns him down because of his agnosticism. By the author's code, his fiction is indeed moral, not without art, and by ending happily substantiates his thesis.

Tourgée and Harris presented their cases in negative terms. Neither had any use for pessimistic realism that showed the brutal and animal side of man, and neither exploited such techniques in his fiction. Tourgée spoke of "emotional transformations" as prime motivators of man's actions and repeatedly illustrated his belief in *Murvale Eastman*. Harris was against passionately unreal romances, literature that dealt with the passions in any form, the theory that style took precedence over content, writing for the tastes of the majority, and the written depiction of any "vile conditions of humanity." He never stated what good literature should be, except by implication. If you turned to the opposites of all the above, you would be hard put to write anything at all. Harris's own *Mr. World and Miss Church-Member* is allegorical, hence abstractly unreal, though it does depict many of the "vile" conditions to which mankind has been subject through the snares of the devil. The book's style by no means overshadows its content, man's evil passions are constantly referred to but never specifically depicted, and it is doubtful that the novel could be said to have appealed to the jaded tastes of the majority of the American public in 1900. Though the author thus did not quite measure up to what seem to be his literary standards, in balance, he seemed pleased with his work. If there were a few lingering doubts, he dismissed them when he gave the hallowed caveat of writers over time and space: "As you read the chapters you may wonder how we became so familiar with the secrets of Satan's work. If you cannot find a solution to the query between the lids of the book, do not seek it from the publisher or the author. Upon a careful perusal of the pages you will find that the book is its own interpreter."[22]

Returning to the generalizations made in the opening pages of this chapter, one can say that the worth of the novels—both as literature and as vehicles for the authors' views—hinges on the authors' abilities in three fundamentals of fiction writing: the development of character, the effectiveness of the author's style, and the logic of his premise. As with any propaganda literature, we can readily sense that one of the reasons why authors of the novels chose the medium of fiction for their appeal was their knowledge that the author of a novel, when arguing from a premise with which his reader may disagree, can sometimes convincingly validate that premise through the reader's sympathetic involvement with the novel's protagonist. Success or failure probably depends upon the author's ability as an artist to make the characters live, and the accurateness of his or her psychological and intellectual logic in directing the ideas and actions of the characters.

While the authors of social Christian fiction knew that some of their readers would not share their views about the causes of and solutions to the economic and social problems of the Gilded Age, they could hope to convince them. If a novelist could establish a rapport between the characters in his fiction and the reader and then strengthen that rapport with logical and convincing arguments for his thesis, he stood, perhaps, a better chance of converting the reader to his way of thinking than did the essayist whose appeal was largely intellectual. The abilities of the social Christian novelists in the art of argument, character realization, and prose are the criteria by which the strengths and weaknesses of individual works can best be evaluated.

The most glaring flaw of the majority of the works is in characterization. Since they are thesis novels, their authors sacrificed artistic achievement for didactic explication. There is an obvious irony here, at least if my evaluation is a valid one. Assuming for the moment that the authors could have rendered whole and believable characters had they wished, their decision not to do so—

to present instead stereotyped, one-dimensional abstractions that were either wholly good or wholly evil—weakened their work both as novel and as propaganda. Of course, secondary characters in novels can effectively represent abstract principles but seldom can the hero or heroine, unless they are well developed.

There are exceptions, however. The primary characters in Florence Converse's *The Burden of Christopher* are well drawn, as are those in Elmore E. Peake's *The Darlingtons* and those in many of the novels of Elizabeth S. Ward, particularly *The Gates Ajar* and *The Silent Partner*. *Philip MacGregor* by William W. Newton, *The Story of a Cañon* by Beveridge Hill, and *John and I and the Church* by Elizabeth Grinnell also present individuals who are multi-dimensional.

There are also instances within some of the novels of an effective, concentrated sketch of a type.[23] One of the best is an extended portrait of the old-fashioned New England Calvinist preacher in Tourgée's *Murvale Eastman*. A scene in which the minister, G. A. Phue, talks to the villain of the novel, Wilton Kishu, portrays a sincere and dedicated man who has outlived his time and is made to be a pawn in a game he does not even know is being played. After lamenting that too many laymen and ministers have moved away from the doctrines, creeds, and confessions of faith of their forefathers, the Reverend Mr. Phue says that it is not enough to follow Christ and His example. That is easy. What men have to believe in, absolutely, is damnation.[24] While depicting hell's fires, Tourgée inserts a footnote:

When these chapters were published serially, some objection was made to the character of Rev. G. A. Phue. These objections were: *First*, that the modern trial for heresy has none of the spirit of persecution about it; *second*, that no one really holds at this time the view of Christianity ascribed to Mr. Phue, at least no one of intelligence, and least of all a minister. The author does not care to discuss either question. Mr. Phue was drawn as a survivor—a type not yet extinct—of which the author has personally known more than one individual. For some of the qualities of this type he even confesses a distinct fondness. He begs to say, however, that the lurid picture of hell, which is put into the mouth of the fervid champion of literalness, has not even the merit of originality, having been taken bodily from the writings of one of the most distinguished living divines. The inquiring reader will find it, and more of the same sort, in *Sermons of Rev. C. H. Spurgeon*, Second Series, No. 17, p. 275.[25]

Mr. Phue then explains his life in terms of martyrdom to an unjust church.[26] At the end of the section, after the minister has announced his intention of driving Murvale Eastman out of the church for heresy and Mr. Kishu has suggested that he seek aid from other ministers of like persuasion to accomplish the deed, the Reverend Mr. Phue replies:

"I need no assistance, sir. . . . I am weak and old, and the Church passes by me in scorn; but in the Lord's cause, battling for the safety of Zion and the preservation of the faith once delivered to the saints, I am armed in triple mail of proof. I shall assail him point-blank, face to face, myself; I shall show his errors and drive him out of the fold whose salvation he endangers.''

"I trust you may, sir," said Mr. Kishu as he handed him a check, which the old man thrust carelessly into his vest-pocket without once glancing at the amount. "Have no fear; it is an unpleasant duty, but it will be faithfully performed."

The Rev. G. A. Phue—in his young days he had written out the first names in full, and his mother had always called him in her piping, sharp New England voice, "God's 'sanynted,'' as if it had been a single word—was a minister without a church, a shepherd without a flock. In fact, he was a shepherd who frightened the lambs and was apt to make even the toughest of the wethers intractable and belligerent. A lean and eager face, pale and deep-lined, with that softness which told that its severity was without hypocrisy or greed, and his zeal only the outcome of a faith which knew no doubt, told the story of his life even better than words could phrase it. His cheeks were cleanly shaven, his high, severe brow with the blue veins showing through the transparent skin, the deep-set, blue eyes, the clean-cut, sharp-pointed nose, thin lips and square chin, told of one to whose soul-life doubt had been a stranger; who being right would never falter, and who starting wrong would never look backward to correct his reckoning, though he should see the breakers of destruction straight ahead.[27]

The portrait is effective. After first repelling the reader with a stereotyped picture of the Puritan breathing fire and brimstone, Tourgée stops and documents the source of his rhetoric—an eminent divine of the day. In his footnote the author also foreshadows his own ambivalence toward the minister, saying in effect that there is much that is good and even noble in the Reverend Mr. Phue, but that he is misguided nonetheless.

The ending of the section is well constructed. The old man swallows a part of his pride and accepts a check from a man who is really his enemy, but whom a particular situation has for the moment made his ally. Yet Phue never looks at the amount; part of his pride is compromised, but only part. Then in the last paragraph Tourgée steps in and gives more background, describes Phue, and evaluates the minister as a man: he had never known doubt or hypocrisy—even when wrong.

Passages like the above from *Murvale Eastman*, while certainly not common in the novels, are to be found, and a number of authors had real ability in presenting "characters" of the Theophrastus variety. In Tourgée's work the Reverend Mr. G. A. Phue is more alive and more understandable than the hero, Murvale Eastman.

It may be subjective to condemn most of these novels for their literary faults, even though the authors clearly preferred their messages to their style of presentation. Among them, the writers of these works committed all the faults that one associates with pompous, vague statements. Samples of these infelicities abound. A sermon gone astray may be seen in the pages of Emma P. Bauder's *Ruth and Marie*.[28] For aggravated pomposity one might choose passages from Henry L. Everett's *The People's Program*.[29] It is much more difficult—as well as much more rewarding—to point out the examples of literary accomplishment.

As has been illustrated previously, the work of Elizabeth S. Ward was often accomplished. Of her works *The Supply at Saint Agatha's*, a shorter work, and *The Silent Partner* are the best. In *The Silent Partner* there is a description of a typical day in the life of a factory mill girl (see quote in Chapter 1). After getting up before dawn, hurrying, and skipping breakfast, the girl has arrived at the mill:

You hang up your shawl and your crinoline, you understand, as you go shivering by gaslight to your looms, that you are chilled to the heart, and that you were careless about your shawl, but do not consider carefulness worth your while by nature or by habit; a little less shawl means a few less winters in which to require shawling. You are a godless little creature, but you cherish a stolid leaning, in these morning moons, towards making an experiment of death and a wadded coffin.

By the time that gas is out, you cease, perhaps, though you cannot depend upon that, to shiver, and incline less and less to the wadded coffin, and more to a chat with your neighbor in the alley. Your neighbor is of either sex and any description, as the case may be. In any event, warming a little with the warming day, you incline more and more to chat. If you chance to be a cotton-weaver, you are presently warm enough. It is quite warm in the weaving-room. The engines respire into the weaving-room; with every throb of their huge lungs you swallow their breath. The weaving-room stifles with steam.
. . . . .

The windows must be closed; a stir in the air will break your threads. There is no air to stir. You inhale for a substitute motionless, hot moisture. If you chance to be a cotton-weaver, it is not in March that you think most about your coffin.[30]

The author continues her impressionistic recital until it is the end of the day when "you" go out into "the wind and dusk":

Perhaps you have only pinned your shawl, or pulled your hat over your face, or knocked against a stranger on the walk. . . . It is cold and you tremble, direct from the morbid heat in which you have stood all day; or you have been cold all day, and it is colder, and you shrink; or you are from the weaving-room, and the wind strikes you faint, or you stop to cough and the girls go on without you. The town is lighted, and people are out in their best clothes. You pull your dingy veil about your eyes. You are weak and heart-sick all at once.[31]

Mrs. Ward's talents are best displayed in passages of this kind. She is excellent in her use of precise detail in order to set mood and tone. The opening paragraph related the cold with death, suicide, and hopelessness, but these qualities were relieved somewhat in the second paragraph, though the squalidness of the weaving-room, and the heat, the steamy hot air filled with cotton lint that the workers breathed did not make the workers' situation any happier in the long run. At the end of the day, back in the cold away from the "morbid heat," the girl is faint and she coughs, left behind by the others. She compares herself to the throng of people around her. She is tired, the song they had all sung earlier in the mill has gone back to the engines, and she recognizes herself as "a miserable little factory-girl with a dirty face."

The use of second person—"you"—manages to effect qualities of objectivity and subjectivity at the same time. Together with the unremitting detail, it makes the passage powerful. Mrs. Ward was one of the best writers encountered.[32]

Akin to the impressionistic realism found in Mrs. Ward's fiction, there are sections of various novels that are suddenly realistic in a twentieth-century sense. Such scenes are rare, and the jolt of running into them is all the greater because in no case is realism sustained in the novels. A novel will unfold in its usual American Victorian way when suddenly a photographic, objective scene will be rendered.[33] Usually euphemism is a cardinal rule of diction in social Christian novels. Authors sometimes no doubt wanted to shock their readers' sensibilities, but ordinarily this was done by indirection, implication, and broad generalities. As a consequence, realistic scenes, when they are used, immediately attract the reader's attention.

Probably the best single novel of the 145 read is *The Burden of Christopher* by Florence Converse. The work is interesting for a number of reasons. First, it is the only work that makes a real hero out of a factory owner and presents a fairly realistic account of his experiment in running a model factory. Second, the characterization of the hero, Christopher Kenyon, his wife Agnes, and his father-in-law—a professor of economics named Gillespie—is much more thorough than is ordinary. The author used a number of unusual literary devices in the novel. The hero's wife, Agnes, for example is smarter than her husband, but she is neither a shrew nor jealous of his position. The picture drawn of her father is one of the best parts of the novel—he is an ivory-tower intellectual with all of the correct sentiments of the professional liberal whose knowledge and sympathies are drawn completely from books. When the chips are down and Christopher's shoe factory is about to go bankrupt because of premeditated, destructive competition by other manufacturers, the professor finally meets the workers about whom he feels so kindly; his reactions, before and after, are expressed in the following accounts:

For a number of years the union principle had been the professor's pet hobby. He had been one of the earliest economists in the country to come round to it; for whatever his defects might be he was a student, and a judge of book matter and written opinions. He had long been in sympathy with the English union movement; and if he got his ideas on the general subject from English publications, rather than from observation of the facts and the workingmen as they were evolved under American conditions, he could hardly be blamed, since all economists were looking towards England as the leader in matters of industrial and economic reform. What the professor did not understand was that the average mortal had no conception whatever of the union principle, and avoided enlightenment concerning it with all the stubbornness and density born of ignorance. Christopher had more than once endeavored to convince him of this fact. . . .

After he [the professor] had heard one or two labor agitators, he experienced a revulsion from the actual. The horny hand of toil irritated his sensitive scholar's palm. The florid oratory, the impossible English, the uncertain logic, and the bad taste—more than all else, the bad taste—of these people whom, in theory, he had come to regard as martyrs

of society, aroused the professor's intellectual distrust, that most alert faculty of his
scholastic mind. Ought a people who were such bad dialecticians to be trusted to think
for themselves? This dumbness of the dispossessed, this chaos of sound which they
emitted, exasperated the fluent professor; they could not explain themselves.[34]

The professor retreats to elitism, and in the process destroys the relationship
between himself and his daughter, who formerly worshipped her father as an
embodiment of intellectual truth unprejudiced by personal bias. The author's
understanding and portrayal of the dilemmas of various kinds of intellectuals
when faced with the grimy facts of lower-class existence are central to making
The Burden of Christopher a psychologically appealing and valid work.

The novel was also the only one encountered that makes extensive use of
symbolism. While it is heavy in some places, it is effective in others. The title
of the work expresses a parallel throughout. Christopher Kenyon, the hero,
becomes the Christopher of the legend; yet, because he refuses to accept Christianity in the formal sense—represented by Kenyon's best friend and Anglican
minister Philip Starr—he does not become a saint nor does he succeed in carrying
the burden of man's inhumanity to man, symbolized by the unfair factory system.
Instead, through the sin of pride he tries to single-handedly reform his factory,
fails, and drowns himself, leaving his burden to his son, also named Christopher.
There is some fine use of water imagery in the novel that parallels the use of
the river in the Saint Christopher legend.[35] The novel opens and closes with the
same scene—a scene that acts as a tragic frame for the action. The hero's suicide
takes place in the same setting where the story had begun.

Some characteristics were peculiar to social Christian fiction: satire, irony,
and allegory. Satire was a favorite technique used by many authors to make their
point.[36] James B. Converse in *Uncle Sam's Bible* does not care for the ideas of
Edward Bellamy, for example, and devotes a long section to satirizing Bellamy's
ideas through a foolish woman who thinks him ''so imaginative and romantic''
and his brand of socialism ''the most sublime, nicest and sweetest thing you
ever dreamed of. . . . Whenever I think of it the symphonies of all the celestial
orbs thrill every vein in me.'' The lady is so impressed she names her neurotic
pet dog after Bellamy.[37]

The Reverend J. B. Logan, promoter of Cumberland Presbyterianism and
archenemy of the Baptist denomination gives an amusing rendition of the Baptist
immersion service of a young girl. She has lead weights sewn into the hem of
her dress to insure decency at all times, but a young boy, in a tree overlooking
the river where the ceremony is to take place, is too heavy for the branch he is
on. He descends at a crucial moment, almost drowning the minister, Mr. Waters,
the girl, and various helpers. The girl's dress somehow gets over her head in
the confusion, and the lead weights insure its remaining in that position for some
time.[38]

The whole of *Deacon Hackmetack* is devoted to the vitriolic ravings of the
Deacon on his deathbed. He has strong feelings about a great many subjects,

all delivered to his niece Betty, and the entire novel is done in a half satiric, half bitter tone. In addition, L. Jonas Bubblebuster's *"Our Best Society"* uses obvious satire throughout. The effect is not generally very amusing, but there is one section of dialogue between villains Mary Annie Bell and Thomas D. AntiLabor in which the two take foolish prenuptial vows that appear to be a takeoff on the famous scene between Millamant and Mirabell in William Congreve's *The Way of the World* (Act IV, scene v).[39]

In other novels fundamentally serious in tone there are passages of satire. In Harriette A. Keyser's *Thorns in Your Sides* there is the following portrait of an effete young man of New York society in the mid–1880s:

He was surmounted with a bell-crowned hat, wore a collar that enclosed his neck like a vise, trousers so tight that they were the wonder of all observers, and a very short coat. He crooked his elbows at a certain angle not to be described in words, and carried a thick stick, horizontally, to the detriment of street passengers, for skillful steering was needed to avoid collision with this fashionable bludgeon. His gait was a slow trot, as if he had started on a hill-top and found it impossible to stop on down-grade. As at this time expression had gone out, his face had as blank an appearance as any thing short of positive imbecility could assume.[40]

The Rev. John Henry, having already informed the reader well in advance of Bruce Barton that Christ was the "first modern business man," also includes a devastating attack by innuendo on upper-class-organized reform societies as being prurient, voyeuristic, and deadly in and of themselves:

It was the especial boast of the Dorcas Society to be engaged in charity of the practical sort. . . . Charity begins at home; and while there were censorious and unreasonable individuals who broadly intimated that the beginnings of the Dorcas Society in the way of charity were too faint to make their *locus* material to the cause, there is no gainsaying that the Dorcas Society had the best of it on principle. There were those indeed who darkly hinted, in speaking of the slumming tours which the Dorcas Society undertook in order to apprise itself of the particular bearings of domestic heathenism in order to take intelligent action for assuagement thereof, that they were prosecuted merely to satisfy somebody's impure curiosity, but who that somebody could be is not imaginable, since none but members of the Society in good and regular standing were allowed to go on the slumming tours. . . .[41]

There is a similar section, though not quite so pungent, in Margaret P. Sherwood's *An Experiment in Altruism*. This novel, like Mrs. Sherwood's *Henry Worthington, Idealist*, is considerably better than most of those read. It combines satire with a serious questioning of social problems of the period, and the combination of self-mockery and quest theme, together with qualities of the author's style, give her work a strikingly contemporary quality.

In the novel she goes to a settlement for young women and describes the leadership as follows:

They were all political economists of the school of Ruskin.

. . . . .

Some of them were fairly well equipped for practical economic study. Others were collecting statistics with the most engaging ignorance.

Every week, a club devoted to the study of social science, the "William Morris League," met at the Settlement. On these evenings the head of the House sat, Lady Abbess fashion, with nun and novice at her side.

. . . . .

I always went away from these discussions with feelings of mingled pride and amusement. These were strong and earnest young women, inspired by no wish for notoriety, but eager to help and to understand.

Yet it was a queer world, where the maidens formed trades-unions, and the young men were making tea!

It was very good tea.[42]

Mrs. Sherwood was shrewd and observant. She could dismiss a certain kind of reformer with a sentence: "An interest in the poor was one of the really important things, like the cut of one's sleeves, or one's knowledge of Buddha." Yet her healthy suspicion of motivation and what was really happening was qualified by her genuine humanitarianism. The last short chapter to the novel seems to sum up the author's feelings:

We are all busy still, and yet the world is not saved.

The Anarchist is perfecting the process that shall bring his millennium to be, and the young Socialists in Barnet House are working out the details of their new economic order. The Altruist still translates the infinite into finite terms; the Young Reformer is on the platform; I toil daily in the self-same Cause, but the world is not saved.

Many times since we closed ranks . . . I have paused, disheartened. Full assurance has not been granted me, and it is my lot in doing battle to strike often in the dark. Yet I have moments when I know that the strife is not in vain. In these I wonder why we are so troubled about our duty to our fellow-man, and about our knowledge of God. The one command in regard to our neighbor is not obscure. And our foreboding lest our faith in God shall escape us seems futile inasmuch as we cannot escape from our faith.[43]

Another work that uses satire as a motif can also serve as a transition to another stylistic device that is common to a whole group of novels. Bailey K. Leach's *Soulless Saints* is a satiric allegory. Allegory both Christian and otherwise was used in many forms in many works. In *Soulless Saints* a Reverend Mr. Daiken Burrom falls asleep in the woods, is awakened (or dreams that he is—the author never specifies) by some "little people" and is conducted through a whole series of other worlds peopled by various kinds of "civilized" monsters. In each world the inhabitants' mores, religions, and ethics satirize their counterparts on earth.

At one point in the novel the hero becomes consort to the queen of the Kingdom of Babbyll because he has fallen under her magic spell of love. He is critical of many aspects of the place, but even as king he has limited power, as he is always subject to his queen's wishes. The religion of his subjects greatly disturbs the Reverend Burrom. He describes it as follows:

In their religious opinions, they were exceedingly peculiar, not to say inconsistent. There was not among them that beautiful harmony so noticeable among the adherents of Christianity, the world over, though their faith was marvelous, nevertheless. They were divided into distinct sects and schisms too numerous to mention, and yet the fundamental principles upon which each was founded were the same. In short, they all believed in the Supreme Noise as the Creator of all things and the Giver of all Good. They argued that noise was life, and in proof they called attention to the fact that as soon as life was extinct no noise could issue from the body—it was silent evermore; hence the noise was out of it altogether; hence it was dead; hence the noise was the life, and life was God; therefore, noise was God.

. . . . .

   All believed that noise was necessary, but as to the manner of the noise was wherein the disputes arose. One sect, the Howlers, believed that howling was according to the will of the Almighty Noise; another sect, the Grunters, advanced the doctrine of grunting as the only acceptable method, and the Warblers taught that singing was the divinely required noise, and were it necessary I could name various other intonations of the voice which were taught by other and lesser sects to be essential to eternal salvation.... However, the differences between the sects referred to produced a bitterness of feeling between the members of each that provoked continual hostilities, which too often resulted . . . in bloodshed.[44]

   Leach satirizes Christianity, labor unions, capitalists, and American society in general throughout the novel without ever intruding in overtly didactic fashion. His criticism is always leveled against the various societies he visits, which he purports to find in contrast to the wonderful excellence of like institutions in America.

   The authors used satire and irony to make their points and though none was a master of either technique, all had the same desire: to question the motives of those who upheld the social and political order, to suggest change in the order, and to objectify their subjects of ridicule just enough to escape libel but make clear nonetheless the object of their scorn. James Converse lacks subtlety in his attack on Bellamy. It is too obvious and too broad. The Reverend Mr. Logan's dramatization of the Baptist baptism, on the other hand, is amusing; it is one of the few moments of comic relief in *Alice McDonald*, and by giving some objective distance to the whole scene—the reader knows none of the participants involved—the author gets his point across quite nicely. While in both of these works the authors use satire sparingly, in works like *An Experiment in Altruism* and *Soulless Saints* it is used throughout. The latter novel is too long, and the combined allegory, irony, and satire grow tiresome because the author has no real focus. As his hero goes from mythical culture to culture, various aspects of nineteenth-century American society are satirized, but the wholesale attack finally weakens the total effect. This is not the case with Mrs. Sherwood's

Experiment in Altruism. The scope of the author's probing of the motivations, actions, and effects of active philanthropists is narrowed to a given set of characters in New York City during a fairly short period, and the plot and point of the author's commentary is strengthened by self-parody. She was a philanthropist too, and wanted to help the poor and the deprived. The question was, how? She saw many flaws in the Lord and Lady Bountiful approach, but she did not know what to do in lieu of it—except be honest and keep trying to teach, learn, and help others in the best way she could.

Leach's *Soulless Saints* uses both satire and allegory. Allegory is used in the novels even more often than satire as a means of dramatizing sins and evils of the time; and, like satire, it has the advantage of lending itself to a wide range of subjects. Also like satire, allegory can objectify problems and speak in terms of abstract evils and abstract reforms. Unlike the conventional novel limited to people, their lives, and their particular problems, allegory can deal with Everyman, Pilgrim, and Gulliver.

Mr. World and Miss Church-Member is a good example of this approach. The two major characters in the novel follow the spiritual road to hell in a pattern similar to that of *Pilgrim's Progress*. Miss Church-Member was originally a good Christian led through missionary zeal to try to draw Mr. World away from the Broad Highway of Satan to the King's Highway to redemption. It was she, however, who was converted to Mr. World's road, and the novel ends with both characters in terror before the Awful River of Damnation. Just before they were pushed in by an agent of the devil they had a "vision of the Shining Pilgrims of the King's Highway, and saw that when they reached the brink of the River of Death they were met by a convoy of angels, on whose snowy pinions they were borne aloft to the very gates of the Celestial City which apparently stood on white clouds."[45]

Albert B. King, author of *Memorable Voyages of Rebel and Victory*, used the same theme as Harris, though in this case the narrative line is more episodic and the battles between good and evil take place primarily at sea between Satan's vessel named *Rebel* and God's good ship *Victory*. All of the names of the crews, ports, and supplies are allegorical, and many evil ports of call are visited— Worldliness, Malady, Supernatural—where *Victory's* crew is tempted and often all but destroyed.

King was fond of animal imagery as a means of depicting various evils. At one point in the novel, after *Victory* had fought a hard fight with an enemy vessel, Captain Spiritual opened the hold of his own ship where he suspected that "things which belonged to the World, the Flesh, and the Devil" had secreted themselves.

Immediately an outcry arose from imprisoned beasts, birds, and reptiles who shrank in terror from the knowledge of God's light. Nor was this fear and hatred lessened, but much increased, when "Love," "Joy," "Peace," and others of the crew sprang into the hold and approached the cages in which these vile and dangerous creatures were confined.

The first cage seen and seized contained the strong lion of "Self-Assertion." This animal was the only one showing no sign of fear. He roared and viciously sought to strike with his claws those who approached him. But the crew quickly got up a tackle on the fore yard-arm, by which the caged lion was hoisted and cast into the sea.[46]

The evils kept coming back, however, and the above process was repeated with variations a number of times during the novel. At the work's end *Rebel* is destroyed and *Victory* gains the safety of the port of New Jerusalem.

An allegory written by William Allen called *Erudia, the Foreign Missionary to our World; or, The Dream of Orphanos* tells of the visitation of Erudia from among the gods of outer space. Her function is to explain to Orphanos, who stands for Everyman, exactly what is the matter with earth. The following describes her at the time of her arrival:

Just as he [Orphanos] reached near the point where the path through the garden meets the grove he saw standing . . . a creature that immediately and deeply impressed him that she did not belong to this world of ours. The dress was female attire, with no attempted display of fashion. . . . She wore a single jewel, beautifully bright, and glittering even in the twilight. It was a *key* which indicated wisdom to unlock the mysteries of the human heart, and to open the doors of right progression for this world of ours. Embracing the upper part of the forehead was a beautiful crescent just large enough to contain in bold type the world *Instructor*. The eyes were exceedingly bright, the face and hands delicately white. The form stood very erect and with so quiet and soft a mien that it afforded entertainment rather than produced alarm. The dress was of the purest white delicately trimmed with glittering ribbon.[47]

The young woman in question—a cross between Diana and Minerva?—must have had a very broad forehead indeed. But no matter. Erudia showed the hero personifications of good and evil through various animals she brought with her and strange jewels into which he could look and see life elsewhere. She assured him that, though his world was small compared to some, it was beautiful and greatly favored by "the Lord God." However, there were many dangers. She praised earth's Christianity, saying that it alone was positive and that all other religions were negative, but that the evils of intemperance, avarice, slander, traveling on Sunday, and concern with fashion threatened Western civilization. At the novel's close Erudia left Orphanos, explaining as she did so that the Golden Rule is man's greatest moral precept and that good in our world would eventually triumph. At that point Orphanos awoke from his dream.[48]

Another allegorical work, William B. Bolmer's *The Time Is Coming*, tells of a Mr. Hilary, a Herculean vegetarian and true man of God and his battles against secular evil. The novel is episodic to the extreme—there is a chapter in which the American navy subdues all of North Africa and then Great Britain, another which tells of the building of a huge Jewish temple in Chicago, and a third attacking the secularization of the Episcopal church. Archeology and philology are also condemned as tools of Satan used to discredit the Bible. The prophet Elijah is a character, announcing the Second Coming of Christ, and with Hilary's help, leading America in a nationwide revival. Near the end of the novel the forces of evil gather under Satan's leadership, throw the country into civil war, and Elijah and Mr. Hilary are captured by the enemy. The heroes are hopeful nonetheless, and the last paragraph of the novel states:

The clouds hang thick and heavy, but some rays pierce the gloom; the distant mountains at least are radiant with sunshine. The movement towards a higher Christianity will not die; Elijah has not spoken in vain, a Remnant at least will be ready to welcome the Lord of Elijah and of Ambrose Hilary when He comes, as come He surely will. "Amen. Even so, come, Lord Jesus."[49]

Another allegory, Charles M. Sheldon's *Robert Hardy's Seven Days; a Dream and Its Consequences*, is a retelling of the Everyman story. Mr. Hardy, a successful man in his middle fifties, is selfish, thoughtless of his family, and a church member but by no means a Christian in the true sense of the term. One Sunday night he has a vivid dream in which God tells him he has seven days to live. The experience is so intensely real that Hardy is convinced of the truth of the premonition. The novel recounts his complete change from his previous way of living to that of a real Christian. During the week Job-like disasters happen to the entire family, most of them due to Hardy's way of living prior to his revelation. All manage to face events, however, and grow in spiritual stature because of them. At the novel's end, Hardy is by and large prepared for his judgment and, in prayer, goes to meet his maker.[50]

The novel is one of Sheldon's poorest. The author intrudes on the narrative so often that the work is more like an extended sermon on how the Christian should prepare for death than a piece of fiction that combines the plots of Everyman and Job.

Three of Mrs. Ward's novels are allegories that form a thematic trilogy on the same subject—the nature of life after death.[51] Originally published over a span of nineteen years, they show the author's continued preoccupation with her theme. Chronologically the first of the three, *The Gates Ajar*, is the least allegorical. Written as a diary in the life of Mary Cabot, it opens with her inconsolable grief over the death of her greatly beloved brother during the Civil War. The standard condolences of friends and her Congregational minister not only give no comfort but make her angry. Her faith in God's justice and mercy is shaken, and her own unhappiness daily increases until an aunt whom she had never met comes for a visit. From that event onward Aunt Winifred and Mary discuss the nature of life after death. Winifred convinces Mary that heaven is much like our earthly existence but without pain and unhappiness. Moreover, there one is united with all those one cared for most on earth.

This element of the Swedenborgian conception of heaven is more pronounced in both of Mrs. Ward's other novels on the subject. *Beyond the Gates* is an extended dream sequence of a young woman in a deep coma during brain fever. Her dream is of heaven where she meets her father, and friends, and leads an active and healthy life, culminating in her reunion with her deceased former lover and their marriage. The ceremony is performed by Christ himself. At the point of the marriage the heroine, to the great joy and pleasure of her family and physician, awakes from her unconscious state. She herself, however, is curiously unhappy. She has seen heaven and longs to be there eternally.

The last novel in the series, *The Gates Between*, was published four years after *Beyond the Gates* and is the poorest and most dogmatic of the author's works read. In dealing with the same subject matter, this time Mrs. Ward makes her hero a worldly physician who had made success in his profession his religion. Killed in a carriage accident, Dr. Thorne can nonetheless see and understand all that takes place about him. He cannot, of course, be seen by others, and it takes him some time to understand that he is actually dead. Such an existence is a kind of hell for him, made worse by his inability to move about freely. He is confined to the business district of his city and can unaccountably not reach his home. At length, after fainting, he awakes in heaven to find that there life is much as it was on earth except that one's social position in heaven's hierarchy is based on spiritual health, not on professional skill and money, as on earth. Finally, after being humbled and seeing the error of his earthly ways he gains spiritual faith, sees Christ, and at the novel's end is united with his wife and small son.

Lester Bodine's *Off the Face of the Earth* tells of a young newspaper reporter's dream on his thirtieth birthday. Pegasus takes him to heaven, where he sees all sorts of allegorical sins and virtues on the way (a Society Mermaid "in the social swim," a character named Influence who has great long arms and is a man with "pull," and the Man with the Marble Heart). The author sought to present a combination of cleverness and high seriousness in his novel. The Unitarian sect is called the broad-gauge line to heaven, and the sinful arrived in hell C.O.D.— cooked on delivery. At the same time Michael Angelo, the young man's guide, cross-examines him about conditions on earth and lectures him on its evils—the corruption of young women seeking work in the big city, the hypocrisy of professed Christians who mouth the Golden Rule on Sunday but bow to the rule of gold the other six days of the week, and prejudice against Jews and Catholics. At the close of the novel Elijah prophesies the imminent destruction of the earth, and the newspaperman is sent back to be condemned with the rest.[52]

Baron Kinatas (Satanik spelled backwards) also foretells the Second Coming. But the plot of this novel deals with the prophesy from Revelation that the Anti-Christ will come first and gain almost absolute control of the world and that at the moment he proclaims himself God, the earth will be consumed by fire. Baron Kinatas is the Anti-Christ, a devil in the form of the Wandering Jew, Cain. The novel is an elaborate treatment of the legend and the only work encountered that is strongly anti-Semitic.[53]

In a number of allegorical works the plot centers on the Second Coming of Christ, or a character in the novel plays the symbolic role of Christ. Almost all of these novels would be classified under the social Gospel heading outlined in Chapter 1. The most famous of them is undoubtedly the best known of all social gospel works, Charles M. Sheldon's *In His Steps*. Especially famous was the scene early in the novel in which the Christ-like wanderer, coming into a church service, speaks to the rich congregation of the city of Raymond about the practical responsibility of man to his fellows and then collapses, a martyr to the actual inhumanity of man to man.[54]

In His Steps was by no means the first to use the Second Coming of Christ, or a Christlike character, as a major fictional device. The pattern is no doubt as old as the recorded Second Coming prophecy in the Bible; but the first of the American novelists in the period from 1865 through 1900 to use it, as far as I could ascertain, was Isaac G. Reed, Jr., in *From Heaven to New York*, published in 1876.

The novel is an odd one. The first half of it is filled with satiric comment on the *nouveaux riches*; then rather abruptly it changes in tone and in its second half is dogmatically serious. The characters are all one-dimensional, either very good, as is the Goodheart family, or very bad, as is the Brownstonefront family. The Goodheart boys all grow up to be fine upstanding Christian men who, each and every one, fail in their chosen professions (law, politics, the ministry) because they insist upon being honest. They fail because they live in a corrupt New York City. There are only two bright spots in this grimness: one is Mary Brownstonefront, the essence of goodness despite her parents, sisters, and upbringing. She marries Melville Goodheart, the minister who fails. The other is Mary's tutor and friend of the Goodheart family, known only as the Mysterious Stranger. When Melville finally sickens and dies, the Mysterious Stranger reveals himself at the funeral to be Christ. He condemns the earth and says He will return to give judgment. *From Heaven to New York* is the only novel in which Christ reveals his identity while on earth a second time.

It was not until 1894 that the next two novels of this type appeared. A rare volume by Milford W. Howard is entitled *If Christ Came to Congress*. Violent and slanderous in tone, it too condemns the state of the nation; the author lashes out at everything from plutocratic, hypocritical congressmen and senators, to Grover Cleveland and his attorney general, Richard Olney. There is even a detailed map of houses of ill fame in Washington, and the author lists them by street, house number, the name of the Madame, her color, and the number of girls on call.[55]

A good example of the author's rhetoric is in his dedication: "This little volume is unwillingly and without permission dedicated to Grover Cleveland, President of the United States, certain corrupt members of his cabinet, and the horde of drunken, licentious, senators and congressmen and their mistresses, herein referred to.''[56]

In the preface and text itself Howard declares that not only would Christ ''find whoremongers and prostitutes holding the destinies of this nation in their grasp,'' but that

if Christ came to this body of plutocrats and asked for bread, he would be scourged to the city prison by the minions of the law, and if he should come pleading for the passage of laws, which will provide work for the starving thousands and enable them to procure food for themselves and helpless families, he would be jeered at as a crank, and insulted and hooted at as a common tramp; and if he asked the right and privilege of presenting the grievances of our people to the law makers, it would likely be said of Him, in the language of a distinguished judge, ''with such a right, all the tramps of the country, would be apt to come and take possession of either House of Congress.''[57]

The other volume that appeared in that year was *The Crucifixion of Philip Strong* by Charles M. Sheldon. His most theologically radical work, it anticipated many of the doctrines expounded in *In His Steps*, published three years later. Strong is a young minister who receives a call from Calvary Church in the growing industrial town of Milton. He goes and, after seeing the terrible plight of the laboring masses and the un-Christian blindness of his rich congregation, tries to induce the congregation to act in a more Christian fashion. He gains both friends and enemies in his church, most notable an individual known only as Brother Man, who plays an allegorical God to Philip's Christ. Finally the opposition element succeeds in asking Philip for his resignation after he has preached a sermon in which he proposes that members of his church give away their wealth and literally go and live among the poor. In his last sermon at the book's close Strong takes on the mantle of Christ himself; while compassionately condemning his congregation, he falls back upon a huge cross built into the altar and dies. As melodrama, no other novel of Sheldon's reaches this intensity. As allegory, no other work is as literal in portraying a Christ-like character.

In 1895, two other novels based on the Second Coming of Christ were published, both considerably less dramatic. Edward E. Hale's *If Jesus Came to Boston* was written in answer to a volume that had caused a sensation the year before, a work by Englishman William T. Stead. In his preface Hale wrote:

Mr. Stead has written a valuable book, under the striking title, *If Christ Came to Chicago*. It has excited much comment and much alarm. It has suggested to ill-informed people that Christ's plans have failed badly, and that, as has been well said, ''we are all going to hell remarkably fast,—as we are not.'' We have no wish to abate the force of any one of its warnings. We have no desire to contrast the cities of Boston and Chicago,—which are, indeed, cities curiously alike in many important regards, though not always thought so. But we believe it so important that every student of life should take all points of view, that we are glad to be able to present another picture, as our friend Dr. Primrose happened to see it. He had noted the title of Mr. Stead's sketch, and, to some notes of his week's experience with his unknown friends, we venture to give the title above, *If Jesus Came to Boston.*[58]

The novel itself is short. Dr. Primrose, a fine Boston clergyman, meets a strange and magnetic Syrian on a boat returning from Europe. The Syrian, going under the name of Benagar, is coming to hunt for a long-lost brother and other relatives, and Dr. Primrose undertakes to help him in his search, all the while showing his friend the fine philanthropic agencies of Boston. Benagar, whom Dr. Primrose never suspects to be Christ, disappears suddenly, leaving the following message: *"I have gone to Chicago. I find I have other sheep there. What you in Boston have been doing to the least of these my brethren and my sisters, you have done it unto me."*[59]

The second allegorical novel published in 1895 is entitled simply, *Lazarus*, by Olla P. Toph.[60] It is a full-scale allegory wherein Lazarus and Christ meet in heaven and discuss the world, which they agree has not sufficiently and rightly practiced the teachings of their "Elder Brother." They decide to return to nineteenth-century America and find a man named Reform, who is trying to effect exactly what Lazarus and Christ had in mind. They appear to Reform and help him as he works to help the poor, the worker, and the church. Hagar and Mary Magdalene also give aid by counseling Reform through dreams. Reform is highly successful in getting Christian legislation passed, and he also gains many followers and friends who promise to maintain and fulfill his work. At the end of the novel Reform joins Lazarus and Christ in heaven.

One of the best of the "If Christ Came" novels is Elizabeth S. Ward's short *The Supply at Saint Agatha's.*[61] Little more than a short story, it tells of a large, wealthy metropolitan church that has asked an aged rural minister, grandson of St. Agatha's founder, to come and preach one Sunday during the absence of the regular minister. The Saturday before he is to preach, the old man is called out in a storm to spend the night with a dying widow and loses his way coming back home. Before he dies, his last words are, "Lord, into thy hands I commit— my supply." The Lord comes Himself. The people are electrified at his sermon, and in the evening's vesper service the huge church is packed with rich and poor alike. No one really knows the identity of the mysterious preacher, but all feel his power. Mrs. Ward's economy of idea and situation are matched by her effective, stark diction and lack of sentimentality.

In His Steps was published in 1897. The title comes from a statement made by St. Peter: "For even hereunto were ye called, because Christ also suffered for you, leaving you an example, that ye would follow in His steps." The initials of the novel's title, IHS, also stand for a commonly used shortened form of the Greek for Jesus. The plot hinges on the Reverend Mr. Henry Maxwell's appeal to his congregation to pledge themselves to try to live exactly as Christ for one year. The major portion of the novel tells of the various members' successes and failures (there is only one of the latter) in attempting to do so. There is little that is sophisticated about the novel; it is not intellectually complex or symbolically difficult; the characters are one-dimensional, and their development is seen on the religious level only. But the emotional appeal of actually being able to be Christlike, to be perfect, was apparently a very strong one, and Sheldon's detailed recounting of how various individuals manage such a feat, told with an almost wholly unselfconscious sincerity, works to the novel's advantage.

One businessman in Maxwell's church resolves to walk in His steps and makes the following list to help him on his way:

"WHAT JESUS WOULD PROBABLY DO IN MILTON WRIGHT'S PLACE AS A BUSINESS MAN."

1. He would engage in the business first of all for the purpose of glorifying God, and not for the primary purpose of making money.

2. All money that might be made he would never regard as his own, but as trust funds to be used for the good of humanity.

3. His relations with all the persons in his employ would be the most loving and helpful. He could not help thinking of all of them in the light of souls to be saved. This thought would always be greater than his thought of making money in the business.

4. He would never do a single dishonest or questionable thing or try in any remotest way to get the advantage of any one else in the same business.

5. The principle of unselfishness and helpfulness in the business would direct all its details.

6. Upon this principle he would shape the entire plan of his relations to his employees, to the people who were his customers and to the general business world with which he was connected.[62]

In conjunction with the rest of the business community of the city, Mr. Wright acts on his principles and is successful.

Two years after *In His Steps*, in 1899, a rather misleadingly entitled novel, *A Dream of Christ's Return*, was published. It tells the story of a minister who is attending a series of church meetings and dreams of seeing a perfect Christian world.[63] Most of the dream sequences relate to the plight of the poor and the necessity of the church's preaching a living, temporal Christianity as well as dealing with the spiritual side of man. Christ himself does not appear in the minister's dream, but the clergyman knows that his visions come from Him. The minister—he is unnamed—gives an impassioned account of his dream at one of the church meetings and convinces a number of his listeners to become involved in the social and economic issues of the time.

Frederic W. Pangborn in his novel *Thou Art the Man. A Suggestion Story for the Christian Church* follows a plot similar to Sheldon's *In His Steps*, the difference being that in this case the minister involved, the Reverend Mr. Johnsbury Jeemax, is made aware of the un-Christian character of a leading portion of his congregation not through a Christlike character's condemnation, but through a series of anonymous letters from a "TJ" that detail the sins of various church members. The Reverend Mr. Jeemax broods on the question of what to do and resolves on a daring move: he preaches a sermon on Christianity in daily life and asks all members to change their ways of living. If not, they will either be dismissed from the church or he will resign. The next Sunday a meeting is held to decide the question. The unknown "TJ" reveals himself as a rich eccentric recluse and tells what he did. A vote is taken on the resignation of the Reverend Jeemax; he wins by a vast majority and the hypocrites leave the church.

One can only speculate about why the particular form of allegory that used Christ literally or symbolically was so popular during the period from the end of the Civil War to the turn of the century, although the idea itself can be traced in America from Samuel Sewall's *Diary* up through the many millenialist sects prior to the Civil War. A probable reason was that since many of the authors stressed the gospel portion of the social gospel movement, they might have been more inclined to follow the parable technique so often used by Christ in the Bible than more conventional forms of fiction. At first glance one might also assume that the tremendous popularity of *In His Steps* precipitated many imitations. Publishing history does not bear out such an assumption, however. Of the nine novels that used this allegorical form at least up through the year 1900, six were published before *In His Steps*. Among them, of course, was William Stead's *If Christ Came to Chicago*, a lurid affair that names names and dates and is full of other documentation of the evils of Chicago. According to Edward E. Hale's preface to *If Jesus Came to Boston*, the Stead book must have caused something of a scandal, and it might well have become the prototype for Second Coming fiction. *If Christ Came to Congress*, for example, published the same year as the Stead volume, is very similar in form and content.

The popularity of the form might also have been one of those periodic fads in publishing similar to that of the dime westerns or the brand of historical fiction associated with Thomas B. Costain and Frank Yerby, popular during the 1940s and 1950s. Whatever the reason, allegories in general and those specifically concerned with comparing Christlike individuals and teachings with the ordinary American and his world in the Gilded Age apparently had considerable appeal.[64]

This chapter has dealt with some aspects of the literary content and quality of social Christian fiction. Prefaces and introductions to the novels give some insights into why their authors chose to express their ideas in fictional form. Likewise various characters in the works sometimes speak for their authors on the same subject and go on to express attitudes about the nature of fiction, aesthetically and as a cultural influence on society.

From the textual evidence, the authors evidently wrote to accomplish one or more of three objectives: to expose some of the wrongs of society and the church in a general fashion and record their concern that something be done to change existing conditions; to pose specific problems and propose specific solutions; and to play the role of Jeremiah in condemning the lax morality of the time, suggesting a return to past institutions and ethical systems. They chose to use narrative prose in the hope of gaining a wider audience for their views, in two cases—*Westbrook Parsonage* and *Alice McDonald*—specifically, young people; for aesthetic shaping and control of the material; and probably because they hoped to gain converts to their point of view by combining the logic of their arguments with an emotional involvement on the part of their readers.

The most unexpected and interesting comments on the nature and role of fiction concerned the aborning techniques of realism. Helen D. Brown's *The Petrie Estate* is the best example of arguing for the new approach, Albion W. Tourgée's *Murvale Eastman* the most vehement against it, and William S. Harris's *Mr. World and Miss Church-Member* the most elaborate in condemning any but the most pure and didactically Christian prose.

Critical evaluation of the literary quality of the novels centers on the validity of the authors' logic and rhetorical skill at argument, their abilities as stylists, and the fullness and depth of the characters created. With noted exceptions the authors are weakest in presenting more than stereotyped, one-dimensional characters. As a whole, their greatest strength lies in arguing their respective theses. Stylistically the majority present mediocre examples of late Victorian-American prose, though again there are some significant exceptions.

The latter half of the chapter has concentrated on stylistic devices and plot patterns widely found in the novels. The use of satire and allegory provide the main focus of attention.

Perhaps the most significant comment about the novels as literature is that the better a given novel in a literary sense, the better it was as propaganda for the author's thesis. The converse, however—the better the propaganda, the better the novel—is not true. In the former case, the stylistic abilities of the author coupled with artistry in delineating the characters in the work helped greatly to enlist the reader's serious consideration of the author's thesis. However, a thinly veiled tract with only the barest outlines of plot and skeleton characters had the effect, at least on this reader, of making him wish the writer had given himself or herself wholly to writing the essay that he or she had in mind instead of weakening the argument by trying to graft the ideas onto a superficial narrative peopled with figures speaking impossible prose. In the latter case the literary product is neither fish nor fowl; as an exercise in persuasion it is blunted by forcing the author's argument to be presented through situations and characters lacking verisimilitude. As literature the work is weakened by inadequate structure and characterization but also because the author's theme becomes an overriding thesis, acceptable in a factual essay, but not in a novel.

When a novel's style and characterization are both successful, as in *The Burden of Christopher*, the author's theme was much more respectfully considered. The novel could then be an effective instrument of propaganda as well as a respectable work of art.

4

Conclusion

The social Christian novel written between the end of the Civil War and the beginning of the twentieth century was but one voice in the chorus of criticism that registered America's uneven shift from agrarianism to industrialization. The novels were first and foremost concerned with how this shift affected Americans' religious beliefs and the nation's institutions. Under the dual impacts of an increasing class of industrial workers and growing cities, the Protestant churches of America were forced to reconsider both Christian dogma and the practical role of the churches in the lives of the people.

On the first level of analysis, the novels registered and reinforced two importantly held beliefs about the period: the Protestant church as an institution had tremendous power during the last half of the nineteenth century and the American industrial revolution caused confusion and upheaval amounting almost to revolt in both spiritual and social spheres. It was in registering and documenting this second statement that one of the most interesting findings of the present study became apparent—that the term social gospel novel, usually given because the novels were assumed to be one aspect of the social gospel movement, was too narrow a term to describe the novels as a whole. It assumed on the part of all the novelists a unified middle-class attitude and point of view, which not all of them demonstrated. Such a misconception is understandable because most of the scholarship done on the subject has identified the work of Charles M. Sheldon—particularly *In His Steps*—as representative of the whole.[1] *In His Steps* does represent a type of social gospel novel, but the social gospel novel is but one type of work within the larger framework of what I have called social Christian fiction. Social Christian fiction during the period from 1865 to 1900 is that in which an author's primary theme deals with some major social problem of the day and then prescribes a solution based on his or her interpretation of Christian morality and ethics.

There are four categories of social Christian fiction, categories made clear by means of defining the point of view of the authors in their interpretation of the problems with which they dealt and the proposed solutions as presented through the actions and statements of the principal characters. The theologically and socially conservative first category stresses the writers' concern with social and economic ferment as a threat to the expanding system of American industrialization. Writers in this mode often thought that those responsible for the difficulties were socialists, foreigners, and/or workers, but seldom proposed specific solutions. Vague generalizations about the usefulness of Christian institutions, the need for ''brotherhood,'' and the responsibilities of *noblesse oblige* on the part of the upper class were common. An allegorical approach that stressed mysticism, transcendentalism, or spiritualism was also popular as a means of expressing that this life is but a transitory vale of tears. All must stoically and righteously endure their position in life—be it good or ill. One's true reward—again be it good or evil—will come in the hereafter.

The second category emphasizes variations of the gospel of wealth. The heroes and heroines are almost all of the upper class, with upper-class values, but their concern leads them to propose more practical procedures for alleviating slum life and the plight of labor as depicted in the novels. Stewardship, philanthropy, and classical charity are the remedies most often suggested, and the protagonists in the novels fall into two main groups: those who are sympathetic but promote reform from afar, instructing subordinates to build model tenements, construct working men's halls and memorial chapels; and those in which the heroines (seldom the heroes) actually go to live in the slums and carry on relief work by trying to gain some real knowledge of the people and problems involved.[2]

Social gospel fiction constitutes the third and largest category of social Christian fiction. The protagonists in this category are either middle class or working class, and the problems and criticism of conditions center on two charges: the principles of social justice expounded in the New Testament are inimical to the practicalities of laissez-faire economics; and too many urban Protestant churches were becoming appendages of the rich—the church as an institution was becoming a secular social club more interested in imposing architecture, choirs, and eloquent speakers than in giving spiritual and temporal comfort to the masses. The authors often charged the churches with being overly preoccupied with the spirit of man while they shied away from the practical teachings of Christianity as stated in the Golden Rule and the Ten Commandments.[3]

The fourth and last category of social Christian fiction is made up of radical Christian works. Novels that announce that Christ was a socialist or that espouse Christian socialism, communism, or anarchism fall under this heading. The primary thesis of these novelists is that since Christian ethics and capitalistic laissez-faire economics are antagonistic to each other, the economic system must be changed to one more in accord with the authors' interpretations of Christianity.[4]

The first two classes of the fiction are thus essentially socially and theologically conservative. Their authors were anxious to draw attention to and remove the threatening aspects of labor unrest—demands for higher wages and shorter hours. The burden of the authors' arguments rested on mitigating some of the effects of the American industrial revolution without changing the basic structure of the economic system that was bringing new wealth to the nation.

The authors of the other two types of social Christian novels directed their attention much more to the causes of economic and theological maladjustment than to their effects. The authors focused their principal arguments on the churches. They felt that the tradition of Protestant dissent and its concern for the moral and physical welfare of all the people had relaxed in the post–Civil War period of economic boom, and they set about to inspire once again ecclesiastical leadership in the cause of social and economic reform.

Aspects of Protestant ferment directly manifest through the novels fall into certain well defined categories. First and foremost are arguments over the pros and cons of social reform sponsored by American churches. The authors who argued against the churches' sponsorship of reform or who offered rationalizations for why this had not been done based their positions on three arguments: the upper class was ignorant of just how bad conditions of those beneath them were; religious ethics are separate from and irrelevant to business ethics, and an attempt to fuse the two would result in chaos for both; and the strength, appeal, and function of Christianity is fundamentally spiritual in nature, and these qualities would be debased and weakened if the churches entered into disputes of the marketplace and the everyday affairs of men.

On the other side are the works in which the authors advocated Protestantism's taking the lead in speaking for the rights of the worker, attacking the abuses of big business, and leading the fight for social humanitarianism in general. The authors' arguments were based on the Golden Rule and the Western tradition of social and political justice.

Directly related to the positions taken by the authors on matters of reform, of how and by whom such measures should be accomplished, are arguments about denominationalism and factionalism due to differences in dogma, ritual, and biblical interpretation. The authors who in their works advocated direct participation of the churches in social reform often maintained that the dogma and ethics of many of the denominations were archaic and unsuited to conditions of the time. Many authors argued for reevaluation and revamping of sectarian tenets as one means of keeping up with social and economic change; others, more militant, maintained that denominationalism itself diminished the vitality and strength of the church—that the churches have to reeducate themselves to changing conditions and thereby redefine the differences between true religion and outdated orthodoxy.[5]

These three elements—the conservative defense and rationale for nonparticipation in reform, the liberal demand for the opposite expounded in the social gospel, and arguments over the role of separate Protestant denominations—are interrelated in some novels and carefully separated in others.

In the novels studied in this monograph, those that are openly sectarian and seek converts through fictional devices are indeed, with very few exceptions, politically, socially, and theologically conservative. However, novels that are evangelical in the cause of the social gospel, that are nondenominational but often published by denominational presses, are almost unanimously liberal in relation to politics, social dislocation, and issues of sectarian dogma. Moreover, as has been made apparent in earlier chapters, to be conservative on Protestant-led reform did not necessarily mean that an author was a strong partisan of a particular denomination or that that author was defensive about preserving the dogmatic purity of his or her brand of Protestantism. Quite often neither of these issues was mentioned in the works read.

Even militant professional evangelists of the period, sectarian or not, resist generalizations about their stands on church-sponsored social reform. Grier Nicholl is correct in the following observation, up to the last sentence quoted. Then he too falls prey to oversimplification.

Although it is true that evangelical Protestantism, in the hands of professional revivalists, tended to confirm the *status quo*, it is not true that evangelism had only a conservative and reactionary cast in the period. Evangelical religion was moderately progressive and reformist as well. What is often neglected in the history of this stream of Protestantism is that evangelicalism of a more moderate cast played an important role in the propagation of the social gospel between 1870 and 1918. Christian social novels, written to dramatize the application of the social gospel to industrial conditions, were the major manifestations of social gospel evangelism.[6]

Aside from a semantic confusion between the words "evangelicalism" and "evangelism," which Nicholl seems to use as synonyms, his argument that "Christian social novels, written to dramatize the application of the social gospel to industrial conditions, were the major manifestations of social gospel evangelism," is an extreme statement that was not verified by my research. It is true that in social Christian fiction there are numerous examples that testify to this equation: liberal orientation and propaganda for reform + arguments against denominationalism = the social gospel message. There are also novels in which the equation reads: conservative orientation and propaganda for traditional charity + positive attitudes toward denominationalism = *implied* resistance to the social gospel. There are also examples of almost every kind of mathematical variation of the two equations.

About the intellectual quality of the novels, two statements can be made. First, as most popular fiction of any period tends to be, it is undistinguished by penetrating and sustained insights about the nature of man in his ambiguous role of living. This said, however, it can be argued, and with good cause, that the

quality and quantity of social, political, and religious sophistication displayed
by the authors in analyzing many of the fundamental problems of the Gilded
Age in America is high. The period from the end of the Civil War to the turn
of the century had been stereotyped as full of simultaneously gross and placidly
self-satisfied people uncritical of pragmatic laissez-faire ethics and the attendant
political corruption. Other stereotypes stress ostentatious wealth and indifference
to poverty and protest. The social Christian novels written during the period do
not validate these stereotypes. Many of the authors of the fiction were not
conservative defenders of their America; they did not rationalize or excuse the
elements of barbarism in our economic and political system. Many saw hypocrisy
between our loudly proclaimed political and theological creeds and our dog-eat-
dog actions, and they were not afraid to specify the hypocrisy. Perhaps no better
example of the essential liberal attitude of the authors of social Christian fiction
is to be found than in their reaction to Darwinism, biologically and socially.
Herbert Spencer we have been told was tremendously popular in America. His
analysis of social Darwinism presumably gave new and welcome strength to the
tired doctrines of laissez-faire. No social Christian novelist had any kind words
for Spencer—in fact, just the opposite. He and his doctrines were roundly attacked by social gospel authors, and the conservatives, even at their most serious,
never evoked his aid.

It is of course true that few of the novelists made direct references to Darwin's
findings, but the vast majority of the authors' arguments for Protestant leadership
in social reform were stated in such a way as to show that they were by definition
against Spencer's passive approach to progress. By Spencerian logic it could be
argued that reform measures sponsored by men were at best meaningless if not
downright harmful, disturbing the balance of nature's gradual changes. Such an
approach was not argued, however. Instead, the widespread spirit of active and
specific demand for reform in the novels constitutes some of the best evidence
that the majority of authors of social Christian fiction were not the purveyors of
pious conservative middle-class tracts that many have assumed them to be. In
sum, the most interesting intellectual aspect of social Christian fiction is its
manifestation of serious questioning and concern over the state and direction of
the American nation during the decades following the Civil War.

In short, these novels support the newer interpretation of the Gilded Age as
a time when discontent was observable. It was a time when "progressive Darwinism" was supplanting the idea of unrestrained competition. It was a time
when literature was playing an important part in identifying the principal problems of urban industrialism and shaping the nascent Progressive Era.

In keeping with this intellectual earnestness, the majority of writers of social
Christian fiction, it is clear, wrote not as literary artists but as propagandists
explaining problems of the time as they understood them and offering solutions.
Comments in the works indicate that most authors considered the function of
fiction to be essentially didactic, and some few were defensive about using the
still suspect form of the novel as a device for expounding their views. In a

number of prefaces and introductions the writers explained that their motives for writing were generally expository, sometimes on the most general level, sometimes exposing some specific evil or abuse. Few made direct statements about why they used the medium of fiction. Of the authors who did so, most agreed with what Harriet B. Stowe propounded in her preface to *Uncle Tom's Cabin*, "The poet, the painter, and the artist, now seek out and embellish the common and gentler humanities of life, and, under the allurements of fiction, breathe a humanizing and subduing influence, favorable to the development of the great principles of Christian brotherhood."[7]

Of course, all the authors hoped they would have Mrs. Stowe's huge success—that by putting their views in fictional form they would reach a much larger audience than if they had used the form of an essay or monograph. Only Charles M. Sheldon was rewarded in this manner, but a writer of social Christian fiction showed that he or she too could do for the cause of labor some of what Mrs. Stowe had done for the cause of abolition, and that the base of both of their arguments was the same—the living Christian ethics of the New Testament.

Contemplating the novels in the light of the standards of literary criticism is difficult. If you believe, along with Wayne C. Booth in *The Rhetoric of Fiction*,[8] that the primary function of creative literature is to argue or reenforce the moral structure of society, and view literature through the glass of history, then you can reasonably argue that the social Christian genre was successful both as propaganda and as literature. If you, with Ortega y Gasset, believe that literature must be judged as *ars artis gratia*, then the works were almost all failures. These two schools may be reconcilable somehow, but that of course is no easy feat. The novels are bad art, but from a historical view they appear to have been effective propaganda. It can be said that the better the novels are when judged by artistic standards, the better they were as propaganda.

Internally the novelists of the genre by and large followed the patterns and standards of late Victorian English—long sentences, asides and direct statements to the reader, Horatio Alger plots with usually happy endings. There were some interesting and distinctive variations, however. A great many authors used the device of allegory to express their attitudes. Animal imagery is abundant in numerous works, and there is a sizeable body of novels in which allegory merges with a mystical impressionism as a means of propagating doctrines of spiritualism, Christian Science, and related occult sciences. Allegory and symbol are also united in a number of works in which a character plays the literal or symbolic role of Christ. Sheldon's *In His Steps* is the best example of successful use of this allegorical technique.[9]

Satire is also employed by the authors. More often than not it is effective, as in *An Experiment in Altruism*, for example. And in many instances allegory and satire are joined in the same work.

Another distinguishing characteristic of the genre is a limited use of realistic technique, sometimes coupled with a discussion between characters of the relative merits of this new European mode of expression. No writer presents a sustained and organized argument for realism as such, and none of the novels is what could be called realistic in the accepted use of the term, though there are scenes in and portions of a number of works that were realistic, often quite effectively. Albion W. Tourgée, one of the few authors who was a professional writer, was vehement in his condemnation of realism, and his criticism, given in 1890 in *Murvale Eastman, Christian Socialist*, was not only extensive but perceptive in anticipating later serious analysis of the weaknesses of realism and naturalism.

Thus, while the social Christian novel is unquestionably in the mainstream of American Victorian prose, it has its unique characteristics—a limited use of realism and a fascination with allegory being the two most notable. It can be postulated that the novels were successful as aids to achieving reform. Almost all of the liberal causes preached in the works have come to fruition, though now, in 1985, we see the wheel turning against some of those very reforms enacted in the cause of equality—attacked, once again, in the name of a particular kind of individual liberty. As a manifestation of the social gospel, social Christian fiction was paradoxical in its impact on American Protestantism. The conservatives who argued that the end result of the churches' entering the marketplace of secular disputes would be a debasement of the lofty position of Christianity as the keeper of humans' souls can now state that that debasement has indeed followed. Sorting out any cause-and-effect relationship, however, is problematic.

The social Christian novel appears to have been an important means of communicating the ideas of social reformers. *Uncle Tom's Cabin* had shown how to do it. *In His Steps* followed the trail of Mrs. Stowe, and thus a tradition was established that runs all the way from *The Jungle* to *The Grapes of Wrath* to *Slaughterhouse Five*. Novels whose aims have been social reformation of one variety or another are seldom judged to be great works of art, but a rendering of ''art'' was probably not their authors' primary purpose. They sought social justice and social change in order to make the American dream of perfect freedom and perfect democracy a reality. That reality is still illusive, but the writers have had their effect—one that defies exact measurement, but that is nevertheless indisputable.

Appendix _____

Annotated List of Social Christian Novels

Out of 1300 novels considered, 145 were chosen as the basis for this work and are described below. To be included a work had to display, as its primary theme, the confrontation of Christian ethics with the social and economic problems of the time; or, to put the matter in another way, each work dramatized in some way the discrepancy between professed religious ideals and socioeconomic inequalities.

Works are listed chronologically according to year of publication. Within each year the order is alphabetical by author's surname. In keeping with the four primary modes of social Christian fiction outlined in the text, at the end of each annotation I have placed one of the letters A, B, C, or D according to the predominant point of view toward Christian sponsorship of social reform expressed by the author through primary characters and themes. Categories A through D are defined as follows:

A. Fictional expressions of vague, abstract, transcendental Christian humanism, usually without proposing any concrete course of action. Most works that used the literary technique of allegory fell under this heading.

B. Social gospel tracts. These are novels that argue for Christian-led secular reform usually based on appeals to social justice, stress on the social teachings of the Bible, and personal fulfillment of the Golden Rule.

C. Works that concentrate on theoretical political radicalism based on Christian ethics—communism, socialism, anarchism.

D. Socially and theologically conservative novels that stress traditional forms of charity as the best means of alleviating social unrest, poverty, and the claims of the working class. The author's themes often stress the responsibility of the upper classes to safeguard traditional forms of Christianity and laissez-faire democracy.

1867

Mitchell, the Reverend Walter. *Bryan Maurice; or, The Seeker.*
Philadelphia: J. B. Lippincott.

The work, pro-Anglican, is a highly intellectualized affair that begins in Italy. There the hero, Bryan Maurice, is a skeptic in search of faith. He meets an Episcopal minister, G. Gardiner, on a trip to Rome and comes to be influenced and fascinated by him. In Rome there are a number of involvements—the death of a Harvard friend, a flirtation with Roman Catholicism, a thwarted love affair with a beautiful Quakeress. Later, when Maurice is on route to England by boat, the vessel sinks. The Quakeress dies, but Maurice is miraculously saved. This brings about his partial conversion to Unitarianism. He goes to a seminary, preaches, but is still unhappy and dissatisfied in his faith. Finally through Gardiner, who has been an influence all along, he is converted to the Episcopal church, falls in love again, marries, and all ends happily. Unitarianism was too sentimentally liberal, Catholicism too traditional and conservative. Episcopalianism is the author's answer. (D)

Wright, Mrs. Julia MacNair. *The Shoe Binders of New York; or, The Fields White to the Harvest.* Philadelphia: Presbyterian Publication Committee; New York: A. D. F. Randolph.

Wealthy Miriam Elliott decides to serve humanity by working in the slums. She finds two young girls—Ruth and Lettie, the latter of whom is deaf and dumb—and after taking them to Sunday School at the local mission, becomes their benefactor. She also meets and reforms one Aunt Nab Wool, a mean and cynical drunkard. Ruth suddenly disappears—she has gone to take care of her father who has escaped from prison—leaving Lettie on Miriam's doorstep. The father conveniently dies, Ruth returns, forgiveness is mutual, and the novel ends with extended praise for Christian philanthropy. (D)

1868

Wright, Mrs. Julia MacNair. *The New York Needle-Woman; or Elsie's Stars.* Philadelphia: Presbyterian Publication Committee; New York: A. D. F. Randolph.

The novel tells the story of the Hart family of five who live in a slum. The father works hard and makes a respectable salary, but virtually every dollar is consumed by the vicious and alcoholic Mrs. Hart. Matthew, the oldest son, resolves to escape his environment and become a gentleman. He goes to board with one Sukey Green. Elsie Ray, the needle-woman of the title, is a Christian living in the same building with the Harts. With the help of wealthy Sophia Randall whom Elsie meets at a religious book store, she resolves to redeem, reform, and aid the Hart family. She does so with dispatch and success, greatly aided by the death of Mrs. Hart, who, drunk, kills her youngest child in her death agony. All ends well: all the remaining Hart children go to night school and become successful members of the churchgoing middle class. (B)

1869

Ward, Elizabeth Stuart Phelps. *The Gates Ajar*. Boston: Fields, Osgood.

This novel is about the question of death. How do we know that the dead are happier in heaven than on earth? Mary Cabot receives word of her brother's death in the Civil War and is grief stricken. The condolences of friends torment her—the rational pieties of the deacon of the Congregational church infuriate her. Her despair and doubt of God's love and mercy grow until her widowed Aunt Winifred arrives. The two have never met before. Winifred leads Mary back to faith through long discussions on the nature and wonder of an afterlife that is a perfection of life on earth. At the end of the novel Winifred dies, leaving Mary the guardian of Winifred's small daughter, Faith. Mary now has a purpose in life as she awaits the joys to come after death. (A)

Wright, Mrs. Julia MacNair. *The New York Bible-Woman*. Philadelphia: Presbyterian Publication Committee; New York: A. D. F. Randolph.

Two seamstresses live together, Christian Mary Ware and shrewish Prussia Wiggins. Mary is always helping her neighbors, and Prussia is always discontented and critical. Among the neighbors is widowed Margaret Wishalow, who has five children and no means of support. Rich Agnes Warren, for whom Margaret used to work, comes to see Margaret and meets Mary Ware. Agnes is so impressed with Mary's goodness that she sets her up as a Bible-woman (i.e., Mary is subsidized and sent to various parts of the city to read the Bible, teach the poor about religious and family duties, care for the sick, take note of destitute cases, and report all to a lady who acts as manager, furnishes relief, and gives advice). The remainder of the novel recounts Mary's successes and accomplishments in this regard, particularly with her fallen son, Richard, who is rescued from drink and eventually becomes a policeman. (D)

1870

McKeever, Harriet Burn. *Westbrook Parsonage*. Philadelphia: Claxton, Remsen and Haffelfinger.

The conflict dealt with here—and in a surprising number of similar novels—is between high and low church Anglicanism. Generally high church proponents sought some measure of rapprochement with the Roman Catholic church and were socially and politically conservative; low church defenders were conversely strongly Protestant and by and large more liberal both socially and politically. This particular novel follows the fortunes of Emily Hastings from the time of her marriage to a young Episcopal minister and their arrival at Westbrook, Massachusetts. Edward, the husband, is militantly low church, and the novel deals with their growing five children's religious crises and conversions, and their neighbors' conversions. Many sermons point out the evils of high Anglican pomp. The novel ends with a maudlin account of Edward Hastings's death. (D)

Ward, Elizabeth Stuart Phelps. *Hedged In*. Boston: Fields, Osgood.

The novelist probes just what the true Christian's approach to the fallen woman should be. Mrs. Ward's answer is the Golden Rule. Nixy is a fifteen-year-old unwed mother, who, in her ignorance, is without any sense of sin. Widow Margaret Purcell, who has a daughter the same age as Nixy, takes the waif in and helps her grow into a respectable adult. Nixy's child dies; she becomes abnormally close to Christina, Mrs. Purcell's daughter, and, at novel's end, dies the same day that Christina is wed. (B)

1871

Ward, Elizabeth Stuart Phelps. *The Silent Partner*. Boston:
James R. Osgood.

Perley Kelso finds herself heir to her father's many mills. A spoiled and petted young woman who has never really thought, felt, or done much of anything, engaged to a man she does not love, she realizes her shallowness when she makes the acquaintance of Sip (Priscilla) Garth, a worker in her mills. Perley breaks off her engagement, becomes the benefactor without fanfare of Sip, Sip's deaf-mute fifteen-year-old sister, and any other mill hands who need help. Eventually she refuses real love when it is offered; she considers her cause of helping others more important. She averts a strike, is instrumental in Sip's becoming a lay preacher, and generally aids the cause of labor and New Testament Christianity. (B)

1872

Author unknown. *Ivy Fennhaven; or, Womanhood in Christ. A
Story of Processes*. Boston: D. Lothrop.

The novel is a strange, almost completely plotless affair built around the theme of the necessary subjection of the individual's will to the will of God. Impressionistic in the extreme, characters enter and leave the plot, live and die, at random. The dialogue is a series of all but incoherent non sequiturs revolving around Ivy, her aristocratic family, and her search for the social and spiritual meaning of Christianity. (A)

1873

Arthur, Timothy Shay. *Cast Adrift*. Philadelphia: J. M. Stoddard.

Edith marries a young man against the will of her evil, domineering mother. The mother resolves to ruin the young husband and, through the fabrication of a forgery, does so. He is sent to prison and then to an insane asylum. Meanwhile Edith has a young son by him. The mother, Mrs. Dinneford, has the child spirited away and tells her daughter that the baby boy is dead. The rest of the plot deals with Edith's growing suspicions of her mother, her search for her child in the slums of Briar Street, Grubb Court, and elsewhere. Then Mrs. Dinneford dies, the husband is cleared, and the baby found. Throughout, Arthur argues that the respectable and influential element of society must be made aware of the evils of the slums—drinking, poor wages, housing, white slavery, and so on—that a large part of the problem is society's ignorance of conditions. Once these social crimes are acknowledged, then society will rectify them. (B)

1875

Murray, William Henry Harrison. *Deacons*. Boston: Henry L. Shepard.

The novel, an attack on the Congregational church for being too conservative and hidebound, is presented through a series of vignettes picturing deacons with allegorical names and characteristics: Deacon Slowup; Deacon Sharpface (the heresy hunter); Deacon Goodheart, kind, corpulent, and full of Christian charity. In the author's preface he states that the story "was written to call the attention of the church and people to the perversion and abuse of an office in our Congregational churches which was created to assist the pastors . . . but which . . . today fulfils no such service." (B)

1876

Chaplin, Mrs. Jane Dunbar. *Mother West's Neighbors*. Boston: American Tract Society.

A series of by and large unrelated vignettes held together by Mother West, who lives in a slum called Guptil Alley. She does good by unpretentiously devoting her life to others and thereby showing to the poor and degraded that there is something for which to live. The last four of twelve chapters are unified through the opening of a mission, Our Door, first by the arrogant Miss Thorne, and finally kept going by Mother West and her neighbors. (B)

Reed, Isaac George, Jr. *From Heaven to New York: or, The Good Hearts and the Brown Stone Fronts. A Fact Founded on Fancy*. New York: Murray Hill.

The problem presented is how to be good, true, and honest, and also successful in the real world where lying and cheating seem the prerequisites for success. Mr. Thomas Swell (an evil man) wants to marry Miss Mary Brownstonefront. The rest of the family wants her to do this also, primarily because Richard Brownstonefront, Sr. and Jr., are in financial difficulties that they think the marriage will resolve. Mary refuses, is disinherited, and marries her true love, Melville Goodheart, with the blessing of her tutor—the mysterious stranger. The story then shifts to the problems of the Goodheart family. One son, Robert, decides to go into business and fails miserably because he will not be dishonest. The same thing happens to Francis, who tries a number of professions—law, medicine, politics, literature. He ends up insane. Melville, as an Episcopalian clergyman, suffers the same fate and dies. At his grave the mysterious stranger reveals himself as Christ. He vows to soon come again and judge this godless, hypocritical world. (B)

1878

Guirey, George. *Deacon Cranky, the Old Sinner.* New York:
Authors' Publishing Co.

The novel deals with the problem of how to achieve a balance between narrow, old style Calvinism and the attacks of transcendental Unitarian liberalism. The church at Plymouth has a new building but is in debt, and the auditorium is unfinished. Moreover the church is without a minister. Deacon Cranky, a hypocritical religious liberal, sponsors a church fair to erase the debt. It is not a success and only widens the split between the liberals and the conservatives. Meanwhile conservative fundamentalist Reverend Mr. Hartman from the Midwest is asked to come and act as minister. He does but becomes embroiled in the factional fighting and is finally forced to resign because of the subversive efforts of Deacon Cranky and company. However, Deacon Cranky and the worldly element lose in the end, and virtue and the old-fashioned faith of fundamentalism are triumphant. (D)

1879

Noble, Annette Lucile. *"Out of the Way."* New York: American
Tract Society.

Mrs. Grey and Mrs. Stuart, both well-to-do Christian ladies, are led into charity work by a seamstress, Miss Hallenbeck, a forceful unmarried woman. All their endeavors take place at the Tombs, an elaborate charity ward outside New York City. While there, Mrs. Grey and Mrs. Stuart also meet a Mrs. Nichols, a kind of Lone Ranger Quakeress saint who disappears immediately after doing her good deeds. The novel tells of these characters' various experiences and focuses primarily on two girls—Mary and Elsie—and how they grow up to be outstanding examples of Christian womanhood because of the efforts of the four ladies involved. (D)

1880

Albert, Bessie. *How Bob and I Kept House; A Story of Chicago*
Hard Times. New York: Authors' Publishing Co.

A short and superficial story of a young couple of wealth and fashion who lose their money in a financial panic. Among other things, they learn that true

Christianity is not the pomp and ritual of the church of their opulent days but is in their little struggling neighborhood church, where "the congregation neither noticed nor cared if our garments were last year's cut and our hats and bonnets a year old." (B)

Buffett, E. P. *Rev. Mr. Dashwell, the New Minister at Hampton.* Philadelphia: J. E. Potter.

The novel is an attack on the Christian church for becoming too secular. The point is personified in the Reverend Mr. Dashwell, who is selfish, vain, and tremendously "liberal"—he smokes, drinks wine, plays pool. In contrast to him is the steadfast but aging Reverend Dr. Woodbridge, who holds the post Dashwell is seeking. The congregation finally sees through Dashwell; Woodbridge is reappointed, and Dashwell, unabashed, seeks a more "acceptable" position elsewhere. More through implication than by statement, the novel is strongly critical of the liberalism implied in the social gospel. (D)

Morgan, the Reverend Henry. *Boston Inside Out! Sins of a Great City! A Story of Real Life.* Boston: Shawmut.

The work is a polemical attack on Roman Catholicism, transcendentalism as permissive nonreligion, clairvoyants, gambling, alcoholism, abortion, and Catholic control of the Democratic Party—and is presumably autobiographical. While the Reverend Mr. Morgan is in Paris, he bitterly complains of the city's immorality; a compatriot tells him that Boston is every bit as bad. Morgan resolves to find out, and with the help of Jonathan Jenks, his chief investigator, finds Boston indeed corrupt beyond Morgan's wildest fears. The evil of the city is recounted with the counterpoint of the destruction of the Gildersleeve family, one of Boston's oldest. At the beginning of the story, the eldest Gildersleeve son is dead from alcoholism. The second son, Frank, also becomes an alcoholic and seducer—he dies insane. The daughter Gertrude becomes involved with an evil Catholic priest, one Father Titus, is seduced by him, and dies, as does the father of the family. Only Mrs. Gildersleeve is left, with her pride and arrogance finally destroyed. There are numerous and lengthy pictures of the underside of Boston life, with special attention to the corruption of the Catholic clergy. The author's social and religious outlook is rigidly Calvinistic. (D)

1881

Anderson, C. H. *Armour; or, What Are You Going to Do About It?* New York: W. B. Smith.

The novel attacks the secularization of the church, its lack of true Christianity, in the form of the hypocritically Christian Malcolm Conyngham, who politically and financially destroys his friend Lawrence Hamilton. The author attacks Jay Gould by name, the social pretensions of lordly Anglican and Presbyterian churches, and false "Sunday Christianity" in general. Conyngham, who rises to power at the expense of Hamilton, is finally unmasked at the novel's end. (B)

1883

Fauntleroy, Henry. *Who's To Blame?* Nashville: Southern
Methodist Publishing House, privately printed.

Penniless Frank Rivers and his young bride Annie come to Chicago from
Lafayette, Indiana, to make good. Frank, after long hunting and close to despair,
gets a job in a dry goods store. He is fired for being honest and refusing to cheat
customers. Annie meanwhile becomes pregnant, and in desperation Frank decides
to rob his former employer. He is caught, blinded by gunfire, and sent to jail.
Annie has her baby while visiting Frank in jail; it dies. Finally Frank regains
his sight and is acquitted of his crime just in time to die a heroic death in the
Chicago fire. The woman he saves befriends Annie, sets up a memorial chapel
for the poor in Frank's name, with Annie as matron. The story ends with a
violent tirade against judicial corruptness and America's loss of Christian principles. (D)

Gladden, Washington. *The Christian League of Connecticut.* New York: Century.

The novel is a tract in fictional form that argues for the consolidation of
Protestantism by means of destroying the barriers between individual denominations. Walter Franklin, banker, and Theodore Strong, minister of the Second
Congregational Church of New Albion, Connecticut, enlist the aid of various
churches in their city in forming a united league whose aim is to reach the
churchless classes and bring them into the Protestant fold. The plan works by
means of a thorough canvass of the entire city: each church is responsible for
seeing that the individuals living in a certain area are contacted and urged to
come to a new nondenominational Church of Christ. At the same time the League
helps to get the First Methodist Church out of debt, sees that temperance laws
are strictly enforced and the poor helped, and establishes three kindergartens.
The League idea spreads to other cities, states, nations, and the novel ends with
a national convention showing all how to do as the Christian League of Connecticut has done. (B)

Ward, Elizabeth Stuart Phelps. *Beyond the Gates.* Boston and New York:
Houghton Mifflin.

Mary, a young woman dying of brain fever, dreams she is in heaven. There
she meets her father and friends, and leads an active and healthy life through
goodness, which is God. Goodness is achieved through Christian unselfishness
on earth and in heaven. In her dream she meets a former lover; they are married
by Christ. At the end of the novel the heroine awakens from her coma, realizes
she is to live after all and is curiously unhappy with the knowledge. (A)

1884

Keyser, Harriette A. *Thorns in Your Sides.* New York: G. P.
Putnam's Sons.

Thorns in Your Sides is a strongly anti-Catholic, pro-Anglican novel that
focuses on the battle between the Reverend Dan Guardian, rector of St. Agnes's

Anglican Church, and Terence O'Farrell, illiterate hod carrier, alderman, and Irish dynamiter. Reverend Guardian and his daughter Sybilla are hated by the Irish in New York in general because they represent renegade Catholicism and work with the poor, and by O'Farrell in particular because their mutual ancestors had fought in medieval Britain and the English had beaten the Irish. A Russian scientist and anarchist manufactures bombs for the Irish, who blow up St. Agnes's Anglican Church. Guardian and his daughter escape, but O'Farrell trails them on a visit to Ireland and kills Guardian; Sybilla immediately falls dead on her father's body. Throughout the novel are various arguments over the labor question and the role of the Church in reform. The author's position is cautiously conservative. (D)

1885

Anderson, Maria Frances Hill. *Mildred Farroway's Fortune; or, Money Not Chief in Christian Work.* Philadelphia: American Baptist Publication Society.

The heroine, Mildred Farroway, finds herself heir to a large fortune at age eighteen. She wants to help others but is not sure of the best method. She tries charity and is repulsed. Through a number of trial-and-error episodes, she learns through her minister friend, Mr. Barton, to do good works on the level of those she seeks to aid. (D)

Chellis, Mary Dwinell. *The Working-Man's Loaf.* New York: National Temperance Society and Publication House.

The work presents a conservative approach to the social problems of the day, stressing the evils of drink, tobacco, and strikes. Young Mary Winter returns to her city house after living in the country with an aunt and uncle. She finds her family gone to ruin: the mother, father, and a twelve-year-old brother all drink; the house is filthy and in a shambles; and self-respect is gone. Mary wants to put things right but is depressed, until her aunt unexpectedly arrives. The aunt begins a reform movement with a vengeance. She confronts her brother in the saloon, who by this time is on strike against the town factory. In shame he takes the pledge to give up beer and tobacco and goes back to work, realizing that the wages are not really bad; he has just spent too much on tobacco and liquor. Eventually all is reconciled: the Winters build a house in the suburbs, and at the novel's end Mary is about to marry a paragon of young manhood. The work is strongly conservative and holds up the Puritan values of the past as the source of happiness on earth and redemption for the future. (D)

1886

Aspinwall, Sherman N. *Garnered Sheaves; An Intensely Interesting Narration of the Good Deeds of a Young Lady of Wealth and Fashion.* Grand Rapids, Mich.: W. W. Hart.

Garnered Sheaves is a good example of the transcendental religious novel of the period. The narrative is all but plotless and revolves around the accomplish-

ments—vast learning, second sight, laying-on-of-hands healing—of Hattie Tha-
ney, who is probably based on Margaret Fuller. Hattie is from a conservative,
well-to-do, high church Episcopalian family that regards her powers with scan-
dalized awe. Eventually she marries her mentor and teacher, Professor Fenton
Lynn; the two of them convert Navine, Hattie's cold and sneering sister, to
transcendental doctrines. The novel ends with the whole family caring for the
poor and sick, happily convinced of Hattie's genius and goodness. (A)

Parsons, Julia Warth [Julian Warth, pseud.]. *The Full Stature of a Man; a
Life Story.* Boston: D. Lothrop.
    The story deals with Milly Burton and her love for John Greenleaf, a minister.
Milly, after the death of her father, who was poor, goes to keep house for her
uncle on the old family farm. There she meets Mr. Greenleaf, a boarder. Her
uncle tries too hard to throw the two together, and Milly leaves for New York
City. On the way the train derails, and Milly takes care of two small children
by the name of Ogden, as their mother has been killed. Milly goes with them
to the family home, where she becomes part of the family. Eventually she and
Greenleaf are reunited and marry.
    There is much discussion of the economic problems of the day, the role of
the church, and class distinctions. It is the author's thesis that the wealth must
be distributed so that all men have enough to live on, and that it should be
distributed on the basis of the teachings of Christ on man's responsibility for his
fellows. (B)

1887

Gill, J. Thompson. *Within and Without, a Philosophical, Lego-
Ethical and Religious Romance in Four Parts....* Chicago: J. T.
Gill.
    Part I of this novel tells of Helen Ray's traumas as a young girl. Her mother
is already dead, her brother dies in an accident, and her father of apoplexy. Her
father was convinced that these dire happenings were divine retribution for his
having cheated his onetime partner, Weir, out of an important invention that
became the basis of the Ray fortune. Mr. Ray is trying to find the Weir heirs
at the time of his death. Part II centers on the Moody Revival in Chicago. There
Helen meets Dr. Paul Corey, a social gospel Christian gentleman, and they fall
in love. Part III deals with Helen's evil Uncle Edward's attempt to get her fortune
by claiming she is illegitimate. In Part IV, the long lost heir, Charles Weir, is
found and restitution is made. Helen is proved to be her father's daughter, and
she and Corey marry. (A)

Post, Mrs. Mary A. *Poverty Hollow, a True Story.* Brooklyn, New York: T. B.
Ventres.
    The novel tells of a Mrs. B—— (possibly the mother of the author, to judge
from the dedication) who decides to reform Poverty Hollow by establishing a

Sunday School, "the best if not the only means of reform." The Hollow is near the end of Manhattan Island on the Old Boston Turnpike and full of highwaymen, thieves, and cutthroats. The local "Dominie" is against her undertaking—he ceases speaking to her—but she goes ahead, and the project is a huge success, causing an eventual reconciliation with the Dominie as well as the regeneration of Poverty Hollow. (D)

Ward, Elizabeth Stuart Phelps. *The Gates Between*. Boston and New York: Houghton Mifflin.

A skilled but vain and worldly doctor "dies" in a carriage accident. His spirit remains on earth, condemned to hear and see all about it but unable to communicate. The "spirit doctor" feels exactly the same as when alive; he is just invisible. Confined to the business section of the city, he cannot even go to his wife. At length he manages to get as far as his house, sees his wife from afar and faints, waking in heaven. There he meets his deceased small son and a long dead eminent physician. They are happy, but the hero is still out of tune with heaven because of his selfishness and pride. At length he gets a menial job in the heavenly hospital (which deals only with spiritual ailments) and slowly starts to build a standing that depends completely on the quality of his spiritual development. The doctor little by little learns faith, sees Christ, and in the end is united with his wife. He has achieved heaven. (A)

1888

Dickinson, Mrs. Ellen E. *The King's Daughters, a Fascinating Romance*. Philadelphia: Hubbard Brothers.

This novel exhibits a fine example of the condescending rich rather awkwardly stooping to help the poor. Marion Fay and her grandmother, Madam Fay, are terribly rich and terribly bored. They find relief through charity work in New York City via the medium of the King's Daughters. The plot is primarily a recounting of Marion's work in a day nursery, visits to shut-ins, organizing the "Truth-Telling Ten," the "Anti-Gossip Ten," and a charity Thanksgiving dinner for New York newsboys. These events are counterpointed with a complex romantic plot. (D)

Hahn, Anna E. *Summer Assembly Days; or, What was Seen, Heard and Felt at the Nebraska Chautauqua. . . .* Boston and Chicago: Congregational Sunday-School and Publishing Society.

A strange, almost essay-like presentation, the story centers on Jean Trevor, who goes to Nebraska to teach and live with her cousins. During the summer of 1888 the family goes to Crete for the Chautauqua. Jean is vaguely troubled in spirit, without being able to define the source. She questions the doctrine of resurrection and life after death in general, and, while she is deeply moved by the sermons of Dr. Pentecost, some of which are of a social gospel sort, the novel ends on an oddly wistful note. Jean is still troubled. There are detailed scenes of what happens at the camp meeting that are objectively graphic and authoritative in presentation. (B)

Hale, Edward Everett. *My Friend the Boss. A Story of To-day.* Boston: J. Stilman Smith.

The novel is a Brahmin approach to the problem of the rich man's going through the eye of the needle to heaven. A Mr. Mellon, temperance leader, arrives at the house of an old college friend to give a temperance speech. The friend, John Fisher, is a rich Christian gentleman who favors Mellon's point of view and is incidentally against unrestricted Chinese immigration. Mellon's speech is given just before a crucial local election; there is a riot, Mellon is heroic, and Fisher wins another victory for Brahmin-led paternalism. The importance of charity and good works is the real theme of the novel. (D)

Keyser, Leander Sylvester. *The Only Way Out.* New York: A. D. F. Randolph.

The novel is a classic presentation of the problem: how can an intellectual believe in reason, science, the Bible, and an anthropomorphic God all at the same time? Leroy Ransom is a well-educated agnostic who resists all religious appeals, even from his mother. In college he is a brilliant success, especially in his attacks on the Bible and Christianity, until he falls in love with Carrie West, who is very much a Christian and just as well educated as Leroy. Most of the novel is concerned with the maturing of their love, Carrie's rejection of Leroy because he is an infidel, and his final conversion by prayer. Graduation, marriage, and presumed happiness follow. (A)

MacDonald, Mrs. M. A. *Deacon Hackmetack.* Philadelphia: Treager and Lamb.

The novel is an odd but often effective monologue delivered by dying Deacon Hackmetack (Baptist) to his niece. He lectures on a great variety of subjects, ranging from communism to free trade to the good old days and the necessity of conservation. He attacks foreigners, newspapers, Latin, women's rights, and foreign missions. Throughout one hears a quarrelsome old man's refusal to accept change, punctuated by a rather touching nostalgia for the past. (D)

1889

Bailey, Reverend Thomas L. *Dr. Wallsten's Way.* New York: National Temperance Society and Publishing House.

The novel is without unity except for Dr. Wallsten's episodic examples of personal Christian charity toward his fellow man in a small country town. His enemy in these endeavors is the hypocritical Deacon Henry, who loves only gold and is the proponent of pride-destroying organized charity of the least expensive variety. (B)

DeWitt, Julia A. W. *How He Made His Fortune*. Boston and Chicago: Congregational Sunday-School and Publishing Society.

Sandy Ferguson is left alone in the world at age eighteen and resolves to become a coal miner in the fields of Pennsylvania. The mines are a hotbed of Molly Maguire agitation connected with the mining unions. Sandy refuses to join, is threatened, and finally loses his job. Meanwhile he has become a friend of Mr. Morgan, superintendent of the mines. Morgan lends Sandy money to start mining on his own. Sandy does so, is enormously successful, and marries Tillie Morgan, the boss's daughter. Moral: The good capitalist is he who climbs the ladder of success by following the Golden Rule. (D)

Lothrop, Mrs. Harriet Mulford Stone [Margaret Sidney, pseud.]. *Our Town, Dedicated to all Members of the Y.P.S.C.E.* Boston: D. Lothrop.

The story deals with Emily Saville's simultaneous growth toward God and Pennington Burr, Christian gentleman and mill owner. Burr institutes radical reforms in his mills—a recreation center, profit sharing, worker stock holders—that make him at the same time a heroic practitioner of social gospel doctrines and an ideal capitalist. (B)

Woods, Katherine Pearson. *Metzerott, Shoemaker.* New York: Thomas Y. Crowell.

Karl Metzerott is a communist and atheist. After his wife dies of overwork, leaving a small son, Louis, Karl, with the help of his housekeeper, Sally Price, and his good friends, the Rolfs, opens a large cooperative restaurant-rooming house called the Prices. By this time Louis is a young man, a shoemaker, and hopelessly in love with spoiled and petted Pinky Randolph, daughter of aristocratic mill owner Henry Randolph. Louis is also an atheist and fights Christianity in the form of Father McCloskey and the Reverend Ernest Clare, a Protestant. He is converted, however, during a disastrous flood that almost destroys the city. Communism, the cause of labor, and atheism—all personified in Karl Metzerott—come into increasing conflict with social gospel Christianity in the form of the ministers, Louis Metzerott, and capital (the Randolphs), which is also supposedly Christian. During a strike the workers, inflamed by the elder Metzerott, set out to burn down the Randolph house; Louis Metzerott is accidentally shot and killed. His father, broken and consumed with remorse, still cannot, at the novel's end, accept a Christian God of love. (C)

1890

Allen, William. *Erudia, the Foreign Missionary to Our World; or, The Dream of Orphanos.* Nashville: Publishing House of the M. E. Church, South.

The novel is in the form of a Spenserian allegory. Erudia is a goddess from outer space who visits Orphanos and explains to him exactly what is the matter with our world. She shows him personifications of good and evil through animals she brings with her, magic jewels in which are shown sublime and evil pictures, and so forth. The novel ends with Erudia assuring Orphanos that the gods consider the Earth one of the most promising of planets and Christianity the best of potential religions. It is to be Orphanos's job to seek to make Christianity completely pure by means of both economic (which are vaguely explained) and spiritual (a return to Puritan severity) reforms. (A)

Bailey, the Reverend Thomas L. *"Nat" the Coal-Miner's Boy; or, One Step at a Time.* New York: The National Temperance Society and Publishing House.

Isaac Cowder, timber man, and his wife Sally live in the deep woods with their daughter Sally. The girl's parents die, and Sally is adopted by an uncle and aunt; she eventually marries Peter Henderson, an honest, upright, and successful miner. They have a son, Nat, who fights for the laboring man's rights, goes to college, becomes a success in business, and marries a millionaire's daughter. All of this is made possible through Nat's Christian living and his preaching of the same. Bailey generally imitates the Horatio Alger pattern of success for his characters. (D)

Bennett, Mary E. *Asaph's Ten Thousand.* Boston and Chicago: Congregational Sunday-School and Publishing Society.

The Milford family, owners of prosperous mills in Massachusetts, is large and varied. Each member has various romantic and psychological problems, but they are not overwhelming. Into this relative peace comes confusion in the form of the rights of the labor movement. Meetings are held; the Champions, a union, is formed; and mutual distrust builds up between the workers and the Milford family. Finally a strike ensues. It is unsuccessful, but each character learns something about himself, other people, and the complexity of social relations in the late nineteenth century. The novel is basically conservative in its social, religious, and economic views. (A)

Gardener, Mrs. Helen Hamilton Chenoweth. *Is This Your Son, My Lord? A Novel.* Boston: Arena.

This work is concerned with establishing one's own religious values without the accepted dogma, cant, and hypocrisy and uses three individuals to express the author's views.

Preston Mansfield illustrates the adage that the wages of sin is death. At an early age he turns into a first rate debauchee, fathers two illegitimate children, drinks, and eventually commits suicide after accidentally being responsible for his true love's death. Much of Preston's plight is the fault of his cynical and hypocritical parents.

Fred Harmon illustrates vain and meaningless superficiality via the medium of a highly satirical portrait of the Anglican church. Harmon eventually takes Anglican orders and marries a girl suitable to his world views.

Harvey Ball expresses the author's bitterness at a soulless Christianity concerned not with men but only with form and dogma. He and his intended are down-to-earth, sensible counterpoints to the mindlessness of Harmon and the hypocrisy of Mansfield. (B)

Porter, Linn Boyd [Albert Ross, pseud.]. *Speaking of Ellen*. New York: G. W. Dillingham.

Ellen is the leader of the factory workers of the Great Central Corporation of Riverfall. All admire and respect her, including the new agent, Philip Westland, who falls in love with her. Wages at the mills are reduced; a combined strike/lockout follows, led by Ellen. The company throws the workers out of their company-owned houses. It is late autumn; the militia arrives, and there are increasing threats of violence. Philip, after much soul searching, joins the workers' cause. Suddenly Ellen's father dies (she is illegitimate), and she falls heir to controlling stock of the Great Central. End of strike, marriage to Philip, and a reorganization of the mills whereby they become a model of corporate socialistic enterprise. (B)

Pounds, Jessie Hunter Brown. *The Ironclad Pledge, a Story of Christian Endeavor*. Cincinnati: Standard.

Donald Kincaid, young Christian gentleman, and his poet friend Philip Darrington decide to go from the Great Lakes to the far West to make their fortunes. Don starts a Young People's Society for Christian Endeavor in a little Western town. It is successful, and Philip gets interested, is converted to Christianity, and becomes an excellent minister and social leader, fighting the forces of evil and sin throughout the West. (D)

Tourgée, Albion Winegar. *Murvale Eastman, Christian Socialist*. New York: Fords, Howard, and Hulbert.

Jonas Underwood is a thoughtful, Thoreau-like man dying of tuberculosis in poverty. Murvale Eastman is the young pastor of the aristocratic Church of the Golden Lilies who sees the evils of the struggle between capital and labor and preaches on them. Eastman also, under the assumed name of Merrill, has been working as a streetcar driver; in this capacity he has been instrumental in ending a strike between the company and the workers, and also saved Underwood's life when the latter took a scab job during the strike. When Eastman begins preaching on social problems, he alienates Wilton Kishu, the most powerful member of his congregation, and consequently Murvale's engagement to Lillian Kishu is broken. Ultimately Lillian's father dies, she settles on another man, and the Church of the Golden Lilies has a religious awakening and organizes a League of Christian Socialists. (C)

Woods, Katherine Pearson. *A Web of Gold*. New York: Thomas Y. Crowell.

The novel presents the argument between benevolent Christian socialism and the philosophy of anarchism. Victor Maurice St. Andre, anarchist, has been sent to the village of Hillborough to gain a responsible position in a flour mill owned by Philip Godfrey: when the time is right, he is to destroy the owner and the mill. All goes well until Victor falls in love with Agatha Godfrey, the owner's daughter. Much inner struggle and melodrama ensues. Finally the organization sets Victor free of his anarchist pledge rather than killing him. Victor marries

Agatha—whose father has died after refusing to join a flour trust—and becomes religious, and Christian socialism blooms in Hillborough. (C)

Wright, Mrs. Julia MacNair. *A Plain Woman's Story*. Philadelphia: Presbyterian Board of Publication and Sabbath-School Work.

The novel is about the plight of the working woman. A young serving girl, Joan Hazzard, who has worked for a number of years for a rich and wise woman is left $6,000 when her employer dies. Joan invests a portion of her inheritance in a philanthropic Working Woman's Bureau, which she manages under puritan and spartan conditions. The novel recounts a series of anecdotes about the good the bureau accomplishes, and also illustrates the pompous Christian virtues of Miss Hazzard at length. (D)

1891

Bartlett, Mrs. Alice Elinor Bower [Birch Arnold, pseud.]. *A New Aristocracy*. New York: Bartlett.

An old scholarly parson dies, leaving his two daughters and small son penniless. The three go from the suburbs of Chicago to the city's slums. Margaret Murchison, the oldest, sets up a sewing school and the Busy Fingers Club for the slum children. She also explains the value and importance of the social teachings of Christ. Meg, Margaret's sister, gets a position as a maid and marries the brother of her rich mistress. All works out for the best, and the new aristocracy of the title is a proud and happy urban working class that the Murchison family embodies. (B)

Benedict, Roswell Alphanzo [John Smith, pseud.]. *Doubting Castle, a Religious Novelette*. New York: John B. Alden.

The novel is a good example of the genre of the period that deals with the battle between religious faith and science. Mary Temple, a young girl, has lost her faith because she relies instead on the logic of science. Two men vie for her: one the son of a minister—he loses—the other a professor of natural science at a local seminary (Boston) who wins her love while also leading her back to faith. (A)

Bogy, Lewis Vital [pseud.?]. *In Office; a Story of Washington Life and Society*. Chicago: F. J. Schulte.

An initiation novel in form, this work tells of a young country girl, Tula Fairleigh, who comes to work as a clerk in the patent office in Washington, D.C. After fighting off the temptations and evil advances of Colonel Letcher Thompson and General Twining, Tula is in despair. Then young, heroic Herbert Brown declares his love for her and all ends well. One section of the novel is a good attack upon fashionable intellectual churches that have no relation to the real-life problems of people. (B)

Buell, Mary E. *The Sixth Sense; or, Electricity; A Story for the Masses.* Boston: Colby and Rich.

The work is cast in an Emersonian, transcendental mold and tells of Aunt Dorothy, a woman of mature years who believes in the "sixth sense" of electrical intuitive knowledge. She seeks to convince her family and fiancé, Judge Abercrombie, of the reality and goodness of her gift, explaining that "to spread such a knowledge as this is . . . to glorify God." The plea of the author is for unorthodox "scientific Christianity" with a strong social orientation. (A)

Chisholm, Belle V. *Stephen Lyle, Gentleman and Philanthropist.* Cincinnati: Cranston and Stowe; New York: Hunt and Eaton.

Stephen Lyle is a rich man who searches throughout the novel for the best way to spend his money for the betterment of mankind. Initially he is thwarted in his efforts by the dignity of the poor that keeps them from accepting charity. He recognizes the value of their pride as a means of avoiding the dangers of socialism and finally sees that the best method of aid is in improving his own property, starting missions, and lending money to those in need. The specific recipient of his help is the impoverished and disintegrating Kent family, whom he helps rescue and put back on its feet. (D)

Cowdrey, Robert H. *A Tramp in Society.* Chicago: F. L. Schulte.

The thesis of this novel is the opposite of Henry George's single tax proposal. Edgar Bartlett, after being helped out of poverty by a former friend, Harold Sears, becomes wealthy because his business has been built on rent-free land. Bartlett, Sears, and a group of businessmen spend considerable time discussing the merits of an economic system of contemporary capitalism and Christianity but without taxes or rent on land. Bartlett eventually builds the city of Freetown to demonstrate the truth of his belief. It is greatly successful, and the novel ends with the whole nation following the pattern of Freetown and moving toward a new utopia. (B)

Curtiss, Alice Eddy. *The Silver Cross, A Story of the King's Daughters. . . .* Boston and Chicago: Congregational Sunday-School and Publishing Society.

Mary is a cripple, a hunchback who lives with her brother and sister-in-law and feels utterly useless, a parasite. On a train while moving with the family to a new city, Mary meets a young lady who belongs to the King's Daughters, a nondenominational charity organization. Mary is converted and from then on does all possible to "lend a hand." She makes friends with her new neighbors, sets up an informal day nursery, organizes the children of the neighborhood into King's Daughters and King's Sons, and actually becomes beautiful by feeling useful. Young, handsome, and widowed Jack Winter falls in love with Mary, and, after numerous difficulties, the novel ends happily with their marriage. (B)

Leland, Samuel Phelps. *Peculiar People.* Cleveland: Aust and Clark.

The story revolves around various arguments for and against socialism as a means of curing the economic ills of the day. The author finally decides against socialism and rather lamely substitutes a watered-down Christianity in its place.

The anonymous narrator meets Lt. Henry Grannis on board a Mississippi steamer on its way to New Orleans. They become great friends, and the narrator goes to visit the southern fort where Henry is stationed. While still on board the boat, both men also meet Professor Wright, a socialist. The professor, after explaining his doctrines at length, invites both men to visit his communist community. They do so in company with Agnes Stanley and her father. Mr. Stanley is also a communist; his daughter, who is in love with Lt. Grannis, is not. Mr. Stanley forbids their marriage unless Grannis embraces communism. After considerable conflict, the Civil War included, the novel ends with uncertain unhappiness, thwarted love, and death. (A)

Martel, Henry. *The Social Revolution. A Novel.* New York: G. W. Dillingham.

This is one of the few novels encountered that, because of the author's sense of righteous Christian outrage, attacks the institution of the church violently and entertains no notion of rapprochement whatsoever.

The story follows the life of young Mark Richardson, who stalks about New York City attacking the inequities of capitalistic laissez-faire in general and the church in particular for letting the system continue. He befriends Anna Fielding, a waitress in a beer garden. She quits her job and goes to work for wealthy Mrs. Luther March, who is unhappy because she married for money, not love. Mr. March tries to seduce Anna and she finally quits to escape his advances. Her new job is as stenographer for equally wealthy Ezra Haynes, who, on a bet, kidnaps her and holds her prisoner in his country house. Mark learns of this and goes to the rescue, but meanwhile one of his converts to social misanthropy has decided to blow up a number of the homes of the wealthy. The Haynes house is on the list. Mark, Anna, all are killed in the explosion. The work is melodramatic and violent in every respect. (C)

1892

Beard, Daniel Carter. *Moonblight and Six Feet of Romance.* New York: C. L. Webster. Reprint. Trenton, N.J.: Albert Brandt, 1904.

(The volume comprises two separate novels: only *Moonblight* is relevant.)

A young man of wealth and fashion decides to go to visit his mills in New England. Suddenly, through a mysterious ancient book he "sees things as they really are"—that is, sees the true character of people. When he looks at his fellow mill owners he sees a fox, a snake, and a vulture. As an effect the young man sets up new mills on a cooperative humanitarian basis and, even though his enemies try to ruin him, he and his plans succeed. (B)

Daniel, Charles S. *Ai; a Social Vision.* Philadelphia: Miller.

The story is set in 1950, though little is made of this. It tells of Ai, a saintly man who becomes an Anglican bishop by popular election and devotes himself to attacking evil in general and the conflicts between capital and labor in particular. Much of the story is made up of transcendental humanistic discussions between Ai and his lifelong agnostic friend, Impey. It is from these discussions that Ai finds his inspiration for trying to better the lot of mankind. (A)

Everett, Henry Lexington. *The People's Program; the Twentieth Century is Theirs... a Romance of the Expectations of the Present Generation.* New York: Workmen's.

This is a crudely presented novel that begins with the establishment of friendship between George Streeter and James Emmet, American students studying in Germany. They have liberal views, meet many influential Americans and Germans in Berlin, are set up in the newspaper business by a Mrs. Ryerson (who has a marriageable daughter), and propagandize for Emperor Frederick William II against Bismarck. Streeter is adopted by the Dowager Empress as a Hohenzollern; international student meetings are planned, whose aims are never stated but presumably have to do with the cause of labor. During the summer of 1892 there is to be a huge meeting in the Sierras "for Jesus Christ and the working man." It takes place, and the establishment of a cooperative labor colony in Kansas is one of the results. Streeter becomes secretary of state and influences the president of the United States to nationalize the railroads and telegraph; he also institutes woman suffrage. At the novel's end Streeter marries Minnie Ryerson. James Emmet has been more or less lost. (A)

Leach, Bailey Kay. *Soulless Saints, A Strange Revelation.* Chicago: American.

A peculiar allegory, the novel tells of the Reverend Daikin Burrom who upon falling asleep is awakened and conducted into a whole series of other worlds populated by "civilized" monsters. In each civilization the mores and religious ethics satirize their various counterparts on earth. The novel, episodic and fragmentary, ends abruptly with the narrator returning to earth. The author does not seem to be attacking Christian religion and social conventions as much as suggesting that such institutions should be approached in a spirit of seriousness and reverence rather than habit. The novel, very possibly influenced by the works of H. Rider Haggard, is unusually subtle in its social Christian commentary. (A)

Schwahn, John George. *The Tableau; or, Heaven as a Republic.* Los Angeles: Franklin.

The novel is a fantasy/allegory that begins with the author's own version of the birth of creation, our solar system, and species; it moves to the Near East, where the reader meets Humanity (a woman) lamenting a Darwinian dog-eat-dog world. Reason (male) comes to her and promises to show her the way to heaven on earth through Invention. They leave her native city of Barbarism, seeking the land of Science. On the way they travel all over the known world, meet Christ, the Medicis, and Luther, and they become embroiled in the Revolutionary War and Civil War in America. The novel ends in a gigantic battle between capital (called Count) and labor. Labor is victorious and accepts the new gods of Reason and Science: they are the true gods of men. (A)

Scott, Milton Robinson. *Henry Elwood, A Theological Novel.* Newark, Ohio: American Print.

The novel is, in comparison with others of the genre, a fairly sophisticated commentary on the effects of higher criticism and German rationalism on the strict Calvinistic dogma of Presbyterianism.

Henry Elwood is just graduating from college at the head of his class and is still undecided as to his profession. He finally decides to become a minister. Along with his friend Homer Vernon he attends Union Theological Seminary, where both are assailed with the skepticism of rationalism, German scholarship, and higher criticism in general. Homer leaves the seminary and becomes a physician. Henry finishes his studies and returns to his college town of Beulah to become minister of the Presbyterian Church. He falls in love, marries, and goes to a larger church. The rest of the novel recounts his life and emphasizes his continued battles against skepticism, which he finally overcomes. The author holds that direct social Christianity is one way to overcome skepticism. (B)

Sheldon, the Reverend Charles Monroe. *Richard Bruce; or, The Life that Now Is.* Boston and Chicago: Congregational Sunday-School and Publishing Society.

Richard Bruce is a young idealistic Christian who has come to Chicago to make his fortune as a writer. His major opus was rejected because it is too full of ideas and ideals and it is accidentally burned in a fire. Meanwhile Richard, with his cynical college roommate, a newspaper reporter, meets a Christ-like evangelist by the name of John King. Tom, the reporter, is converted by King, who also stops a big railroad strike by preaching brotherly love. Richard leaves for two years, to go to North Dakota to care for destitute relatives. By this time he has rewritten his book in serial form, and it becomes a best seller. Before his return to Chicago, with three small orphaned cousins in tow, he is assured of a career of fame and fortune as editor of the nation's first religious daily under King's guidance. (B)

1893

Bailey, the Reverend Thomas. *In the Pine Woods.* New York: American Tract Society.

Hugh Dalton, a mining engineer somewhere in the southern pine country, becomes the manager of a newly opened mine in this fairly primitive region. He brings his wife, three children, niece, heroine Effie Lane, to live there. Effie brings religion and progress with her and is the main force for peaceful civilized progress—that is, no liquor is allowed in the camp, a mission school is started, a church built and converts claimed. Effie emerges in stereotypic fashion as being inhumanly perfect, loved by all, and a model of Christian womanhood. (D)

Bishop, the Reverend R. F. *Camerton Slope, A Story of Mining Life*. Cincinnati: Cranston and Curts; New York: Hunt and Eaton.

The novel tells the story of the good Scotchmen versus the bad Irishmen in a coal-mining town in Pennsylvania. Algerian hero Archie, after a number of unhappy experiences—thrown rocks, false accusations of stealing, violent struggles with the Molly Maguires—is finally victorious over all obstacles because he has declared his faith and vowed his life to Christ. (D)

Brown, Helen Daws. *The Petrie Estate*. Boston and New York: Houghton Mifflin.

This novel is one of the classic examples of social gospel fiction. Charlotte Covendale is a poor young school teacher who unexpectedly inherits a large sum of money. She wants to use it in the best way for the betterment of mankind but is not sure how. Through a liberal journalist, Richard Waring, whom she eventually marries, she finds the solution in meeting the poor on their own terms, being their friend, and helping them by means of lower rents and providing better living conditions. (B)

Bubblebuster, L. Jonas [pseud.?]. *"Our Best Society" and The Rise and Fall of Boomtown Between the Years 1880 and 1910*. Chicago: Chicago Press.

Advertized on the cover as ''the Uncle Tom's Cabin of the Labor Movement,'' the novel tells the story of evil Thomas D. AntiLabor and his family's attempt to make a fiefdom of Boomtown. Theodore Warren, foreman in one of the AntiLabor works, foils their plot through Christian action helped by discovering gold on his property. The AntiLabors one and all are destroyed and Christian virtue triumphs. (B)

Chisholm, Belle V. *Consecrated Anew; a Story of Christian Endeavor Work*. Philadelphia: Presbyterian Board of Publication and Sabbath-School Work.

The Reverend Joseph Holland is despondent over his parish in Glendale. Attendance is small, those who do come are primarily old-guard critics, and there is a dearth of young people. Helen Priest, a rather indifferent Christian, is unexpectedly elected to represent the church at the socially oriented Young People's Society of Christian Endeavor in Chicago. While there, Helen is indeed consecrated anew and upon her return revitalizes her family, the church, and the community, in line with a conservative social conscience. (D)

DeWitt, Julia A. W. *Life's Battle Won*. New York: Hunt and Eaton; Cincinnati: Cranston and Curts.

The thesis of this novel is that slum conditions and high rents can be overcome by building good houses with space around them and renting them at a small profit.

After the Civil War Margaret Fleming is left a widow consumed with guilt because while she went searching among the battlefields for her husband, her little son died of malnutrition. As penance she goes to work in the slums of New York—Neversink Court, Murderer's Row, Ghost Court, the House of Blazes.

Margaret interests wealthy Elsie Peters in the slum work, and Elsie builds ideal tenements, rents at five percent profit, and becomes a model for all those interested in charity work. The novel is sanctimonious in the extreme. (D)

Gardner, Hattie Sleeper. *The Endeavorers of Maple Grove*. Omaha: Megeath Stationery.

Gertrude Marsden, her brother Horace, her best friend Ruth Malcolm, and Ruth's brother Fred are all leading members of the local Young People's Society for Christian Endeavor, an organization that promotes the social gospel. By means of a petition they are responsible for stopping the local trolley service on Sundays, closing all the town saloons, and saving numerous young people from sin. The plot includes various involved romances—all of which work out happily. The novel is a good example of conservative social gospel propaganda. (D)

Holding, Elizabeth E. *Joy the Deaconess*. Cincinnati: Cranston and Curts.

The story starts with young Hettie, an orphan, being rescued from her mean guardians by an elderly country couple. She then goes to live with a rich aunt, gets a fine education, and resolves to become a nurse. She does so, and refuses a doctor's proposal of marriage because she wants to dedicate herself and her skills to the poor and underprivileged. By this time Hettie is going by a new name, Joy, given her by her grateful patients. She hears a sermon by one of the Deaconesses (an interdenominational women's charity organization) and decides to devote her life to the Deaconesses. The rest of the novel outlined her great and wonderful successes in the Deaconess organization. (D)

Howard, Mrs. C. B. *Annie Cooper's Friends. . . .* Nashville: M.E. Church, South.

Annie Cooper is an invalid because of a railroad accident, but instead of being embittered she is a perfect Christian, the power behind the local King's Daughters Society, and the organizer of an Epworth League. The novel is episodic, presenting one form of Christian charity after another—a King's Daughters charity hospital, rural holidays for factory children, help to the sick—with Annie always the prime mover. (D)

Petersilea, Carlyle. *Mary Anne Carew: Wife, Mother, Spirit, Angel*. Boston: Colby and Rich.

The novel is a combination of transcendental and Swedenborgian propaganda. Mary Anne, a young Catholic mother, dies and goes to heaven. There she meets her deceased children and sister. All things in heaven are just as they are on earth, even unpleasant human traits (hell and heaven are only within us), but this ''reality'' is actually spiritual and can appear and disappear as an individual's effort of will demands. Those in heaven can visit earth, in invisible form, and even communicate with certain receptive individuals (there is considerable propaganda for mediums and spiritualists).

The bulk of the novel is made up of Mary Anne's spiritual growth, including finding a literal soul mate by the name of Solon. At length, through their mutual love and wisdom (an individual must learn both—many originally have only love, not wisdom) they enter the kingdom of heaven. (The reader is left to assume that all that preceded this took place in a kind of ante-room of the *real* heaven.) The author presents liberal social propaganda as one outgrowth of her new, true religion. (A)

Willey, Mary B. *Tending Upward.* Philadelphia: American Sunday-School Union.

The story deals with the maturing of the children of the Sherman family, particularly with the eldest daughter, Arminta. Among other things Arminta becomes a Christian leader of the community and is instrumental in changing her lover's choice of profession from law to the ministry. His decision in turn changes Arminta from a selfish and introspective individual to just the opposite— one who is socially and spiritually fit to be the wife of a minister of the Lord. The novel ends with their marriage and departure for the western prairie. (D)

Winslow, Helen Marie. *Salome Shepard, Reformer.* Boston: Arena.

The plot of the novel follows the awakening of the social conscience of Salome Shepard, owner of the Shawsheen Mills. As the story opens Salome has no knowledge of the mills whatsoever. They are under the extremely conservative management of Otis Greenough. A strike, the mills' first, is in progress. Greenough dies suddenly, and Salome, having to become involved, gradually sees the justice of the workers' claims and the larger social gospel light. The strike is settled in the workers' favor, and Salome marries the new superintendent of the mills, stalwart Christian John Villard. (B)

Wright, Mrs. Julia MacNair. *Mr. Grosvenor's Daughter. A Novel of City Life.* New York: American Tract Society.

Deborah Grosvenor is the spoiled and pampered only daughter of wealthy parents killed in a carriage accident. Her Uncle Amos tells her that her fortune is lost. She moves to a slum with her old nurse and uncle, finds Christ, and becomes a Christian philanthropist on a small scale even before she learns that her uncle was only withholding her inheritance in an attempt to make a true woman of her. The novel is a fine example of the lady bountiful theme. There is a curious preface to the work, which makes a farfetched analogy between the evil city and a microscopic creature made entirely of stomach. (B)

1894

Bamford, Mary Ellen. *Jessie's Three Resolutions.* Philadelphia: American Baptist Publication Society.

The novel, set in California, presents an unusual combination: an attack on Roman Catholicism (they are more to be pitied than censured), a plea for available translations of the Bible into foreign tongues (in this case Chinese and Portuguese, the two groups with whom Jessie worked), and vivid appeals for home and foreign missions. Jessie wishes to become a missionary but has to support her aged mother by giving music lessons. The plot of the novel follows Jessie's adventures and sermons on the virtues of Baptist Protestantism, missionary work, and the evils of Catholicism and ignorance. (D)

Bech-Meyer, Mrs. Nico. *A Story from Pullmantown*. Chicago: C. H. Kerr.

The story opens with the arrival of a Mr. and Mrs. Wright in Pullmantown, where Mr. Wright intends to open a grocery store. Evil Mr. Hoard owns the town, and along with his deputies (Mr. Hog and cohorts) runs it with complete despotism—fixing prices, running company stores, refusing to sell land. At the instigation of Mrs. Ada Wright the men start to organize. They finally present their requests, couched in terms of Christian humanism, to Mr. Hoard. He refuses to listen to them, and the novel ends with the beginning of the Pullman strike and a paean of praise for the cause of labor and the social gospel. (B)

Bodine, Lester. *Off the Face of the Earth, A Story of Possibilities*. Omaha: Festner.

Roger Rush is a fairly average young newspaperman who, on his thirtieth birthday, has a remarkable dream. Pegasus takes him to heaven, where he sees a great variety of allegorical sins and virtues—a society mermaid in the social swim; a man called Influence with tremendously long arms; Prude, a man with a marble heart. Just before Roger wakes up, Elijah prophesies the destruction of earth by fire, which takes place. Roger is condemned to stay on earth and be consumed with the rest—such is the judgment of God on man for betraying Him and His church for the love of Mammon. (A)

Crawford, Theron C. *A Man and His Soul*. New York: Charles B. Reed.

A cynical young newspaper man meets a man who is completely happy, Captain Harcourt. Fascinated, the reporter seeks to discover Harcourt's secret. It is simple: The Captain has "the double power of seeing things exactly as they are in contrast with what they should be." The medium for this feat is a literal ability to see and converse with one's soul, an absolute perception of oneself. After the reporter proves his true idealism and Christian goodness via a political battle in Washington, he meets his soul and becomes a convert to the Captain and his mentor, a shadowy Dr. Longman who lives on the island of Nolos. The Captain departs for the island, leaving the reporter to carry on his work— establishing a perfect America built along socialist lines. Among other things there is a marvelous scene in which Captain Harcourt introduces President Grant to his soul. The event is not a success. (A)

Dement, Isaac Strange. *Baron Kinatas, a Tale of the Anti-Christ*. Chicago: M. T. Need.

The novel presents the story of the second coming of Christ at the time when the devil, in the form of the wandering Jew, Cain, is on the verge of controlling the world. Baron Kinatas (Satinik spelled backwards) comes to Chicago, performs miracles, convinces men that they can become gods, builds a magnificent Temple of Truth, and virtually becomes king of the world. During an elaborate ceremony at which the Baron finally proclaims himself God, he and all his followers are destroyed. There are righteous men who battle the Baron, but the novel essentially deals with Kinatas's activities. He, among other things, hates and fears labor as a stronghold of belief in New Testament Christian teachings. (B)

Doubleday, E. Stillman. *Just Plain Folks; a Story of "Lost Opportunities."* Boston: Arena.

This work is a disjointed, vague novel primarily concerned with the problems of the hero, John Hardhand, a poor farm boy who tries to make enough money to marry his sweetheart, Theoretta Vick. He leaves the farm and goes to the city, where he finally finds work, is slandered and arrested for stealing, is finally cleared, gets another job, loses it because of his "past," and finally returns to the farm, no wealthier but somewhat wiser in the ways of the world. He constantly tries to be a good Christian, is dimly made aware of social problems broader than his own through a speech at the Cooper Union, and supports Henry George's single tax. At length, after many events relating to John's title to his farm, all ends well. John becomes rich through the suddenly increased value of his property, and he and Thetty finally marry. (B)

Howard, Milford Wriarson. *If Christ Came to Congress.* Washington and New York: Howard.

If Christ came to the American Congress, he would be appalled and destroy it is the thesis of Howard's novel. Pretty young Jenny Harmon comes to Washington, D.C., to get a job so that she can support her aged parents. She is preyed upon and corrupted by the Honorable Mr. Snollygoster, loses her virtue and her job, and commits suicide. Much of the novel is told in the form of a combined religious/sociological allegory attacking the loss of moral and ethical principles among the presumed great leaders of the country. The author's social gospel orientation is strongly presented. (B)

McConnell, Alice Barber. *Richard Rogers, Christian.* Philadelphia: Presbyterian Board of Publication and Sabbath-School Work.

The problem posed here is how, in a little prairie town of the West, can one Christian bring Christ to about three hundred infidels? Richard Rogers, owner of the lumberyard in Boom City, Nebraska, is faced with this problem. He decides to hold a gospel meeting, which is a success, though marred by the attacks of Lou Dietrich, owner of the major local saloon. Dietrich is eventually converted when his small son dies. A school teacher, Hennella Geddes, comes to Boom City; she is a Christian, as are many others arriving. Rogers falls in love with Hennella and they eventually marry. There are lectures on geology versus the Bible (there is no real conflict between science and Christianity—it will just take time to work things out), attacks on immigration of other than white Anglo-Saxon Protestants, and descriptions of prairie storms. The religious outlook is fundamentally conservative Calvinist. (D)

McCowan, Archibald. *Christ, the Socialist*. Boston: Arena.

The story follows the friendship and dialogues between two friends, the Reverend David Burkley, Presbyterian, and Robert Stewart, principal of the local high school in Springfort, Connecticut. Stewart argues Christian socialism and Burkley orthodox Calvinism. Stewart's principles are dramatized through a portrayal of the autocratic and unchristian management of the local mill. An employee is discharged for no reason after sixteen years' service. Another, exhausted by her work, goes mad and drowns herself. A third drinks because he cannot face the problems of economic hardship. The social system has been the major factor in the destruction of all three.

A fire destroys the mill, and the economic distress grows worse. At the same time Stewart suddenly dies of pneumonia. The two events combine to convert Burkley to the cause. The men of the mill strike and Burkley supports them even to a martyred death. The last section of the novel is a polemic presentation of the last two essays written by Stewart before his death: "Socialism and Christianity" and "Christ the Socialist." (C)

Sheldon, the Reverend Charles Monroe. *The Crucifixion of Philip Strong*. Chicago: A. C. McClurg.

The Reverend Philip Strong simultaneously gets two calls from two different churches—one in the old university town where he went to the seminary, the second in Milton, a growing industrial town that represents the challenges of modern industrial life. He chooses the latter, and the remainder of the novel deals with his growing concern over the plight of the masses and the unchristian blindness of his congregation. After meeting a godlike figure called Brother Man and asking the members of the church to give away their wealth and literally go and live among the poor, he is asked to resign his pastorate. By this time Philip has become an obvious Christ figure. He dies while giving his last sermon, literally framed against a gigantic cross on the altar in an imitation of Christ. The novel is Sheldon's most radical fictional religious and social statement. (C)

1895

Baker, Josephine R. *Gee's Trap; or, The Lambs and Field Street*.
Boston and Chicago: Congregational Sunday-School and
Publishing Society.

This novel is representative of the gospel of wealth through stewardship. Aster Lamb is the youngest member of a large, wealthy family. The family home is separated from a slum by a high wall. Aster meets a slum girl, formidable Lize Clawson, by the wall and soon after comes down with scarlet fever, from which she almost dies. Lize becomes her friend and strives successfully to become a Christian like Aster. Philip Lamb, Aster's brother, becomes interested in the slum—where Gee's Trap, a dilapidated tenement owned by a man named Gee, is located—and makes friends with Lize's invalid brother Nate. Nate had been crippled when he fell from Lamb's wall while trying to steal grapes. Philip more or less adopts Nate and educates him. Through self-help and the Lambs's money the slum is cleared up. A play room and a day nursery are installed; the Brothers House, a place for workers' rest and recreation, is built; and the Lamb family realizes what it means to be their brother's keeper. (D)

Barton, Catherine Josephine. *Evangel Ahvallah; or, The White Spectrum. A Novel Whose Incidents are Linked Together by a Chain of Metaphysical Deductions.* Kansas City, Mo.: Privately published.

This novel is an odd combination of sharp frontier naturalism contrasted with considerable mystical erudition and half-knowledge. The plot is disjointed and fragmentary, unified through the adventures of Evangel Ahvallah, the heroine. The reader first sees Evangel as a little girl having her first vision, followed by much biblical explication. The scene then shifts to a frontier revival, murder, and witch hunt; soon after, Evangel causes a Mrs. Bleevneevl to be raised from the dead. At length the heroine goes to college, meets her soul mate, and the two of them travel all over the world spreading their own particular interpretation of the word of God: perfect freedom and perfect democracy through a utopian change of social institutions. (A)

Bauder, Emma Pow Smith. *Ruth and Marie: A Fascinating Story of the Nineteenth Century.* Chicago and Philadelphia: American Bible House.

Ruth Mansfield, who used to be wealthy but whose father lost all through drink, is a ladies maid to petulant, willful, but noble-underneath-it-all Marie Ernestine. Marie's devilish cousin, "the pitfall of many a working girl," Harry Rumsford is interested in Ruth, who rejects him. He dies of drink. This is the prelude to Marie's disastrous marriage. Her husband drinks, steals her wealth, goes mad, is locked up, cured, and finally there is a happy ending. Meanwhile Ruth takes the path of female reformer: women's rights, the plight of the worker, the irresponsibility of the church, prison reform. She marries a cardboard Christian hero at the novel's end. (D)

Beach, David Nelson. *How We Rose.* Boston: Roberts Brothers.

The novel tells of a young woman who has tuberculosis, dies, and is for some time unaware of her demise. In time she is illuminated by an angel who becomes her guide in heaven. She meets Christ, who explains that heaven is an extension of the idea of perfection known on earth: men are still capable of achieving this perfection if they will just follow God. A band of angels had gone to teach earth and found it in a huge "civil war"; the angels, defeated, return to heaven, but there is still hope for earth's future. Throughout the novel there is expressed the belief that all religions actually worship the same God. He is just called by different names. (A)

Benson, Percival R. *The Rev. John Henry; Incidents Which Deeply Concerned One Life and Were Not Without Their Bearing Upon Others.* New York: A. S. Barnes.

This novel is a strong attack on the fashionableness and hypocrisy of many late nineteenth-century American churches. The story opens with the firing of a young New England school teacher because he does not give religious instruction in his school. John Henry, one of the teacher's pupils, ultimately becomes a minister and is called to his first pastorate in a large, well-to-do metropolitan church. There he sees hardship and evil, want and callousness, hypocrisy of the worst sort among the members of his church. The effect of all this drives Henry to question his faith, even though he meets his old teacher, who has become a strong believer through personal revelation. At the novel's end John Henry has regained his belief, but it is ambivalent, resting not so much on the institution of the church as on his individual dedication to Christ and belief in His teachings. (B)

Bross, Edgar Clifton [Eduard DeBrosé, pseud.]. *A Modern Pharisee*. New York: G. W. Dillingham.

Willard Millard, after establishing his heroism by saving Judge Caryle and his daughter Charlotte from a runaway horse, goes off to school at Columbia. He loses Charlotte, who falls into the evil clutches of Egbert Makepeace. After betrayal and lengthy brain fever, to escape her father's demands that she marry Makepeace Charlotte runs away to New York where she experiences hardship. Willard finally finds her, and they marry happily. The chief interest of the novel is in two subplots: one concerns the hypocrisy of Reverend Madison, who secretly likes girlie shows; the other follows the decline of George Waymont due to drink and un-Christian living. Men who practice the social gospel, like Millard, are contrasted with those who are corrupt—Makepeace and Minister Madison. (B)

Clark, Susie Champney. *Pilate's Query*. Boston: Arena.

Pilate's Query is a propaganda novel that advocates a socialized spiritualism in general and Christian Science in particular. The story opens with the perfect marriage of Reginald and Hope. She is a devout Catholic, he a nominal one. After much pressure from his wife, Reginald becomes interested in his soul and begins delving into theosophy, then spiritualism. He makes contact with his recently deceased mother, along with Mozart, via automatic writing and is elated. Hope learns of his sinful doings; they quarrel and separate—he goes to Europe and Asia, she to her former home and a mentally ill sister. The remainder of the novel chronicles Hope's eventual conversion to spiritualism (it alone cures her sister) and in the end husband and wife are reconciled and become missionaries of spiritualism to the world. The novel is an example of preaching social utopianism through mysticism. (A)

Conover, James Francis. *"Church Amusements"; The Church Dramatic and Terpsichorian Association, (Limited), Promoters of Novity. A Satire*. Detroit: Raynor and Taylor.

This work is a heavy-handed attack on the use of church theatricals to retain the younger members of a congregation. Two old actor friends, Noah Playfair and Aubrey Ransom, unexpectedly meet somewhere in Michigan and exchange laments about the decline of their profession. They decide that the chief cause for complaint is the fashion for amateur theatricals—particularly those under church sponsorship—and finally decide to go into business together producing professional church amusements. They do so with limited success at Episcopal St. Dubious under the sponsorship of the Reverend Arius Volney Fogg, D.D. The production is raucous, the church splits over the degradation of a house of God, and the Reverend Dr. Fogg resigns for reasons of poor health. Playfair and Ransom set out for greener pastures. (D)

Davis, Harold McGill. *The City of Endeavor; a Religious Novel Devoted to the Interests of Good Citizenship in the City of Brooklyn, New York*. Brooklyn: Collins and Day.

Carl Berg, a small shopkeeper in Brooklyn, and his wife used to be good Christian churchgoers but have drifted away from the fold. One morning Berg suddenly decides to go to a sunrise service sponsored by the Endeavor Society. He and his wife attend the Endeavor Convention and are reconverted, believing that Brooklyn could become a New Jerusalem. A Gideons Band is established for this purpose. Berg's two sons, Horace and Stephen, are converted—not without a struggle. The former gives up drink, becomes an Endeavor leader, and marries his former sweetheart, a devout Christian. The Gideons band is tremendously successful; all the saloons in Brooklyn are closed and the New Jerusalem is well on the way toward being a reality by the work's end. The novel has a strong social gospel orientation. (B)

Hale, Edward Everett. *If Jesus Came to Boston*. Boston: Lamson, Wolffe.

This short novel is a conservative attempt to answer British writer William T. Stead's attack on social maladjustment in the United States, entitled *If Christ Came to Chicago*, by presenting Boston's excellent and successful attempts at organized charity.

On a boat returning from Europe Dr. Primrose meets a strange and magnetic Syrian. The Syrian is coming in search of a long-lost brother. Primrose helps him and in the process shows the great philanthropic and Christian concern of Boston for the poor and downtrodden. The Syrian, who is most favorably impressed, is Christ. Dr. Primrose realizes this only after He has left Boston for Chicago to continue His search. (A)

Hill, Beveridge. *The Story of a Cañon*. Boston: Arena.

If men lived by Christian principles, there would be no injustice, no rich and poor: such is the thesis of this novel. The story takes place in a Colorado mining town and is told by Philip Martston, who has a series of Socratic dialogues with fellow miners on a variety of topics—the lot of the working man, bimetalism, life in the city, the nature of the Protestant church, and so on. He slowly wins the love of Miriam Howard, daughter of his childhood friend, John Howard. The last half of the novel concentrates on Howard, who is slowly dying because he has never been a success. The general corruption of American ideals, and the Sherman Silver Act in particular, is what is killing him. (B)

King, the Reverend Albert Barnes. *Memorable Voyages of Rebel and Victory*. Boston: James H. Earle.

Memorable Voyages is an allegorical version of John Bunyan at sea. The story, without characters as such, is made up of a series of tales in the form of sermons showing the battles between the vessels Rebel (Satan) and Victory (the ship of God). First one wins a battle, then the other; all the names of the crews, ports, supplies are allegorical—the ports of call are Worldliness, Malady, Supernatural, and the like. In each, Victory (also a character) is repeatedly tempted and often all but destroyed. At last Victory gains the city of New Jerusalem, Rebel is destroyed, and God is pleased. Throughout the work there are violent tirades against the Roman Catholic church, the Jews, Hinduism, all "false" religions. The author is strongly conservative on both religious and social questions. The evils depicted are in grisly animal allegorical form. (A)

Newton, William Wilberforce. *Philip MacGregor*. Hartford, Conn.: Student Publishing.

This novel presents a rather sophisticated story of Philip MacGregor, an intelligent, intellectual man who loses his faith, falls from high estate to low, dabbles in theosophy, and is reduced to stealing. He also has an adulterous affair with a modern Jezebel, and finally, at the end of the novel and at the point of death, is redeemed by a combination of Catholic, Anglican, and Unitarian tenets. The plot itself is complex, full of numerous events and characters. Throughout, the social as well as the spiritual role of Christianity is debated without any clear resolutions. (A)

Prentice, Dwight S. *Revelations in Politics. A Story; Illustrating Thirty Years of American Political History*. Findlay, Ohio: Populist Publishing.

A Christian approach to politics is the theme of the novel. Charles Hayward (Common Sense Hay) is sent from a small farming community in Ohio to Washington to ascertain just what is the cause of the plight of the western farmer—his poverty, the power of trusts, liquor trafficing. After an interview with Senator John Sharp, who explains all the evil ways and means of the powerful, and being invited to join in, Hay meets Mr. Facts, the liberal spokesman for reform (initiative and referendum, the single tax, women's suffrage, government ownership of natural monopolies), who also asks his aid. Hayward of course joins Facts's cause because he is an American and a Christian gentleman. The novel is one of the few that combine Populism with social gospel propaganda. (B)

Scott, Milton Robinson. *Ernest Marble, the Labor Agitator*. Newark, Ohio: Tribune Book Print.

Ernest Marble is a well paid minister who is in love with Lucy Penrose, daughter of the man who owns the town. Slowly Ernest becomes aware of the shady practices and social injustices for which Mr. Penrose is responsible. Finally the men in Penrose's plants strike, and though they lose, public sentiment turns against Penrose and Company. At the end of the novel Mr. Penrose—who is not really a bad man, just weak—fires his evildoing vice-president, and reorganizes his factories along social gospel lines. Ernest and Lucy marry. (B)

Sherwood, Margaret Pollock [Elizabeth Hastings, pseud.]. *An Experiment in Altruism*. New York and London: Macmillan.

An unnamed young lady comes to the big city determined to help humanity. Very soon she meets a series of stereotypical individuals who are seeking the same objective—the Transcendental Altruist; a Woman Doctor; the Lad, a Greek hero and mechanical genius; a Precocious Teenager; the Anarchist; and Janet, unhappy girl cynic. The novel is highly satirical and episodic, focusing on the strengths and weaknesses of each individual's attempt to better humanity's lot. The tone is brittle, self-mocking, yet searching. The effect is rather uncomfortably modern in some ways. (B)

Toph, Olla Perkins. *Lazarus*. Indianapolis: Indianapolis Printing.

Lazarus and Christ meet in heaven. Both bemoan the world that did not sufficiently and rightly practice the teachings of the "Elder Brother." They decide to return unseen to earth and try to rectify the situation. They return and find a man named Reform, who knows and understands the plight of the poor and the blindness and insufficiency of the Christianity currently practiced. Reform becomes the instrument of Christ and Lazarus, and they help him with good council via dreams as he labors for the betterment of the working man and regeneration of Christianity. At the novel's close Reform joins Lazarus and Christ in heaven. (B)

Warner, Charles Dudley. *The Golden House. A Novel*. New York: Harper and Brothers.

The Golden House is a complex story that offers that Golden Rule and true Christianity as the means of establishing a meaningful life. There are two major plots in the novel, only one of which, the relationship between physician Ruth Leigh and Catholic priest Father Damon, is relevant here. Ruth and the priest, she the scientist, he the religious idealist, meet while working in the slums of a large city. He runs a mission, and she is a physician to the poor. They fall in love, recognize the impossibility of their situation, and finally part, but not before each gives spiritual and physical aid to the other so that they can better carry on their individual efforts for reform and apply Christianity. (B)

Wright, Mrs. Julia MacNair. *A New Samaritan. The Story of an Heiress*. New York: American Tract Society.

Persis Thrale, a young girl who has recently inherited a large fortune, finds that her money might morally belong to two spinster sisters, Rebecca and Susan North. Their claim is obscure and related to a lawsuit of long ago that was questionably settled. For some reason left unexplained, this knowledge leads Persis to give up her dilettante literary life, and, with the help of the sisters North—upon whom she has bestowed $10,000—she reconditions one of her houses, rents the rooms to poor girls, gives dressmaking classes, opens a day nursery, enlists the help of her friends, and converts many to Christianity. The novel is primarily filled with anecdotes and adventures illustrating Persis's great worth in the cause of Christian work. (D)

1896

Armstrong, Minnie L., and Sceets, George H. *The Social Crime*.
New York: W. L. Allison.

This novel deals with the plight of the working man and seeks a solution of social gospelism and Christian socialism. Richard Hardman is the owner of iron mines and an enemy of labor, who is pitted against Phillip Comstock, Dr. Berkman, and Baroness Von Waldmere, a former poor girl seduced by Hardman, now titled and an anarchist. Through a fantastic and complex plot Hardman is destroyed and righteousness and labor triumph. (B)

Boteler, Mattie M. *The Conversion of Brian O'Dillon*. Cincinnati: Standard.

Brian O'Dillon is a Horatio Alger hero. Beginning as a humble worker, he has been prudent and is the owner of the Franshaw Shoe Works. While he is an honest man, he has the reputation of being somewhat hard on his men and of being sour in disposition. He is not a Christian; his mother was an alcoholic Catholic under the malevolent influence of the parish priest, and since his childhood Brian has never had more than a cynical regard for Christian doctrine. He meets Agnes Bond at a temperance meeting, immediately falls in love with her, and proposes. While Agnes loves him, she rejects him because he is not a Christian. In desperation Brian decides to read the whole Bible; the process converts him. He gains Agnes's hand, which gives the shop owner a new humanitarian outlook. The novel provides a good example of a man coming to believe in the social gospel by means of a personal conversion. (B)

Bolmer, William Brevoart. *The Time is Coming*. New York: G. W. Dillingham.

The plot of the novel is a fairly incoherent combination of allegory, melodrama, and ultranationalistic utopianism. Dr. Ambrose Hilary is a Herculean vegetarian and a true man of God. When Elijah comes to announce the Second Coming, Hilary acts as his right-hand man in conducting a nationwide revival against corrupt monopolists who degrade their men and have gained control of God's churches. The forces of evil have been gathering, however, and are symbolically represented as being ensconced in a gigantic Jewish temple in Chicago. Civil war ensues; both Hilary and Elijah are captured, but they remain stoically calm—the Master is coming. (A)

Sheldon, the Reverend Charles Monroe. *His Brother's Keeper; or, Christian Stewardship*. Boston and Chicago: Congregational Sunday-School and Publishing Society.

In orthodox social gospel terms, the novel treats of the conflicts between labor and capital in a strike situation. Stuart Duncan returns from college and a year abroad to find a strike threatening the coal mines he is about to inherit. The leader of the strikers is Stuart's closest boyhood friend, Eric Vassall. Stuart's father dies, Stuart has a religious conversion, and the remainder of the novel is concerned with the eventual settlement of the strike by means of an appeal to the Golden Rule. Along the way Stuart falls in love with a Salvation Army woman who was formerly a society belle. They marry at the book's close. (B)

Ward, Elizabeth Stuart Phelps. *The Supply at Saint Agatha's*. Boston and New York: Houghton Mifflin.

This novel is a short and effective treatment of the Second Coming. St. Agatha's is a large, fashionable and secular church in a large city. While the regular pastor is on vacation in France, a series of substitutes or "supplies" are needed. One of them is an aged rural minister, grandson of the founder of St. Agatha's. Before the old man can come, he dies from exhaustion while serving one of his parishioners. His last words are, "Lord, into thy hands I commit— my supply." The Lord himself comes. The congregation is filled with terror, wonder, and exhilaration. St. Agatha's Church has been supplied. (A)

1897

Barr, Mrs. Amelia Edith Huddleston. *The King's Highway*. New York: Dodd, Mead.

Nicholas Lloyd is a scheming business tycoon who marries for his wife's money. He has two children, a boy and girl, both of whom rebel against their father's evil teachings and become model Christians. The plot is involved, but periodically it stops for the author to expound on the social gospel and the need for reform. (B)

Ellison, Nina E. *Nadine: a Romance of Two Lives*. Nashville: Gospel Advocate.

Extremely beautiful Nadine is besieged by suitors. Finally she pledges herself to Earle Desmond, but through the trickery of a rejected admirer they break off. Nadine is suddenly left a penniless orphan, which results in her becoming a Christian. She is just about to fall in love again when her suitor is mysteriously shot and killed. (The rejected admirer again.) In her grief Nadine decides to travel. There follow long descriptions of the West, Salt Lake, and Alaska—and in Alaska she is reunited with Desmond, who just happens to be there. All ends happily; the villain has been taken care of along the way. Throughout, Nadine's primary consolation in her woes has been her faith and good works for those less fortunate than she. (A)

Grinnell, Elizabeth. *John and I and the Church*. New York: Fleming H. Revell.

This book concerns the author's views of how, ideally, the Protestant churches and ministers should conduct themselves. Those in prayer meetings should avoid the use of personal pronouns, particularly when relating their past sins. Church gossip, factions, unfair demands on the minister and his wife are all wicked. The story is told in the first person by the wife of a parson and relates the various problems and joys of their service to God. John, her husband, is a good man with a good church, but the church becomes worldly, goes into debt for a more stately mansion, and dismisses John. After a year of farming he takes a new parish with many troubles and scandals of its own. Eventually his influence and work are crowned with success, and the novel ends with a long sermon on just what makes a good congregation and a good minister: humility before God and mutual respect among men built upon brotherly love. (D)

Parkman, Susan. *Two Noble Women*. New York: American Tract Society.

Mrs. Baldwin, while having some work done by a tinsmith, Jim Burris, hears the man's life story, which is mainly about his wonderful wife Nancy who saved him from the curse of drink. Mrs. Baldwin is so impressed that she goes to see Nancy, and they in turn go to see a young unwed mother. The father of her child is in jail for stealing. He comes to trial before Judge Baldwin, is given a light sentence, and marries the girl. Meanwhile Mrs. Baldwin tries to persuade her husband to accept Christ, which he finally does after seeing how Burris retains his strength and faith after Nancy dies. Mrs. Baldwin and Nancy Burris are the two noble women of the title. (D)

Sheldon, The Reverend Charles Monroe. *In His Steps; "What Would Jesus Do?"* Chicago: Advance.

In His Steps was the most famous and widely read of the social gospel genre. The story tells of a minister, Henry Maxwell, whose anguish over the social and economic injustices of the day lead him to ask the members of his congregation in the city of Raymond to ask themselves, before performing any single act, what they think Jesus would do if He were in their place. The people do as the Reverend Maxwell asks, and the results represent a social revolution built on Christian principles. The experiment is then successfully tried in Chicago and, it is assumed, will soon spread all over the Western world. (B)

Smith, Marion Couthouy. *Dr. Marks, Socialist*. Cincinnati: Editor Publishing.

Dr. Alpheus Marks, M.D., argues socialist nationalization of all natural monopolies and distribution of wealth so that all men will have at least the essentials to maintain daily life. He preaches his doctrines to all levels of society, though he practices his profession among the poor. In the process of presenting the doctor's views the author also manages to present almost every major contemporary idea on methods of reform. Dr. Marks, after falling in love with a rich and intelligent woman who does not share his views, is eventually killed by an insane anarchist. (C)

Wells, Amos Russel. *Elijah Tone, Citizen. A Story of Christian Citizenship*. Boston and Chicago: United Society of Christian Endeavor.

This work is a social gospel novel primarily concerned with the responsibilities of democratic citizenship. Elijah Tone has just graduated from college with a teacher's certificate when he is suddenly asked by Mr. Sanders Hackerman to be editor of a newspaper to be published soon in his home town. He accepts and heads the *Danford Citizen*. The rival *Danford Bee*, under Caspar Griffith, wrecks the office of the *Citizen* as soon as it opens. A political fight ensues in which Elijah and the "better Christian" citizens of the town fight the corrupt mayor and general political apathy of the citizenry. The Endeavor Society of Elijah's church comes to his aid, as finally do the professors and students of the local college. A coming political election is fought over in the rival newspapers until Hackerman suddenly sells the *Citizen* to the owner of the *Bee*. Elijah finally prints the last issue on a toy printing press he had as a boy, is shot during the voting, and survives. The forces of Christian citizenship are victorious. (B)

Wright, Mrs. Julia MacNair. *The Cardiff Estate. A Story*. New York: American Tract Society.

Jean and John Cardiff, twins, inherit a huge estate when they are but children. Spoiled and petted, they do not at all like their Aunt Prudence, who comes to take care of them. Slowly Jean is converted to her aunt's Christian principles, and both then set out to clean up the notorious Cardiff slums, the basis of the family fortune. John, however, goes the way of dissipation, almost dies of his excesses, and is sent to sea to recuperate. He is shipwrecked and during this crisis becomes a man and a Christian. After existing for some time in Robinson Crusoe fashion on a deserted island, he is rescued and returns home to join his sister and aunt in their philanthropic work. (D)

1898

Coulter, James W. *The Larger Faith, a Novel*. Chicago: Charles H. Kerr.

The Larger Faith presents a combination of romantic Christian humanism and a love story set in Colorado. The hero, Bill Young, is a Christlike figure who helps all who come in contact with him, from a small orphan boy whom he saves from lynching and subsequently adopts, to a Presbyterian minister harried by the narrow dogmatism of his church elders. Young finally finds his lost love; the boy grows up to be a fine young man; and the minister leaves the Presbyterian Church to teach nondenominational universal brotherhood built on the New Testament doctrine of Christ's love. The novel is better written than most of the genre. (A)

Farnell, George. *Rev. Josiah Hilton, the Apostle of the New Age*. Providence, R.I.: Journal of Commerce Co.

A thinly veiled tract urging socialism built on Christianity, the work is arranged as a series of monologues presented by Mr. Charles Trevor, who argues a socialist solution to the major problem of the day. His approach is orthodox Marxian economics, though he never mentions Marx by name. One of Trevor's listeners and periodic questioners is the Reverend Josiah Hilton. The Reverend Hilton eventually renounces his pastorate and goes West to preach the gospel of Christ through the economics of socialism. (C)

Johnston, James Wesley [Annan Dale, pseud.]. *Dwellers in Gotham; a Romance of New York.* New York: Eaton and Mains; Cincinnati: Curts and Jennings.

The novel is a fairly well written example of social gospel fiction that emphasizes the waste of formal charity: "Don't throw the human dog a bone; change society so that the dog becomes a human being once more."

The plot centers around three young men who are former college classmates— Edward Vaughan, an unrealistic romantic socialist; John Disney, also an idealist, but who uses the mask of cynicism as a means of hiding his confusion about what he wants to do; and wealthy Hugh Dunbar, who runs a mission in one of the slum sections of the city. Each has various sisters. Love affairs develop, as do financial crises. Through each individual's difficulties comes a growing awareness of the pressing need for social justice built on the principle of the Golden Rule. (B)

Martyn, Carlos. *Sour Saints and Sweet Sinners.* London and New York: F. Tennyson Neely.

A story of how an enterprising young minister, the Reverend Van Dyke Earl, slowly but effectively lifts his wealthy parish from self-satisfied, hypocritical complacency and to genuine concern for the social welfare of all through Christian principles. The Reverend Earl has to deal with such characters as Miss Medusa Gorgon, Miss Selina Soft, and Elder Jeremiah in the process, but he wins the battle, as well as the hand of his beloved Giulia Zaldiva. (B)

Sheldon, the Reverend Charles Monroe. *The Redemption of Freetown.* Boston and Chicago: United Society of Christian Endeavor.

Claude Vernon, eminent Judge Vernon's son, is killed in Freetown, a black ghetto in the city of Merton, on his way home from a drinking party. It is assumed—wrongly—that an escaped black, whom the judge that morning had sentenced to twenty years imprisonment, had killed Claude. The effect of the murder on the young man's fiancée and his parents is unexpected. They determine to clean up Freetown by means of Christian philanthropy. The local minister, along with the Ladies' Club, takes the lead in the campaign and the rich and respected follow. All ends well with a reporter's glowing account of the great success of the city in redeeming a minority slum ghetto. (B)

1899

Converse, James Booth. *Uncle Sam's Bible; or, Bible Teachings About Politics.* Chicago: Schulte.

There is almost no plot to this novel. The Reverend Jacob Jones delivers a whole series of commentaries on practically every social and political problem then current. After outlining a difficulty, he invariably resorts to the Bible—

usually the Old Testament—for his principle of action. The novel is an exercise in Socratic procedure, save that the Reverend Jones answers the final question each time. The above takes place at the various homes of six church members (denomination unspecified) who meet to discuss political and social conditions. The only plot as such concerns Jenny Smith and Jack Robinson, who are in love, fight over free silver, and almost break up. Jack recants (he was for gold), and they marry to live happily ever after. The novel is an almost perfect example of social gospel tract in the guise of fiction. (B)

Fuller, Hulbert. *God's Rebel*. Chicago: Regan.

The novel compares well with *The Jungle* as a mixture of sardonic satire and romantic outrage. The story centers on liberal, well educated Dr. Kenneth Moore. After completing his studies in economics he is vacationing in Monte Carlo. While there he receives word of his father's death and returns to the United States to accept a teaching position in a Chicago university liberally supported by the Saviour Oil Company. After publishing information damning to the oil company, and expounding radical economic and religious views, Moore is fired and his wife leaves him. In desperation he takes a job as an editorial writer for a large conservative newspaper but quits when he can no longer tolerate the paper's social and political hypocrisy. The novel ends with Moore's leaving to die in the Spanish American War. (C)

Griffith, Mrs. Susan M. *The Ladder of Promise*. Richmond, Virginia: Presbyterian Committee of Publication.

Stalwart young Christian Merril Merton takes a young boy, Tom Knox, to a Thanksgiving Day service at fashionable St. Paul's. Tom, an orphaned street urchin with no intellectual or Christian training, is impressed and resolves to become a Christian gentleman. Merton and the Bible become his mentors, and the novel recounts Tom's successful efforts to convert other homeless boys, his recognition of humility through the social gospel, and the development and training of his unusual musical ability. After spurning a secular career in grand opera, the hero eventually becomes a music professor and gospel singer. (D)

Morgan, David. *A Dream of Christ's Return*. Chicago: Curts and Jennings.

Morgan's work is a novelette that tells of a minister's going to a church conference. Between heated sessions on the role of the church in facing social problems, he dreams of how things should be, as opposed to how they are: long and unfair working hours make the masses literally too tired to come to Sunday morning services; too many ministers are so concerned with their congregation's spiritual welfare that they do not understand or comprehend the day-to-day problems of the people. The minister explains his dream at the next meeting and is instrumental in convincing many that the church must teach a living, temporal Christianity with full involvement in the social and economic problems of the time. (B)

Sheldon, the Reverend Charles Monroe. *Robert Hardy's Seven Days; a Dream and Its Consequences.* New York: Street and Smith.

The novel is a modern retelling of the everyman story. Robert Harding is a man in his middle fifties, selfish, successful, a church member but hardly a Christian in the true sense. One Sunday night he has a vivid dream in which God tells him he will die in seven days. In those seven days that follow, Robert becomes a different man, a real Christian, at the same time that a series of shattering misfortunes befall him. A daughter is seriously injured in a train wreck; his eldest son, it is learned, drinks and gambles to excess and is on the way to becoming a criminal. The whole family is eventually redeemed. Meanwhile Robert spends every minute trying to make amends for his past. On the seventh day he is prepared and, in prayer, goes to meet the Lord. (B)

Sherwood, Margaret Pollock [Elizabeth Hastings, pseud]. *Henry Worthington, Idealist.* New York and London: Macmillan.

The novel poses the question of what the role of the scholar and the university should be in relation to the social and economic inequities of the day. Henry Worthington, just back from getting a Ph.D. in economics from Germany, takes a position at Winthrop University, where his father is a professor of biology. Henry offends everyone by giving a lecture condemning the university's taking bequests from capitalists who made their wealth at the expense of the poor. The lecture is couched in general terms, but everyone knows that Henry is attacking Samuel Gordon, who has just given a large amount to the biology department. Gordon's daughter, Annice, feels as Henry does. They fall in love, Henry is fired by the board of trustees, his father dies, and Annice is disinherited by her father when she marries Henry. At the novel's end the lovers have only each other, but they smile bravely as they begin their life in the West. (B)

1900

Alleman, Julia Suesserott. *Postmarked "Colima."* Philadelphia: Lutheran Publication Society.

The novel is a story of love thwarted through lost letters. Lawrence Howe loves Frances Stuart, presents his case, and is told she will give him her answer in three months. He goes to sea. Frances writes her acceptance, but the letter is lost. When she in turn hears nothing, she is broken hearted but finds salvation in the Lutheran Church—faith and good works. It is this section of the novel that preaches the social gospel. After many twists of the plot, all ends happily when Lawrence claims his bride after a twenty-five-year delay. (B)

Bess, Elmer Allen. *Our Master's Church; a Parable.* New York, Chicago, London: Neely.

A "what would Jesus do" novel, the work is split into two fairly unrelated parts. The first half of the story deals with the decision of the Reverend James O'Rourke to accept a call from a small western church. After going to the city in disguise he decides that, yes, the church definitely needs him. The attendance is small, indifferent, cool. After O'Rourke's arrival the rest of the novel deals with the conversion, through social gospel and spiritual appeals, of four individuals—corrupt, rich, handsome Thaddeus Covington; Grace Glover who loves Thad and is converted after one sermon; heroic, ugly, heavy drinking Labe Incoln; and the girl he loves, Annie Arlington. These four in turn lead other members of the town into the Christian fold. (B)

Converse, Florence. *The Burden of Christopher.* Boston: Houghton Mifflin.

Of those read, this novel is the best in a literary sense. Christopher Kenyon is a reform idealist who inherits his father's shoe factory in New England. He tries to pay decent wages, have an eight-hour work day, and aims at cooperative profit sharing. The competition of other manufacturers slaughters him. To keep going he uses money left in his trust, is found out, and ultimately commits suicide.

There are good characterizations: Christopher; his best friend, Episcopal minister Philip Starr; Christopher's wife Agnes, smarter than he; and his father-in-law, an academic idealist who fails him by retreating to abstractions when Kenyon is trapped by financial failure. The work is an excellent argument for the social gospel while also pointing up a number of problems with such a philosophy. (B)

Goss, Charles Frederic. *The Redemption of David Corson.* Indianapolis: Bowen-Merrill.

Goss's novel is an elaborate and highly complicated retelling of Adam's bliss, fall, and final redemption. The story revolves around a young Quaker who loses his faith, sinks into all kinds of degradation (from an Ohio Eden to the evil city), and is finally redeemed by means of a Saul-to-Paul conversion. The novel ends with the hero's return to his Eden and his first true love. Its interest lies in the hero's reconversion by means of seeing the necessity of Christ's teachings on a broad social level as well as on an individual spiritual level. (A)

Grinnell, Elizabeth. *For the Sake of a Name; a Story of Our Times.* Elgin and Chicago: David C. Cook.

The novel's unity is gained through place—a slum called Deep Gutter. Alfred Slocomb is a rich man dying of heart disease and without heirs; he is fascinated by the lives of the poor and suddenly seeks to gain some kind of immortality through philanthropy. At first he tries charity, which the people are too proud to accept. Finally he realizes that only through Christianity can he be worthy of helping others. He is converted and becomes a benefactor to all who know him. (D)

Harris, the Reverend William Shuler. *Mr. World and Miss Church-Member; or, The Secret Service of Satan. An Allegory.* Cleona, Pa.: G. Holzapfel.

The work is a bad combination of *Pilgrim's Progress* and Dante in the form of a thorough attack on "liberal" Christian attitudes—a tale of terror by allegory.

Presented in the omniscient third person, the story tells of the slow corruption of Miss Church-Member by Mr. World as they travel the road of life toward the heavenly kingdom. Miss Church-Member, originally on the King's Highway, is led through missionary zeal to try and convert Mr. World, traveling on the Broad Highway of the Devil. Mr. World convinces her that he just cannot muster the strength to walk on the King's Highway all at once—won't she accompany him for a time on the Broad Highway? In her mistaken hope of saving him, Miss Church-Member does so, and the rest of the novel is concerned with the decline and ultimate fall of them both. Allegorical devices full of graphic horror abound. (A)

Hill, Mrs. Grace Livingston. *A Daily Rate.* Philadelphia: Union Press.

Celia Murray and her Aunt Hannah have been living with a niece and her family but are made to feel unwanted. Celia goes to the city, gets a job as a ribbon girl in a department store, and lives in a rundown boarding house. Life is hard until she unexpectedly inherits a modest fortune from an unknown uncle. Immediately Celia sends for her aunt; they buy the boarding house, fix it up, and start redeeming its inhabitants for Christ. They save a little shop girl well on the way to sin, a would-be drunkard, and a sick old lady. Soon a young clergyman moves in; he and Celia fall in love, marry, and all ends happily. (B)

Logan, the Reverend J. B. [James the Less, pseud.]. *Alice McDonald; or, The Heroine of Principle; a Story of the Early Cumberland Presbyterian Church.* Rev. ed. Nashville: C. P. Publishing House.

The novel begins with the conversion of the whole McDonald family—except the father, John—from Old Presbyterianism (symbolized in the doctrine of the Elect) to Cumberland Presbyterianism (all men can be saved through the martyrdom of Christ; he died for all) by means of a camp meeting. Alice, the youngest of the McDonald family, is the most militant for the new faith. After going to school in Philadelphia she returns to her hometown of Nebo and marries Mr. Wiseman, who becomes a circuit-riding Cumberland minister. The remainder of the novel relates Alice's brilliant victories in Biblical argument—particularly over Baptist churchman Mr. Waters, concerning total immersion versus sprinkling—the growth of the Cumberland Presbyterian Church, and its growing strength and virtue. The religious liberalism in the novel carries over into the social sphere, though this is more implied than stated. (B)

Meyer, Mrs. Lucy Jane Rider. *Deaconess Stories.* Chicago: Hope.

As the title indicates, this is not really a novel but a series of stories that do, however, have a unifying theme of Deaconess work. Many of the same characters reappear, and vignettes are grouped under headings such as "In the Slums," "Caring for the Sick," "In the Sunday School," "Saving Souls," "Homes for Orphans," "In the Jails and Police Stations," and "Making Calls." (D)

Miles, Austin. *About My Father's Business.* New York: Mershon.

Dr. Hamilton Jay Lovett becomes pastor of a Methodist Church in a new city. Arriving at the same time is Raymond Chester, homeless and jobless. The latter is taken in by Mr. Bushwick, a member of the Methodist Church. Bushwick gets Chester a job in Mr. Goodtime's electrical factory, and all goes well until Chester refuses to work on Sunday and is fired. Meanwhile Dr. Lovett is described as a worldly and superficial man and is contrasted with Episcopalian Mr. Petrow, who stops a strike through preaching a sermon on Christ as a socialist. Lovett's church becomes more and more formal, and the mission that Bushwick is in charge of is closed for being too unseemly. Finally the good Methodist people dismiss the pastor. They have had enough of Roman pomp. Dr. Lovett never understands why. Raymond Chester marries a beautiful and rich girl. The author's orientation is reformingly liberal on both social and religious issues. (B)

Myers, Cortland. *Would Christ Belong to a Labor Union? or, Henry Fielding's Dream*. New York: Street and Smith.

Yes, Christ would be a union member. It was also the author's thesis that the church and all of its parts had to become actively involved in helping to solve the differences between capital and labor. By the end of the nineteenth century the church could no longer concern itself with soul saving alone; it had to adjust itself to a broader context.

Henry Fielding lives with his sister in New York City where he works hard. Intrigued by the title of a sermon (that of the novel) to be given by David Dowling, he goes to church for the first time in many years and is very impressed. He tells of the sermon at the next union meeting; a tremendous argument about the relationship between labor and Christianity ensues, and Fielding is delegated to ask Dowling to speak at the next meeting of union members. Dowling does with huge success. Meanwhile Henry has met rich Grace Chalmers at Dowling's mission and falls immediately in love with her. They eventually marry. The story ends with Henry setting up a profit-sharing factory, completely converted to Christian socialism. (C)

Pangborn, Frederick Werden. *Thou Art the Man. A Suggestion Story for the Christian Church*. London and New York: Wright.

An anonymous and highly critical letter comes to the Reverend Johnsbury Jeemax of the Church of the Good Saint Paul. The letter is about the hypocrisy of many in this congregation. The minister broods on the letter and sees that it is true—an elder owns the worst slums in the city, another sells watered stock, a third bribed voters in an election. The list is long. The Reverend Jeemax almost puts the whole thing aside but keeps getting letters from the mysterious author, who signs himself "T. J.," telling more and more. Finally the minister preaches a sermon on Christianity in daily life and asks that all members change their ways. If they choose not to, they will either be dismissed from the church or he will resign as pastor. The next Sunday rich Tackabury Jones, author of the letters, reveals himself. A vote is taken on the proposed resignation of Reverend Jeemax, and seventeen of the worst hypocrites are overwhelmingly outvoted and leave the church. Living social gospel Christianity wins another battle. (B)

Peake, Elmore Elliott. *The Darlingtons*. New York: McClure, Phillips.

A fairly well-written novel dealing with the plea for liberalizing Christian doctrine (specifically within the Methodist Church) if its appeal is to remain vital in a changing America. Carol Darlington is an intelligent and rich woman, ethically Christian but without strong denominational alliance, who falls in love with Stephen Kaltenborn, a rich, liberal Methodist minister. The conflict for both individuals in the novel revolves around the difficulties of finding a suitable balance between Christian humanism and the parochial fundamentalism of the Methodist Church at the turn of the century. While the two finally marry, the problem is not solved. (B)

Robinson, Margaret Blake. *Souls in Pawn; a Story of New York Life*. New York and Chicago: Fleming H. Revell.

Katherine Irving, daughter of a mission leader, is beloved by Richard Masterson, an Irish rake who feigns conversion and is unmasked, and John Pierce, true-blue Christian hero. ''Christian Merchant Grey,'' a corrupt man who seduces working girls in the guise of bringing them to Christ, tries to produce a scandal over Katherine and Richard. He is foiled, but not before he disfigures Katherine with acid. Ultimately, John and Katherine marry, Richard is truly converted, and all ends well. There is much throughout the novel about the brotherhood of man under the fatherhood of God. (B)

Stiles, the Reverend William Curtis. *The Master's Mission; or, The Minister Who Dared*. New York: Street and Smith.

This novel tells of the Reverend Terence Virgil's attempts at soul saving in the town of Newvane, New England, the home of Phailor College. Virgil's good work among the ''wards'' is primarily through fighting the liquor interest, whereby he saves the drunk, down-and-out Jeremiah, who had formerly been a brilliant student at the college. The Reverend fears the same thing will happen to impetuous Phil Remington. It almost does—Remington accidentally kills a policeman during a student brawl—but he is converted to Christianity while in jail and is released a model Christian. Meanwhile Virgil marries his true love and becomes president of the college. Traditional Christian charity is the author's theme and solution to all problems. (D)

Notes

Chapter 1

1. Charles S. Daniel, *Ai; a Social Vision* (Boston: Arena, 1893), p. 198.

2. Nina E. Ellison, *Nadine: A Romance of Two Lives* (Nashville: Gospel Advocate, 1897).

3. Samuel P. Leland, *Peculiar People* (Cleveland: Aust and Clark, 1891).

4. Alice B. McConnell, *Richard Rogers, Christian* (Philadelphia: Presbyterian Board of Publication and Sabbath-School Work, 1894), p. 105.

5. Edward E. Hale, *My Friend the Boss. A Story of To-Day* (Boston: J. Stilman Smith and Co., 1888), pp. iii–iv.

6. Mary E. Bennett, *Asaph's Ten Thousand* (Boston and Chicago: Congregational Sunday-School and Publishing Society, 1890), pp. 131–34.

7. Ibid., p. 38.

8. Julia M. Wright, *The New York Needle-Woman; or Elsie's Stars* (Philadelphia: Presbyterian Publication Committee; New York: A. D. F. Randolph, 1868), p. 223.

9. William C. Stiles, *The Master's Mission; or, The Minister Who Dared* (New York: Street and Smith, 1900), p. 71.

10. Susan Parkman, *Two Noble Women* (New York: American Tract Society, 1897), pp. 67–68.

11. Helen D. Brown, *The Petrie Estate* (Boston and New York: Houghton Mifflin, 1893), pp. 76–77.

12. A particularly good sustained example of a character that acts as a foil in this way is in a novel by Julian Warth [Julia W. Parsons], *The Full Stature of a Man; a Life Story* (Boston: D. Lothrop, 1886), pp. 135 ff.

13. Novels that basically follow the plot outlined are Maria F. H. Anderson, *Mildred Farroway's Fortune; or, Money Not Chief in Christian Work* (Philadelphia: American Baptist Publication Society, 1885); Julia A. W. DeWitt, *Life's Battle Won* (New York:

Hunt and Eaton; Cincinnati: Cranston and Curts, 1893); Ellen E. Dickinson, *The King's Daughters, A Fascinating Romance* (Philadelphia: Hubbard Brothers, 1888); Mrs. C. B. Howard, *Annie Cooper's Friends*. . . . (Nashville: Publishing House, Methodist Episcopal Church, South, 1893); Austin Miles, *About My Father's Business* (New York: The Mershon Co., 1900); Mary A. Post, *Poverty Hollow, A True Story* (Brooklyn, N.Y.: T. B. Ventres, 1887); Charles M. Sheldon, *His Brother's Keeper; or, Christian Stewardship* (Boston and Chicago: Congregational Sunday-School and Publishing Society, 1896); Helen M. Winslow, *Salome Shepard, Reformer* (Boston: Arena, 1893); and two novels by Julia M. Wright, *Mr. Grosvenor's Daughter. A Story of City Life* (New York: American Tract Society, 1893); *The Cardiff Estate. A Story* (New York: American Tract Society, 1897).

14. Elizabeth S. P. Ward, *The Silent Partner* (Boston: J. R. Osgood, 1871), pp. 34–35. Mrs. Ward probably was the best writer of those dealt with in this study. A number of her novels will be touched on in other discussions of social Christian fiction, and she is discussed at greater length in Chapter 3. The selection quoted almost surely owes some of its inspiration to Poe's "The Bells" (1848–49).

15. Ibid., pp. 94–95.

16. Ibid., pp. 127–28.

17. Parsons, pp. 199–200; DeWitt, pp. 307–8.

18. Howard, p. 240.

19. Miles, pp. 160–61.

20. The following novels, not all of which will be separately commented upon, are examples: (Note: Because of the number of novels, when a second citation occurs many pages after the first, both author and short title will be given. Some of the novels listed have been previously cited in full.) Maria F. H. Anderson, *Mildred Farroway's Fortune*; Thomas L. Baily, *Dr. Wallsten's Way* (New York: National Temperance Society and Publication House, 1889); Josephine R. Baker, *Gee's Trap; or, The Lambs and Field Street* (Boston and Chicago: Congregational Sunday-School and Publishing Society, 1895); Belle V. Chisholm, *Stephen Lyle, Gentleman and Philanthropist* (New York: Hunt and Eaton, 1891); Robert H. Cowdrey, *A Tramp in Society* (Chicago: F. L. Schulte, 1891); Henry Fauntleroy, *Who's to Blame?* (Nashville: Southern Methodist Publishing House, 1883); Hulbert Fuller, *God's Rebel* (Chicago: Regan Publishing House, 1899); J. Thompson Gill, *Within and Without: A Philosophical, Lego-Ethical and Religious Romance*. . . . (Chicago: J. T. Gill, 1887); Elizabeth Grinnell, *For the Sake of a Name; A Story for Our Times* (Elgin and Chicago: David C. Cook, 1900); Grace L. Hill, *"A Daily Rate"* (Philadelphia: The Union Press, 1900); David Morgan, *A Dream of Christ's Return* (Chicago: Curts and Jennings, 1899); Jessie H. B. Pounds, *The Ironclad Pledge: A Story of Christian Endeavor* (Cincinnati: Standard, 1890); Milton R. Scott, *Ernest Marble, The Labor Agitator* (Newwark, Ohio: Tribune Book Print, 1895); Margaret P. Sherwood, *An Experiment in Altruism* (New York and London: Macmillan, 1895); Ward, *The Silent Partner*; Charles D. Warner, *The Golden House* (New York: Harper and Brothers, 1895); Amos R. Wells, *Elijah Tone, Citizen. A Story of Christian Citizenship* (Boston and Chicago: United Society of Christian Endeavor, 1897); and four novels by Julia M. Wright, *A New Samaritan. The Story of an Heiress* (New York: American Tract Society, 1895); *The New York Bible-Woman* (Philadelphia: Presbyterian Publication Committee; New York: A. D. F. Randolph, 1869); *A Plain Woman's Story* (Philadelphia: Presbyterian Board of Publication and Sabbath-School Work, 1890); *The Shoe Binders*

of New York; or, the Fields White to the Harvest (Philadelphia: Presbyterian Publication Committee; New York: A. D. F. Randolph, 1867).

21. Wright, *The Shoe Binders of New York*, pp. 102–3.

22. Wright, *A New Samaritan*, pp. 48–49. I have used the spelling and punctuation of the novels as published and have not put "*sic*" after every curious usage.

23. Wright, *The New York Bible-Woman*, pp. 79–80.

24. Ibid., p. 278. I mention the diction of this passage. Throughout, but especially in this opening chapter, I have resorted to much direct quotation; often, to paraphrase would have meant losing much of the point and presentation of the authors and their views. Better to let an author speak directly, I have felt, than summarize in words that would not give the flavor of the original.

25. Wright, *A Plain Woman's Story*, p. 49.

26. Ibid., p. 133.

27. See Appendix.

28. Stanley Kunitz and Howard Haycroft (eds.), *Twentieth Century Authors: A Biographical Dictionary of Modern Literature* (New York: H. W. Wilson, 1942), pp. 1273–74; Charles M. Sheldon, *Charles M. Sheldon: His Life Story* (New York: George H. Doran, 1925).

29. For a biography of Sheldon, see Glenn Clark, *The Man Who Walked in His Steps* (St. Paul, Minn.: The author, 1946).

30. Kunitz and Haycroft, p. 1274.

31. See John W. Ripley, "*In His Steps*," *Kansas Historical Quarterly* 34, no. 3 (1968): 241–65, for an essay that demolishes many of the myths surrounding Sheldon and *In His Steps*.

32. Charles M. Sheldon, *His Brother's Keeper*, pp. 8–9. After the "Amen" Sheldon has a footnote: "This incident is based on fact. The writer of this story was witness to a gathering of iron miners in the great strike of July, 1895, where one of the miners offered just such a prayer as the above, at Nagaunee, Mich., July 24, 1895."

33. Ibid., pp. 238–39.

34. James B. Converse, *Uncle Sam's Bible; or, Bible Teachings About Politics* (Chicago: Schulte, 1898), pp. ix–xi, xiv–xv.

35. Ibid., pp. 221–22. The above points are specific statements that affirm the religious and secular evangelism explained by Ralph H. Gabriel in *The Course of American Democratic Thought*, 2d ed. (New York: Ronald Press, 1956). In the foreword, Gabriel stresses that by 1815 Americans had formulated three basic beliefs: the dignity and freedom of the individual as expressed in his ability to participate in decisions fundamental to him; second, that there are certain basic principles universal to man in society and that these principles make possible freedom and dignity. Third, that the United States as an indivisible body has for its raison d'être the extension of freedom and the humane life both at home and abroad (pp. vi-vii). Gabriel's principles are again explained, in specific Christian terms, on pages thirty-eight and thirty-nine of his work. He stresses the rule of moral law implicit in Converse and summarizes his view by saying that "the mission of American democracy to save the world from the oppression of autocrats was a secular version of the destiny of Christianity to save the world from the governance of Satan" (p. 38). This latter statement of Gabriel's could be taken as the credo of the majority of social Christian fiction and is quoted in the epigraph to this volume.

36. Beveridge Hill, *The Story of a Cañon* (Boston: Arena, 1895), pp. 230–33.

37. Marion C. Smith, *Dr. Marks, Socialist* (Cincinnati: Editor Publishing, 1897), p. 191.

38. Jane D. Chaplin, *Mother West's Neighbors* (Boston: American Tract Society, 1876), preface, pp. 1–2. Four other novels representative of this variety of social gospel appeal are Annan Dale [James W. Johnston], *Dwellers in Gotham; A Romance of New York* (New York: Eaton and Mains; Cincinnati: Curts and Jennings, 1898); Dwight S. Prentice, *Revelations in Politics. A Story; Illustrating Thirty Years of American Political History* (Findlay, Ohio: Populist, 1895); Emma P. S. Bauder, *Ruth and Marie. A Fascinating Story of the Nineteenth Century* (Chicago and Philadelphia: American Bible House, 1895); Ward, *The Silent Partner.*

39. Mrs. Nico Bech-Meyer, *A Story from Pullmantown* (Chicago: C. H. Kerr, 1894), p. 95. The book is, incidentally, unique in social gospel fiction in two ways—first, in the author's description of the union movement as a means of Americanizing first-generation foreign labor, and second, for the publisher's insertion at the end of the novel of the following highly unusual advertisement:

WANTED—MEN AND WOMEN

Men and women who believe in human rights, who can see how human rights are now endangered, and who want to do their part in the defense of human rights, are urged to let us know where we can find them.

Our work is the publishing of books of social reform; books like this one that expose acts of oppression and injustice, and books that point to some way for bringing about better social conditions.

We need fifty thousand agents for this book, to bring it before the American people, that the lessons of Pullman may not be forgotten. Hundreds of agents already are earning good pay in the circulation of the book.

If you do not need to make money in this way, circulate the book and give the profit to the Pullman sufferers.

Write us for prices by the dozen, hundred and thousand, and write for our list of other books of reform. We want particularly the address of every reform lecturer in the United States.

Charles H. Kerr & Company, Publishers
175 Monroe Street, Chicago

The advertisement was unique in the novels dealt with, although many had front and back pages advertising everything from other books on the publishers' lists to foot powder and patent medicines. It would be of interest to know the social, political, and religious stance of many editors and publishing houses. I have done no specific research on the question, but work in this area might well be worth doing.

40. Charles M. Sheldon, *His Brother's Keeper*, p. 240.

41. L. Jonas Bubblebuster [pseud.?], *"Our Best Society" and the Rise and Fall of Boomtown Between the Years 1880 and 1910* (Chicago: Chicago Press, 1893), pp. 31–33. The author has a footnote at the close of this passage: "The reader is asked to note the fact that this is not intended for a reflection on the Christian religion, but on the abuse of it."

42. Hulbert Fuller, *God's Rebel*, pp. 43–44.

43. Ibid., p. 194.

44. Ibid., p. 129.

45. Cortland Myers, *Would Christ Belong to a Labor Union? or, Henry Fielding's Dream* (New York: Street and Smith, 1900), p. 32.

46. Ibid., p. 30.

47. Ibid., p. 37.

48. Florence Converse, *The Burden of Christopher* (Boston and New York: Houghton Mifflin, 1900), p. 51.

49. Ibid., p. 52.

50. Margaret Sidney [Harriet M. S. Lothrop], *Our Town, Dedicated to All Members of the Y. P. S. C. E.* (Boston: D. Lothrop, 1889), p. 368.

51. Ibid., pp. 366–67. Three other novels also stress the question of the Protestant denominations' role in the worker versus owner controversy: Birch Arnold [Alice E. B. Bartlett], *A New Aristocracy* (New York and Detroit: Bartlett, 1891); Mattie M. Boteler, *The Conversion of Brian O'Dillon* (Cincinnati: Standard, 1896); Charles M. Sheldon, *The Crucifixion of Phillip Strong*, 2d ed., rev. (New York and Boston: H. M. Caldwell, 1899).

52. James F. Conover, *"Church Amusements." The Church Dramatic and Terpsichorean Association, (Limited,) Promoters of Novity. A Satire.* (Detroit: Raynor and Taylor, 1895), p. 52.

53. Ibid., pp. 42–43.

54. George Guirey, *Deacon Cranky, the Old Sinner* (New York: Authors' Publishing Co., 1878), p. 35.

55. William H. H. Murray, *Deacons* (Boston: Henry L. Shepard, 1875), pp. 31–32.

56. Austin Miles, *About My Father's Business*, p. iv.

57. Other novels of this type that attack the decline of spirituality and growing worldliness of the church are William B. Bolmer, *The Time is Coming* (New York: G. W. Dillingham, 1896); E. P. Buffett, *Rev. Mr. Dashwell, the New Minister at Hampton* (Philadelphia: J. E. Potter, 1880); Elizabeth Grinnell, *John and I and the Church* (New York, Chicago, and Toronto: Fleming H. Revell, 1897); Beveridge Hill, *The Story of a Cañon*; James W. Johnston, [Annan Dale, pseud.], *Dwellers in Gotham; a Romance of New York* (New York: Eaton and Mains; Cincinnati: Curts and Jennings, 1898).

58. Daniel, pp. 258–59.

59. C. H. Anderson, *Armour; or, What Are You Going To Do About It?* (New York: W. B. Smith, 1881), pp. 172–73.

60. Eduard DeBrosé [Edgar C. Bross], *A Modern Pharisee* (New York: G. W. Dillingham, 1895), pp. 171–82.

61. Julia W. Parsons, *The Full Stature of a Man*, pp. 143–47.

62. Other works already cited and relevant in this area as well are by Chisholm, DeWitt, Fuller, Gill and Myers. See also Mrs. Ward's *The Silent Partner*.

63. Lewis V. Bogy [pseud.?], *In Office; A Story of Washington Life and Society* (Chicago: F. J. Schulte, 1891), pp. 153–55.

64. Lucy J. R. Meyer, *Deaconess Stories* (Chicago: Hope, 1900), pp. v–viii.

65. Elizabeth E. Holding, *Joy the Deaconess* (Cincinnati: Cranston and Curts, 1893).

66. Alice E. Curtiss, *The Silver Cross, A Story of the King's Daughters . . .* (Boston and Chicago: Congregational Sunday-School and Publishing Society, 1891). The volume also includes another novel, *Miss Marigold's Tithes*, by the same author, that is not relevant. Previously cited works include, Dickinson's *The King's Daughters*; Mrs. C. B. Howard's *Annie Cooper's Friends*; Mary B. Willey, *Tending Upward* (Philadelphia and New York: American Sunday-School Union, 1893).

67. Dickinson, p. 41.

68. Curtiss, pp. 17–18.

69. Harold M. Davis, *The City of Endeavor* (Brooklyn, N.Y.: Collins and Day,

1895); Hattie Sleeper Gardner, *The Endeavorers of Maple Grove* (Omaha: Megeath Stationery, 1893); Wells, *Elijah Tone, Citizen.*

70. Gardner, p. 230.

71. Archibald McCowan, *Christ, the Socialist* (Boston: Arena, 1894).

72. Ibid., p. 8.

73. Ibid., p. 30.

74. Miles, p. 148.

75. Bross, p. 17.

76. Katherine P. Woods, *Metzerott, Shoemaker* (New York: Thomas Y. Crowell, 1889). One other novel is relevant here; however, the author was considerably more concerned with political socialism than he was with Christian socialism, and the work will be discussed under that heading. The reference is to George Farnell, *Rev. Josiah Hilton, the Apostle of a New Age* (Providence, R.I.: Journal of Commerce Co., 1898).

77. Ibid., pp. 45–46.

78. Minnie L. Armstrong and George N. Sceets, *The Social Crime* (New York: W. L. Allison, 1896); Mrs. Amelia E. H. Barr, *The King's Highway* (New York: Dodd, Mead, 1897); Myers, *Would Christ Belong to a Labor Union?*; Albert Ross [Linn B. Porter], *Speaking of Ellen* (New York: G. W. Dillingham, 1890); Charles M. Sheldon, *The Redemption of Freetown* (Boston and Chicago: United Society of Christian Endeavor, 1898); Albion W. Tourgée, *Murvale Eastman, Christian Socialist* (New York: Fords, Howard and Hulbert, 1890).

79. Barr, pp. 291–94.

80. Ibid., p. 173. Unfortunately, Mrs. Barr gives no music to go with her lyrics.

81. Tourgée, p. 319. For the full wording of all nine principles, see pp. 318–19.

82. Charles M. Sheldon, *The Redemption of Freetown*, pp. 40–41. Contemporary politicians are still asking the same question and using the same techniques. Not many years ago the mayor of San Francisco did exactly as Sheldon asked "the best people of Freetown" to do.

83. Armstrong, pp. ii–iii.

84. Farnell, *Rev. Josiah Hilton.*

85. Katherine P. Woods, *A Web of Gold* (New York: Thomas Y. Crowell, 1890), p. 281.

86. Ibid., p. 282.

87. Julia W. Parsons, pp. 116–17.

88. Harriette A. Keyser, *Thorns in Your Sides* (New York and London: G. P. Putnam's Sons, 1884).

89. Ibid., pp. 152–53.

90. James B. Converse, *Uncle Sam's Bible*, pp. 70–71.

91. Henry Fauntleroy, *Who's to Blame?*, pp. 145–46.

92. Marion C. Smith, *Dr. Marks, Socialist*, p. 227.

93. Ibid., pp. 64–65.

94. Alice E. B. Bartlett, *A New Aristocracy.*

95. Ibid., pp. 220–23.

96. Ibid., pp. 229–32. A novel previously cited, Samuel P. Leland's *Peculiar People* also deals at length with the pros and cons of socialism. Leland thought the social gospel idea had a much greater chance of success in righting the social and economic inequities of the time because it was a positive philosophy and socialism was negative and pessimistic.

97. Wallace E. Davies, "Religious Issues in Late Nineteenth-Century American Novels," *Bulletin of the John Rylands Library* 41 (March 1959): 328–59.

98. Ibid., p. 358.

99. The quotations from Beveridge Hill's *The Story of a Cañon*, Linn B. Porter's *Speaking of Ellen*, and George Farnell's *Rev. Josiah Hilton* are good examples of expressions of working-class attitudes.

100. A full discussion of this attitude will be presented in Chapter 3 when the novels are discussed in literary terms.

101. By middle class I mean those who were neither white- nor blue-collar workers, those belonging to the professions—lawyers, ministers, doctors—and the bourgeois who owned small businesses or shops and were striving to move into the upper class, a class made up of bankers, railroad magnates, and steel tycoons who owned or controlled many businesses or financial empires.

Chapter 2

1. James W. Johnson, *Dwellers in Gotham*, pp. 361–62.

2. Katherine P. Woods, *A Web of Gold*, pp. 188–89.

3. Archibald McCowan, *Christ, the Socialist*, pp. 43–44.

4. Marion C. Smith, *Dr. Marks, Socialist*, p. 73. See Chapter 1.

5. Percival R. Benson, *The Rev. John Henry; Incidents Which Deeply Concerned One Life, and Were Not Without Their Bearing Upon Others* (New York: A. S. Barnes, 1895), pp. 166–69.

6. Cortland Myers, *Would Christ Belong to a Labor Union?*, pp. 134–35.

7. Charles M. Sheldon argued the same point, though not as succinctly, in *His Brother's Keeper*, pp. 295–97.

8. Albion W. Tourgée, *Murvale Eastman, Christian Socialist*, pp. 316–17.

9. Ibid., p. 273.

10. Robert H. Cowdrey, *A Tramp in Society*, p. 207.

11. Ibid., p. 208.

12. Ibid., p. 210.

13. Ibid., p. 211.

14. Ibid., pp. 216–17.

15. Hulbert Fuller, *God's Rebel*, p. 155.

16. Ibid., p. 156.

17. Henry Martel, *The Social Revolution. A Novel* (New York: G. W. Dillingham, 1891), pp. 22–23.

18. Ibid., pp. 152–54.

19. Austin Miles, *About My Father's Business*, pp. 72–73.

20. Albion W. Tourgée, *Murvale Eastman*, p. 21.

21. Amelia E. Barr, *The King's Highway*, pp. 115–16.

22. Sidney E. Ahlstrom, *A Religious History of the American People*, vol. 2, pp. 238–42.

23. Julia S. Alleman, *Postmarked "Colima"* (Philadelphia: Lutheran Publication Society, 1900), p. 259. It is unusual for these authors to advocate the study of the new field of sociology; and here it is even more surprising since in this particular novel the author is fairly conventional about almost everything else.

24. Helen H. C. Gardener, *Is This Your Son, My Lord? A Novel* (Boston: Arena, 1890), pp. 176–77.

25. Isaac G. Reed, Jr., *From Heaven to New York: or The Good Hearts and the Brown Stone Fronts. A Fact Founded on a Fancy* (New York: Murray Hill, 1876), pp. 92–95.

26. Ibid., pp. 95–98.

27. James W. Coulter, *The Larger Faith; a Novel* (Chicago: Charles H. Kerr, 1898), pp. 130–31.

28. Ibid., p. 232.

29. Elmore E. Peake, *The Darlingtons* (New York: McClure, Phillips, 1900), pp. 202–3.

30. Ibid., p. 341–43.

31. The inclusion of this work was the only exception to a rule I otherwise followed. In order to avoid confusion and controversy over what is and is not fiction, I used the Library of Congress classification (PZ3) as my guide. Gladden's *The Christian League*, though presented in narrative form, is classified under BX (philosophy and religion) at the Library of Congress. I have included the volume because of its uniqueness as an example of a particular social Christian approach to reform and because a number of secondary works on the period have considered it fiction.

32. Washington Gladden, *The Christian League of Connecticut* (New York: Century, 1883), pp. 22–23. Gladden, along with Josiah Strong and Walter Rauschenbusch, was one of the premier architects of the whole social gospel movement. After attending Williams College when Mark Hopkins was president, and studying privately with Moses Coit Tyler, he entered the Congregational ministry in 1860.

33. Florence Converse, *The Burden of Christopher*, p. 105. James W. Coulter, *The Larger Faith*, p. 265. Helen M. Winslow, *Salome Shepard, Reformer*, pp. 95–96.

34. Amelia E. H. Barr, *The King's Highway*, pp. 294–95.

35. Margaret B. Robinson, *Souls in Pawn; A Story of New York Life* (New York and Chicago: Fleming H. Revell, 1900), pp. 24–25.

36. Ibid., pp. 95–96.

37. James B. Converse, *Uncle Sam's Bible*, pp. 157–58.

38. L. Jonas Bubblebuster [pseud.?], *"Our Best Society,"* pp. 52–53.

39. Elizabeth Grinnell, *John and I and the Church*, pp. 19–21.

40. Anon., *Ivy Fennhaven; or, Womanhood in Christ. A Story of Processes* (Boston: D. Lothrop, 1872); Timothy S. Arthur, *Cast Adrift* (Philadelphia: J. M. Stoddard, 1873); Helen H. C. Gardener, *Is This Your Son, My Lord?*; Albert B. King, *Memorable Voyages of Rebel and Victory* (Boston: James H. Earle, 1895); Walter Mitchell, *Bryan Maurice; or, The Seeker* (Philadelphia: J. B. Lippincott, 1867). William W. Newton, *Philip MacGregor* (Hartford, Conn.: Student Publishing Co., 1895). These latter two, written almost ten years apart, are strikingly similar in tone and plot. Both deal with intellectual young men seeking faith. Both begin in Europe and end in the United States, and both heroes go through phases of Unitarianism. In Newton's novel, however, the hero ends up a Roman Catholic. In Mitchell's work, Bryan Maurice, after becoming a Unitarian minister, eventually finds his true home in the Episcopal church.

41. William S. Harris, *Mr. World and Miss Church-Member; or, The Secret Service of Satan. An Allegory* (Cleona, Pa.: G. Holzapfel, 1900).

42. Ibid., Introduction, p. 15.

43. Ibid., pp. 60–61.

44. Ibid., pp. 236–37.

45. Ibid., pp. 241–42.

46. Ahlstrom, *A Religious History of the American People*, vol. 2, pp. 274–97.

47. Grier Nicholl, "The Christian Social Novel and Social Gospel Evangelism," in *Religion in Life: A Christian Quarterly of Opinion and Discussion* 34 (Autumn 1965): 548–49.

48. Ibid., pp. 549 ff. He was probably right in regard to evangelical activity in the northern urban slums; beyond that, May et al. (including Ahlstrom) probably have the better part of the argument.

49. Ahlstrom, vol. 2, p. 254.

50. Helen H. Gardener, *Is This Your Son, My Lord?*; James the Less [J. B. Logan], *Alice McDonald: or, The Heroine of Principle; A Story of the Early Cumberland Presbyterian Church*, 4th ed. (Nashville: C. P. Publishing House, 1900; first published in 1870); Harriet B. McKeever, *Westbrook Parsonage* (Philadelphia: Claxton, Remsen and Haffelfinger, 1870); Walter Mitchell, *Bryan Maurice*; William W. Newton, *Philip MacGregor*.

51. Gardener, pp. 230–31.

52. Aaron Abell, *The Urban Impact on American Protestantism*, p. 11.

53. Ibid., p. 65.

54. Ibid., p. 137. As an illustration of these last two quotations, the mystical hero of a novel by Theron C. Crawford, *A Man and His Soul* (New York: Charles B. Reed, 1894) says: "Look at the churches of to-day—great fortresses, representing millions of capital, but closed during the greater part of the time, and, with the single exception of the Catholic Church, never open for the poor," (pp. 192–93).

55. R. F. Bishop, *Camerton Slope, a Story of Mining Life* (Cincinnati: Cranston and Curts; New York: Hunt and Eaton, 1893).

56. Gardener, pp. 239–40.

57. Albert B. King, *Memorable Voyages*, p. 235. More will be said of this particular novel in Chapter 3. This quotation is representative of its flavor. Other works that present a neutral or limitedly positive attitude to Catholicism are Alice E. Curtiss's *The Silver Cross*, p. 121; Elizabeth Grinnell's *John and I and the Church*, p. 123; Margaret B. Robinson's *Souls in Pawn*. See preceding quotations, footnotes 35 and 36 of this chapter.

58. Julia M. Wright, *A Plain Woman's Story*, pp. 98–99.

59. Austin Miles, *About My Father's Business*, pp. 186–87.

60. Milton R. Scott, *Henry Elwood, a Theological Novel* (Newark, Ohio: Newark American Print, 1892), pp. 304–5.

61. Mary Ellen Bamford, *Jessie's Three Resolutions* (Philadelphia: American Baptist Publication Society, 1894), pp. 14–15.

62. Ibid., p. 52.

63. Ibid., p. 60.

64. Henry Morgan, *Boston Inside Out! Sins of a Great City! A Story of Real Life* (Boston: Shawmut, 1880).

65. Ibid., pp. 206–9.

66. Ahlstrom, vol. 2, p. 316.

67. Helen H. C. Gardener, *Is This Your Son, My Lord?*; William S. Harris, *Mr. World and Miss Church-Member*; Leander S. Keyser, *The Only Way Out* (New York: A. D. F. Randolph, 1888); Milton R. Scott, *Henry Elwood*; John Smith [Roswell A. Benedict], *Doubting Castle, A Religious Novelette* (New York: John B. Alden, 1891).

68. Milton R. Scott, *Henry Elwood*, pp. 224–25.

69. Ibid., pp. 265–68.

70. Ibid., p. 274.

71. Gardener, p. 232.

72. Scott, p. 184. Questions and comments on the "Higher Criticism"—the study of the Bible by scientific and historical techniques—are also touched on lightly by Elizabeth Grinnell in *John and I and the Church* and in a novel by Carlos Martyn, *Sour Saints and Sweet Sinners* (London and New York: F. Tennyson Neely, 1898). This latter work will be discussed in Chapter 3.

73. The following touch on the controversy in one manner or another: Armstrong and Sceets, *The Social Crime*, Bartlett, *A New Aristocracy*; Bauder, *Ruth and Marie*; Daniel C. Beard, *Moonblight and Six Feet of Romance*, 2d ed. (Trenton: Albert Brandt, 1904). Beard's book was originally published in 1892; Benedict, *Doubting Castle*; Percival R. Benson, *The Rev. John Henry*; Bolmer, *The Time is Coming*; F. Converse, *The Burden of Christopher*; Crawford, *A Man and His Soul*; Daniel, *Ai*; Davis, *The City of Endeavor*; Dickinson, *The King's Daughters*; Farnell, *Rev. Josiah Hilton*; Fauntleroy, *Who's To Blame?*; Fuller, *God's Rebel*; Grinnell, *For the Sake of a Name* and *John and I and the Church*; B. Hill, *The Story of a Cañon*; Leander S. Keyser, *The Only Way Out* (New York: A. D. F. Randolph, 1888); McCowan, *Christ, the Socialist*; Meyer, *Deaconess Stories*; Myers, *Would Christ Belong to a Labor Union?*; Margaret B. Robinson, *Souls in Pawn*; Scott, *Henry Elwood*; Tourgée, *Murvale Eastman*; Woods, *Metzerott, Shoemaker* and *A Web of Gold*.

74. Robinson, p. 100.

75. Davis, pp. 19–20.

76. Grinnell, *For the Sake of a Name*, p. 38. In Mrs. Grinnell's other novel, *John and I and the Church*, there is an inconclusive section on how one should rightly interpret the findings of Darwin in a social context.

77. Beard, p. 78.

78. Dickinson, p. 83.

79. F. Converse, p. 27. There is also a passage from Roswell A. Benedict's *Doubting Castle* voicing the same theme but using the phraseology of eighteenth-century Deism:

"And God himself does not look at me kindly any more from the blue sky in the day-time and from the stars at night. He has gone away somewhere far beyond my thought and imagination. I think of him sometimes as a great engineer, with his hand on the lever that stops and starts the machinery of the whole universe; for he no more seems to me a father to every one of his creatures, not to any one of them, but only the first cause that put the principle of life into matter, and then let it work out its own results. I myself seem to have come from nowhere, and to be destined for nothing in particular" (p. 10).

What is missing in 1891, the date of the book's publication, is Lockean optimism. Instead, the quotation is modern in its existential pessimism.

80. Fauntleroy, pp. 211–13.

81. Ibid., pp. 215–17.

82. Grinnell, *John and I and the Church*, pp. 74–76.

83. Fuller, p. 86.

84. Ibid., p. 230.

85. McCowan, pp. 138–39.

86. John Dewey's *The Influence of Darwin on Philosophy* (New York: Holt, 1910) elucidates this thesis in detail.

87. Benson, *The Rev. John Henry*, p. 125.

88. Daniel, pp. 62–65.

89. Bauder, pp. 204–5.

Chapter 3

1. Most of the novels are set east of the Mississippi, and a large proportion in either New York City, Chicago, or some other metropolis. Very few of the works deal with rural problems—land speculators, the hardships of farming, problems with the railroad. Almost all the authors were concerned with the new urban worker and his or her problems, spiritual and temporal.

2. Charles M. Sheldon, *In His Steps, "What Would Jesus Do?"* 1961 ed. (New York: Grosset and Dunlap; Chicago: Advance, 1897), pp. v–vi.

3. Elizabeth S. P. Ward, *The Silent Partner*, pp. v–vi.

4. Henry Morgan, *Boston Inside Out*, introduction, pp. 5–6.

5. Thomas L. Bailey, *Dr. Wallsten's Way*, p. iv. See also Harold M. Davis, *The City of Endeavor*, p. vii. The prefaces to James B. Converse's *Uncle Sam's Bible* and Elizabeth Grinnell's *For the Sake of a Name* are of the same nature, except that in the latter volume the author also suggests that "poor boys and girls and older folk may sympathize with the lonely rich if they stop to give the matter a thought. All are in need of something, and poverty has no exclusive patent on misery" (p. 1).

6. Ellen E. Dickinson, *The King's Daughters*, p. i.

7. See for example the editorial note to Mrs. C. B. Howard's *Annie Cooper's Friends* and the introduction by the Rev. A. E. Dunning to Anna E. Hahn's *Summer Assembly Days; or, What Was Seen, Heard and Felt at the Nebraska Chautauqua. . . .* (Boston and Chicago: Congregational Sunday School and Publishing Society, 1888). The fourth edition of J. B. Logan's *Alice McDonald*, the novel praising the Cumberland Presbyterian Church, along with a new preface, also reprinted the prefaces to all three other editions. Each made quite clear that the novel was written for proselytizing, propagandistic purposes. Yet one of the curiosities of many of the novels is the fact that a great number were published by denominational presses that either made no overt sectarian plea or actually advocated nonsectarianism.

8. Harriet B. McKeever, *Westbrook Parsonage*, p. v.

9. J. B. Logan, *Alice McDonald*, pp. 7–9.

10. James B. Converse, *Uncle Sam's Bible*, p. 64.

11. Edgar C. Bross, *A Modern Pharisee*, p. 34. This hammering away, perhaps all too apparent from the many passages I have reproduced, was a general hallmark of social Christian fiction. Subtlety, on any level, was not.

12. Helen D. Brown, *The Petrie Estate*, pp. 176–77.

13. Ibid., p. 172.

14. Ibid., pp. 119–20.

15. Elizabeth Grinnell, *John and I and the Church*, pp. 67–68.

16. Leander S. Keyser, *The Only Way Out*, pp. 66–68.

17. Albion W. Tourgée, *Murvale Eastman, Christian Socialist*, p. 113.

18. Ibid., pp. 165–66.

19. Ibid., p. 214.

20. William S. Harris, *Mr. World and Miss Church-Member*, pp. 147–49.

21. Ibid., pp. 151–52.

22. Ibid., p. 5.

23. William H. H. Murray gives a good portrait of the New England Yankee in 1875 in *Deacons*, pp. 10–11, and James W. Coulter presents "the genus cow-boy" of 1898 on pp. 75–76 of *The Larger Faith*. There is also a section of C. H. Anderson's *Armour* (pp. 215–16) portraying Jay Gould that is a minor masterpiece of character assassination. And in Margaret P. Sherwood's *Henry Worthington, Idealist*, there is a fine presentation of the taciturn but idealistic New Englander who fought institutions in the name of individual, independent thinking (pp. 236–39).

24. Tourgée, pp. 346–47.

25. Ibid., p. 347.

26. Ibid., pp. 348–49.

27. Ibid., p. 351.

28. Emma P. S. Bauder, *Ruth and Marie*, pp. 131–32.

29. Henry L. Everett, *The People's Program: The Twentieth Century is Theirs . . . A Romance of the Expectations of the Present Generation* (New York: Workmen's, 1892), pp. 38–40.

30. Ward, *The Silent Partner*, pp. 72–74.

31. Ibid., p. 77.

32. Mrs. Ward could also make excellent use of dialogue and render the uneducated speech of a New England mill girl. See pp. 287–88 in the same novel, for example.

33. See for example Percival R. Benson, *The Rev. John Henry*, pp. 115–18, and Susan Parkman, *Two Noble Women*, pp. 25–26. In the same vein, there is a surprising section in Elizabeth Grinnell's *John and I and the Church* in which the minister of the title does not kiss and hold an attractive six-year-old girl upon his knee because he is afraid of his own impulses. As his wife candidly says to the child's perplexed mother: "John is peculiar, you know. His inclination to kiss the child, winsome little thing that she is, yielded to his principle. . . . It was for her sake. What is the little girl but a little woman?" (p. 154). The dramatization and discussion of the scene is extended, covering almost four pages.

34. Florence Converse, *The Burden of Christopher*, pp. 176–77, 196.

35. The background to the legend itself is interesting. Its origins are pagan, related to the stories of Atlas and Hercules. In Christian form it appeared in the third century A.D., at which time the story was transformed into its present form—Christopher carrying Christ across a river during a storm. The Albrecht Dürer engraving is perhaps the most famous rendering of the scene.

36. All of the following works contain elements of satire, and in some the device carries the real burden of expressing the author's ideas: Benson, *The Rev. John Henry*; Lester Bodine, *Off the Face of the Earth. A Story of Possibilities* (Omaha: Fester, 1894); L. Jonas Bubblebuster, *"Our Best Society"*; James B. Converse, *Uncle Sam's Bible*; Hulbert Fuller, *God's Rebel*; Gill, *Within and Without*; James W. Johnson, *Dwellers in Gotham*; Harriette A. Keyser, *Thorns in Your Sides*; Bailey K. Leach, *Soulless Saints, A Strange Revelation* (Chicago: American, 1892); Logan, *Alice McDonald*; Mrs. M A. MacDonald, *Deacon Hackmetack* (Philadelphia: Treager and Lamb, 1888); Carlos Martyn, *Sour Saints and Sweet Sinners*; Isaac G. Reed, *From Heaven to New York*; Margaret P. Sherwood, *An Experiment in Altruism*; Elizabeth S. P. Ward, *Hedged In*, 28th ed. (Boston: Houghton Mifflin, 1897; first published in 1870).

37. James Converse, pp. 68–70.

38. Logan, p. 22 ff.

39. Bubblebuster, pp. 4–6.

40. H. Keyser, pp. 83–84.

41. Benson, pp. 130–33.

42. Sherwood, *An Experiment in Altruism*, pp. 46–50.

43. Ibid., pp. 214–15. Almost all of the characters in the novel instead of having names in the usual sense are known only by abstractions—the Altruist, the Butterfly Collector, The Man of the World, the Anarchist, etc.

44. Leach, pp. 108–13.

45. Harris, p. 307.

46. Albert B. King, *Memorable Voyages of Rebel and Victory*, p. 132. Daniel C. Beard's *Moonblight and Six Feet of Romance*, which was partially allegorical, also uses the same device. The hero mill owner, through a magic book, sees his fellow stockholders as they really are—snakes, foxes, pigs.

47. William Allen, *Erudia, the Foreign Missionary to Our World; or, The Dream of Orphanos* (Nashville: M. E. Church, South; privately printed, 1890), pp. 8–9.

48. Ibid., p. 238.

49. William B. Bolmer, *The Time is Coming*, p. 282.

50. Charles M. Sheldon, *Robert Hardy's Seven Days; a Dream and its Consequences*, rev. ed. (Elgin, Ill.: David C. Cook, 1900; originally published in 1893).

51. Elizabeth S. P. Ward, *The Gates Ajar* (Boston: Fields, Osgood, 1869); *Beyond the Gates* (Boston and New York: Houghton Mifflin, 1883); *The Gates Between* (Boston and New York: Houghton Mifflin, 1887). In 1964 the Belknap Press of Harvard University Press put out an edition of *The Gates Ajar* with an excellent thirty-page introduction by Helen Sootin Smith. Christine Stanwell has also written an interesting biographical piece on Mrs. Ward that briefly deals with *The Gates Ajar*: "Elizabeth Stuart Phelps: A Study in Female Rebellion," *Massachusetts Review* 13, nos. 1 and 2 (1972): 239–56. The essay as a whole is not germane to this study; it does, however, detail various feminist aspects of the author's life and work.

52. Lester Bodine, *Off the Face of the Earth. A Story of Possibilities* (Omaha: Festner, 1894).

53. Isaac S. Dement, *Baron Kinitas, a Tale of the Anti-Christ* (Chicago: M. T. Need, 1894).

54. Sheldon, *In His Steps*, pp. 6–10.

55. Milford W. Howard, *If Christ Came to Congress* (Washington and New York: Howard, 1894), pp. 320, 324–26.

56. Ibid., dedication.

57. Ibid., p. 97.

58. Edward E. Hale, *If Jesus Came to Boston* (Boston: Lamson, Wolffe, 1895), preface, pp. 3–4.

59. Ibid., p. 45.

60. Olla P. Toph, *Lazarus* (Indianapolis: Indianapolis Printing Co., 1895).

61. Elizabeth S. P. Ward, *The Supply at St. Agatha's* (Boston and New York: Houghtonl Mifflin, 1896).

62. Sheldon, *In His Steps*, p. 75. Sheldon's *Richard Bruce; or, The Life that Now Is* (Boston and Chicago: Congregational Sunday-School and Publishing Society, 1892) also made some use of the "If Christ Came" theme. For an interesting and pertinent rein-

terpretation of the former work, see Paul S. Boyer, "*In His Steps*: A Reappraisal," *American Quarterly* 23, no. 1 (Spring 1971): 60–78. Boyer argues that *In His Steps* is really about temperance and that the novel is more revealing about late nineteenth-century middle-class fears of the new immigrant working class than it is about the tenets of the social gospel. I find his argument on the last point unconvincing; and while his psychological interpretation of middle-class fears seems valid, such fears were, part and parcel, one of the reasons for the whole social gospel movement and certainly not unique to *In His Steps*. Forebodings concerning immigration were common to the social Christian fiction of the entire period.

63. David Morgan, *A Dream of Christ's Return*.

64. There are nine other works that use various allegorical techniques to get across their respective points: Daniel's *Ai*; Everett's *The People's Program*; three make use of allegory to argue pantheism: David N. Beach, *How We Rose* (Boston: Roberts Brothers, 1895); Theron C. Crawford, *A Man and His Soul*; and John G. Schwahn, *The Tableau; or, Heaven as a Republic* (Los Angeles: Franklin, 1892); Susie C. Clark, in *Pilate's Query* (Boston: Arena, 1895), argues spiritualism and Christian Science; Sherman N. Aspinwall, *Garnered Sheaves. An Intensely Interesting Narration of the Good Deeds of a Young Lady of Wealth and Fashion* (Grand Rapids, Mich.: W. W. Hart, 1886). These last two novels were strongly influenced by Swedenborgianism and advocate Swedenborg's doctrines; Mary E. Buell's *The Sixth Sense; or, Electricity: A Story for the Masses* (Boston: Colby and Rich, 1891) is an argument for "scientific Christianity" as opposed to orthodox Christianity; and Catherine J. Barton's *Evangel Ahvallah; or, The White Spectrum. A Novel Whose Incidents are Linked Together by a Chain of Metaphysical Deductions* (Kansas City: Privately printed, 1895); among other things, tells how Evangel achieves a spiritual union with God.

Chapter 4

1. There are two exceptions: Grier Nicholl's unpublished Ph.D. dissertation entitled "The Christian Social Novel in America, 1865–1918," University of Minnesota, 1964, and Elmer F. Suderman's unpublished Ph.D. dissertation entitled "Religion in the American Novel, 1870–1900," written on the subject.

2. Both of these types of novels present characters generally satisfied with the modes and attitudes of Protestant Christianity during the Gilded Age. Elmer F. Suderman's thesis in his article "Criticisms of the Protestant Church in the American Novel: 1870–1900," *Midcontinent American Studies Journal* 5, no. 1 (1964): 17–23, that "American novelists writing between 1870 and 1900 were, on the whole, critical of the American Protestant church" (p. 17) is only partially correct. His misconception is understandable; evidently he just ran on to the more militant social gospel works or radical Christian novels in his reading. Generally, those works designated as falling either into category "A" or category "D" as listed in the Annotated List of Social Christian Novels tend to diminish the validity of Suderman's assumptions.

3. In another article by Suderman, "The Social-Gospel Novelists' Criticisms of American Society," *Midcontinent American Studies Journal* 7, no. 1 (1966): 45–60, he makes a distinction between reform religious fiction that was aimed at reformation of individuals—"convert the factory owner, not primarily that he might help his employees in times of trouble but that he might go to heaven and take his employees with him" (p. 46),

and social gospel fiction that was not so much orientated toward individuals as toward change of social institutions.

4. In Grier Nicholl's study, referred to earlier (fn 1, this chapter) he came up with similar categorizations and parallel conclusions.

5. About the Roman Catholic church the writers of social Christian fiction had surprisingly little to say. Only a fraction of the number of works read had any comment on Catholicism, and of the twenty that did, almost half were either neutral or well disposed toward the church. Only four novels took the incipient menace of Catholicism as a principal theme.

6. Grier Nicholl, "The Christian Social Novel and Social Gospel Evangelism," *Religion in Life: A Christian Quarterly of Opinion and Discussion* 34, no. 4 (1965): 549.

7. Harriet B. Stowe, *Uncle Tom's Cabin* (1852; reprint New York: Washington Square Press, 1963), p. xix.

8. Wayne C. Booth, *The Rhetoric of Fiction* (Chicago and London: University of Chicago Press, 1961).

9. Elmer F. Suderman, thoughtful scholar that he is, also has an article on the Christ motif in religious fiction of the period, "Jesus as a Character in the American Religious Novel: 1870–1900," *Discourse: A Review of the Liberal Arts* 9, no. 1 (1966): 101–15. He deals only with "the straightforward and unsophisticated depiction of the undisguised Jesus as a character in [the] fiction" (p. 101), not with symbolic or allegorical portrayals of Christ, and he covered works in which Christ came to earth in the present day, those in which He was among those present in a work set in heaven (such as Ward's *The Gates Ajar*) and those biblical novels set in the time of Christ. Most of the article was concerned with the latter historical novels. Suderman could find only one novel in which Christ appeared on earth, Edward E. Hale's *If Jesus Came to Boston*. There were four others that I encountered: William S. Harris's *Mr. World and Miss Church-Member*, Issaac G. Reed's *From Heaven to New York*, John G. Schwahn's *The Tableau*, and Elizabeth S. P. Ward's *The Supply at St. Agatha's*. In general Suderman lamented the character of the various Christs portrayed, noting that they were almost uniformly sweet and gentle to a consumptive fault. The Jesus that drove the moneychangers from the temple was seldom encountered. Such a picture was accurate in Hale's and Ward's work, though not in Harris's (where the character may have been either Christ or God Himself) or Reed's. In the latter especially Christ foretold of His return and earth's judgment in tones not far removed from Jonathan Edwards's.

Bibliography of Interpretive Works

BOOKS

Abbott, Lyman. *Silhouettes of My Contemporaries*. Garden City, N.Y., and Toronto: Doubleday, Page, 1921.

Abell, Aaron Ignatius. *The Urban Impact on American Protestantism, 1865–1900*. Cambridge: Harvard University Press; London: H. Milford, Oxford University Press, 1943.

Adadourian, Reverend Haig. *If Jesus Came to Manomet*. Printed for Private Distribution. Plymouth, Mass.: Memorial Press, 1898.

Adair, Ward William. *Vital Messages in Modern Books*. New York: Association Press, 1926.

Ahlstrom, Sidney E. *A Religious History of the American People*. New York: Doubleday, 1975.

Bacon, Leonard Woolsey. *A History of American Christianity*. New York: Christian Literature, 1897.

Baker, Ernest A. *A Guide to the Best Fiction in English*. London: G. Routledge, 1913.

Baldwin, Charles Crittenton [George Gordon, pseud.]. *The Men Who Make Our Novels*. New York: Moffat, Yard, 1919.

Ballou, Adin. *History of the Hopedale Community, from its Inception to its Virtual Submergence in the Hopedale Parish*. Edited by William S. Heywood. Lowell, Mass.: Thompson and Hill, 1897.

————. *Practical Christian Socialism: A Controversial Exposition of the True System of Human Society; in Three Parts, viz: I. Fundamental Principles. II. Constitutional Polity. III. Superiority to Other Systems*. Hopedale, Mass.: Author; New York: Fowlers and Wells, 1854.

Banks, Louis Albert. *White Slaves; or, The Oppression of the Worthy Poor*. Boston: Lee and Shepard, 1892.

Barnes, William Eddy (ed.). *The Labor Problem: Plain Questions and Practical Answers*. New York: Harper and Brothers, 1886.

Barr, Amelia E. *Maids, Wives and Bachelors*. New York: Dodd Mead, 1898.

Bartol, Cyrus Augustus. *Radical Problems*. Boston: Roberts Brothers, 1872.

Bascon, John. *The Philosophy of English Literature, a Course of Lectures Delivered in the Lowell Institute*. New York: G. P. Putnam's Sons, 1874.

————. *Social Theory. A Grouping of Social Facts and Principles*. New York and Boston: T. Y. Crowell, 1895.

Bates, Daniel M. *Christ in Modern Thought*. New York: Thomas Whittaker, 1889.

Bellamy, Edward. *Equality*. New York: D. Appleton, 1897.

————. *Looking Backward, 2000–1887*. Boston: Ticknor, 1888.

Bernays, Edward L., *et al.* (eds.). *The Broadway Anthology*. New York: Duffield, 1917.

Betts, Lillian Williams. *The Leaven in a Great City*. New York: Dodd Mead, 1902.

Bierbower, Austin. *How to Succeed*. New York: R. F. Fenno, 1900.

————. *The Morals of Christ. A Comparison with Contemporaneous Systems*. Chicago: W. E. Wolcott, 1885.

————. *Socialism of Christ; or, Attitudes of Early Christians Toward Modern Problems*. Chicago: C. H. Sergel, 1890.

Bliss, William Dwight Porter (ed.). *The Encyclopedia of Social Reform. . . .* New York and London: Funk and Wagnalls, 1897.

Blotner, Joseph Leo. *The Political Novel*. Garden City, N.Y.: Doubleday, 1955.

Bodein, Vernon Parker. *The Development of the Social Thought of Walter Rauschenbusch*. New York: N.p., 1937.

Boyer, Paul S. *Urban Masses and the Moral Order in America, 1820–1920*. Cambridge: Harvard University Press, 1978.

Boyesen, Hjalmar Hjorth. *Literary and Social Silhouettes*. New York: Harper and Brothers, 1894.

Bradford, Amory Howe. *The Return to Christ*. New York: Dodd Mead, 1900.

Bremner, Robert Hamlett. *American Philanthropy*. Chicago: University of Chicago Press, 1960.

Brooke, Stopford Augustus. *Religion in Literature and Religion in Life*. New York: T. Y. Crowell, 1901.

Brown, Herbert Ross. *The Sentimental Novel in America, 1789–1860*. Durham, N.C.: Duke University Press, 1940.

Brushingham, John Patrick. *Catching Men; Studies in Vital Evangelism*. Cincinnati: Jennings and Graham; New York: Eaton and Mains, 1906.

————. *Spiritual Electrology*. Cincinnati: Jennings and Graham; New York: Eaton and Mains, 1912.

Buck, James Smith. *The Chronicles, of the Land of Columbia, Commonly Called America. . . .* Milwaukee: F.W. Stearns, 1876.

Buckham, John Wright. *Progressive Religious Thought in America; A Survey of the Enlarging Pilgrim Faith*. Boston and New York: Houghton Mifflin, 1919.

Burroughs, John. *The Light of Day; Religious Discussions and Criticisms from the Naturalist's Point of View*. Boston and New York: Houghton Mifflin, 1900.

Bushnell, Horace. *An Oration, Pronounced Before the Society of Phi Beta Kappa, at*

New Haven, on the Principles of National Greatness, August 15, 1837. New Haven, Conn.: Herrick and Noyes, 1837.

Byer, John. *Christ on Wall Street: A Meditation.* Louisville: J. P. Morton, 1896.

Carey, Henry Charles. *Principles of Social Science.* Philadelphia: J. B. Lippincott, . . . 1858–59.

Carnegie, Andrew. *The Gospel of Wealth, and Other Timely Essays.* Edited by Edward C. Kirkland. Cambridge: Harvard University Press, Belknap Press, 1962.

Carwardine, William Horace. *The Pullman Strike.* Chicago: C. H. Kerr, 1894.

Casson, Herbert Newton. *The Red Light.* Lynn, Mass.: Lynn Labor Church Press, 1898.

Catalogue of the General Theological Library. . . . Boston, Massachusetts. Boston: The Fort Hill Press, 1913.

Chaffee, Edmund Bigelow. *The Protestant Churches and the Industrial Crisis.* New York: Macmillan, 1933.

Chamberlain, John. *Farewell to Reform, Being a History of the Rise, Life and Decay of the Progressive Mind in America.* New York: Liveright, 1932.

Cherouny, Henry William. *Socialism and Christianity, Sober Thoughts for All Who are Concerned in the Welfare of Our Industry.* New York: Privately printed, 1882.

Clark, Francis Edward. *Our Business Boys. (What Eighty-three Business Men Say).* Boston: D. Lothrop, 1884.

Clark, Glenn. *The Man Who Walked in His Steps.* St. Paul, Minn.: Privately printed, 1946.

Clemens, William Montgomery (ed.). *Sixty and Six Clips from Literary Workshops.* New York: New Amsterdam, 1897.

Coan, Otis W., and Lillard, Richard G. *America in Fiction; an Annotated List of Novels that Interpret Aspects of Life in the United States.* Stanford: Stanford University Press, 1941.

Coates, Jacob B. *God and Our Country. The Financial Question of Our Country as Seen by an American Citizen Abroad.* N.p., 1895.

Cole, Charles Chester. *The Social Ideas of the Northern Evangelists, 1826–1860.* New York: Columbia University Press, 1954.

Combs, George Hamilton. *The Christ in Modern English Literature.* St. Louis: Christian Publishing Co., 1903.

Commons, John Rogers. *Social Reform and the Church.* New York: T. Y. Crowell, 1894.

Conwell, Russell Herman. *Acres of Diamonds. . . .* Philadelphia: J. Y. Huber, 1890.

Cook, Dorothy E., and Munroe, Isabel S. (comps.). *Fiction Catalog.* New York: H. W. Wilson, 1942.

Cook, Joseph. *Labor, with Preludes on Current Events.* Boston: Houghton Mifflin, 1880.
———. *Socialism, with Preludes on Current Events.* Boston: Houghton Mifflin, 1880.

Cooper, Frederic Taber. *Some American Story Tellers.* New York: Henry Holt, 1911.

Crafts, Wilbur Fisk. *National Perils and Hopes; a Study Based on Current Statistics and the Observations of a Cheerful Reformer.* Cleveland: F. M. Barton, 1910.
———. *Practical Christian Sociology. . . .* New York: Funk and Wagnalls, 1895.
———. *Successful Men of To-day and What They Say of Success. Based on Facts and Opinions . . . From Five Hundred Prominent Men. . . .* New York: Funk and Wagnalls, 1883.

Crooker, Joseph Henry. *Jesus Brought Back. Meditations on the Problem of Problems.* Chicago: A. C. McClurg, 1889.

Darnell, Calvin Robinson (comp.). *Scholastic Literature*. Nashville: Southern Methodist Publishing House, 1870.

Davies, Trevor H. *Spiritual Voices in Modern Literature*. New York: George H. Doran, 1919.

Dewey, John. *The Influence of Darwin on Philosophy*. New York: Holt, 1910.

Dillistone, Frederick William. *The Novelist and the Passion Story*. New York: Sheed and Ward, 1960.

Dombrowski, James. *The Early Days of Christian Socialism in America*. New York: Columbia University Press, 1936.

Dorchester, Daniel. *The Problem of Religious Progress*. Rev. ed. New York: Eaton and Mains; Cincinnati: Jennings and Pye, 1900.

Dunlap, George Arthur. *The City in the American Novel, 1789–1900; a Study of American Novels Portraying Contemporary Conditions in New York, Philadelphia, and Boston*. New York: Russell and Russell, 1965.

Eggleston, Edward (comp.). *Christ in Literature.* . . . New York: J. B. Ford, 1875.

Featherstun, Henry Walter. *The Christ of Our Novelists*. Nashville: M. E. Church, South, 1904.

Fine, Sidney A. *Laissez-faire and the General-welfare State; a Study of Conflict in American Thought, 1865–1901*. Ann Arbor: University of Michigan Press, 1956.

Fiske, Horace Spencer. *Provincial Types in American Fiction*. Chautauqua, N.Y.: Chautauqua Press, 1903.

Flory, Claude Reherd. *Economic Criticism in American Fiction, 1792–1900*. Philadelphia: University of Pennsylvania Press, 1936.

Foster, Charles I. *An Errand of Mercy; The Evangelical United Front, 1790–1837*. Chapel Hill: University of North Carolina Press, 1960.

Fraser, Alexander N. *The Social Gospel and the Bible; a Business Man Turns to His Bible to Learn the Truth Concerning the Social Gospel*. Pittsburgh: Privately printed, 1939.

Gabriel, Ralph Henry. *The Course of American Democratic Thought*. 2d ed. New York: Ronald Press, 1956.

Garrison, Winfred Ernest. *The March of Faith; the Story of Religion in America Since 1865*. New York and London: Harper and Brothers, 1933.

Gladden, Washington. *The Christian League of Connecticut*. New York: Century, 1883.

Glicksberg, Charles Irving. *Literature and Religion: A Study in Conflict*. Dallas: Southern Methodist University Press, 1960.

Griswold, William McCrillis. *An Analytical Index to the Political Contents of "The Nation"* . . . *Forming a Record of Politics and Politicians in the United States, 1865–1882*. N.p., 1883.

———. *A Descriptive List of Names and Tales Dealing with the History of North America*. Cambridge, Mass.: Privately printed, 1895.

Gunn, Giles B. *The Interpretation of Otherness: Literature, Religion and the American Imagination*. New York: Oxford University Press, 1979.

——— (ed.). *Literature and Religion*. London: SCM Press, 1971.

Hale, Edward Everett. *How They Lived in Hampton.* . . . Boston: J. Stilman Smith, 1888.

Hall, Thomas Cuming. *The Religious Background of American Culture*. Boston: Little Brown, 1930.

Halstead, William Riley. *Christ in the Industries*. Cincinnati and New York: Curts and Jennings, 1898.

Hamilton, William Thomas. *Lecture: On the Indebtedness of Modern Literature to the Bible.* . . . Mobile, Ala.: F. H. Brooks, 1844.

Handlin, Oscar. *The Americans; a New History of the People of the United States.* Boston: Little Brown, 1963.

Hart, James David. *The Popular Book; a History of America's Literary Taste.* New York: Oxford University Press, 1950.

Headley, Phineas Camp (ed.). *God and Home and Native Land: A Crown of the World's Choicest Gems, in Prose and Verse.* . . . Boston: Eastern, 1891.

Herron, Ima Honaker. *The Small Town in American Literature.* Durham, N.C.: Duke University Press, 1939.

Higham, John. *Strangers in the Land; Patterns of American Nativism, 1860–1925.* New Brunswick, N.J.: Rutgers University Press, 1955.

Hillis, Newell Dwight. *Great Books as Life Teachings; Studies of Character, Real and Ideal.* 16th ed. Chicago and New York: Fleming H. Revell, 1901.

Hobson, John Atkinson. *God and Mammon; the Relations of Religion and Economics.* New York: Macmillan, 1931.

Hofstadter, Richard. *Social Darwinism in American Thought.* 2d ed., rev. Boston: Beacon Press, 1955.

Hopkins, Charles Howard. *The Rise of the Social Gospel in American Protestantism, 1865–1915.* New Haven, Conn.: Yale University Press; London: H. Milford, Oxford University Press, 1940.

Jamison, Albert Leland, and Smith, James Ward (eds.). *Religion in American Life.* Princeton: Princeton University Press, 1961.

Johnson, Frederick Ernest. *The Social Gospel Re-examined.* New York and London: Harper and Brothers, 1940.

Kahoe, Walter. *Book Titles from the Bible.* Moylan, Penn.: Rose Valley Press, 1946.

Knight, Grant Cochran. *American Literature and Culture.* New York: Ray Long and Richard R. Smith, 1932.

———. *The Critical Period in American Literature.* Chapel Hill: University of North Carolina Press, 1951.

———. *The Strenuous Age in American Literature.* Chapel Hill: University of North Carolina Press, 1954.

Kort, Wesley A. *Narrative Elements and Religious Meanings.* Philadelphia: Fortress Press, 1975.

Leaming, James. *Prince Emmanuel.* Des Moines, Iowa: Christian Index Publishing Co., 1900.

Leary, Lewis Gaston. *Articles on American Literature, 1900–1950.* Durham: Duke University Press, 1954.

Lenrow, Elbert. *Reader's Guide to Prose Fiction.* . . . New York and London: D. Appleton-Century, 1940.

Lingenfelter, Mary Rebecca, and Hanson, Marie Alice. *Vocations in Fiction; an Annotated Bibliography.* Chicago: American Library Association, 1932.

Literature and Society, 1950–1955, A Selective Bibliography. Coral Gables, Fla.: University of Miami Press, 1956.

Little, Lawrence C. (comp.). *Bibliography of Doctoral Dissertations in Character and Religious Education.* Pittsburgh: University of Pittsburgh, 1960.

Long, Mason. *The Bible and English Literature.* State College, Penn.: Pennsylvania State College Press, 1935.

Loomis, Samuel Lane. *Modern Cities and Their Religious Problems*. New York: Baker and Taylor, 1887.

Luccock, Halford Edward. *Contemporary American Literature and Religion*. Chicago and New York: Willett, Clark, 1934.

McCullough, Esther Morgan (ed.). *As I Pass, O Manhattan; an Anthology of Life in New York*. North Bennington, Vt.: Coley Taylor, 1956.

McIntyre, Willard Ezra. *Baptist Authors; a Manual of Bibliography, 1500–1914*. Montreal and Toronto: Industrial and Educational Press, 1914.

McKelvey, Blake. *The Urbanization of America, 1860–1915*. New Brunswick, N.J.: Rutgers University Press, 1963.

Malcom, Howard. *An Index to the Principal Works in Every Department of Religious Literature. Embracing Nearly Seventy Thousand Citations, Alphabetically Arranged Under Two Thousand Heads*. 2d ed. Philadelphia: J.B. Lippincott, 1870.

Mann, Arthur. *Yankee Reformers in the Urban Age*. Cambridge: Harvard University Press, Belknap Press, 1954.

Marchant, James (ed.). *Anthology of Jesus*. New York and London: Harper and Brothers, 1926.

Mathews, Shailer. *Christianity and Social Process*. . . . New York and London: Harper and Brothers, 1934.

―――. *The Individual and the Social Gospel*. New York: Missionary Education Movement of the United States and Canada, 1914.

―――. *Jesus on Social Institutions*. New York: Macmillan, 1928.

―――. *The Social Gospel*. Philadelphia and Boston: Griffith and Rowland Press, 1910.

May, Henry Farnham. *Protestant Churches and Industrial America*. New York: Harper, 1949.

Mayer, Frederick Emanuel. *The Religious Bodies of America*. 3d ed. St. Louis: Concordia, 1958.

Merriam, Charles Edward. *American Political Ideas; Studies in the Development of American Political Thought, 1865–1917*. New York: Macmillan, 1929.

Mode, Peter George. *The Frontier Spirit in American Christianity*. New York: Macmillan, 1923.

―――. *Source Book and Bibliographical Guide for American Church History*. Menasha, Wis.: George Banta, 1921.

Monfort, Francis Cassatte. *Applied Theology*. Cincinnati: Monfort, 1904.

Morgan, Howard Wayne (ed.). *The Gilded Age, a Reappraisal*. Syracuse, N.Y.: Syracuse University Press, 1963.

Moseley, Edwin M. *Pseudonyms of Christ in the Modern Novel: Motifs and Methods*. Pittsburgh: University of Pittsburgh Press, 1963.

Mosher, William Eugene. *The Promise of the Christ-Age in Recent Literature*. New York and London: G. P. Putnam's Sons, 1912.

Mott, Frank Luther. *Golden Multitudes; The Story of Best Sellers in the United States*. New York: Bowker, 1960.

Munger, Theodore Thornton. *The Freedom of Faith*. Boston and New York: Houghton Mifflin, 189?.

Nash, Henry Sylvester. *Genesis of the Social Conscience; the Relation Between the Establishment of Christianity in Europe and the Social Question*. New York: Macmillan Co.; London: Macmillan, 1897.

Neff, Merlon L. *Keepers of the Flame*. Mountain View, Calif.: Pacific Press, 1943.

Niebuhr, Helmut Richard. *The Kingdom of God in America*. Chicago and New York: Willett, Clark, 1937.

Noel, Mary. *Villains Galore; the Heyday of the Popular Story Weekly*. New York: Macmillan, 1954.

Olmstead, Clifton E. *History of Religion in the United States*. Englewood Cliffs, N.J.: Prentice-Hall, 1960.

Papashvily, Helen Waite. *All the Happy Endings; a Study of the Domestic Novel in America, The Women Who Write It, The Women Who Read It, in the Nineteenth Century*. New York: Harper, 1956.

Parrington, Vernon Louis, Jr. *American Dreams; a Study of American Utopias*. Providence, R.I.: Brown University Press, 1947.

Pattison, Robert Bainbridge (comp.). *Book Titles from the Bible*. New York: American Bible Society, 1942.

Peabody, Francis Greenwood. *Jesus Christ and the Social Question; a Examination of the Teaching of Jesus in its Relation to Some of the Problems of Modern Social Life*. New York: Macmillan Co.; London: Macmillan, 1900.

Pegasus Club, Philadelphia. *The Year Book of the Pegasus*. No. 1. Philadelphia: J. B. Lippincott, 1895.

Pierson, Arthur Tappan. *Forward Movements of the Last Half Century; Being a Glance at the More Marked Philanthropic, Missionary, and Spiritual Movements Characteristic of Our Time*. New York and London: Funk and Wagnalls, 1900.

Potter, Henry Codman. *God and the City*. 2d ed. New York: Abbey Press, 1900.

Rauschenbusch, Walter. *Christianity and the Social Crisis*. New York: Macmillan Co.; London: Macmillan, 1907.

————. *A Theology for the Social Gospel*. New York: Macmillan, 1917.

Richardson, Ernest Cushing, *et al. Periodical Articles on Religion, 1890–1899*. 2 Vols. New York: Scribner's Sons, 1911.

Richmond, Wilfrid John. *Christian Economics*. London: Rivingtons, 1888.

Roads, Charles. *Christ Enthroned in the Industrial World; a Discussion of Christianity in Property and Labor*. New York: Hunt and Eaton; Cincinnati: Cranston and Curts, 1892.

Roberts, Evelyn Harvey. *The Pure Causeway. A Religious Story*. Chicago: Charles H. Kerr, 1899.

Roberts, Richard. *That One Face; Studies in the Place of Jesus in the Minds of Poets and Prophets*. New York: Association Press, 1919.

Robins, John B. *Christ and Our Country; or, A Hopeful View of Christianity in the Present Day*. 2d ed. Nashville: M. E. Church, South, privately printed, 1889.

Rowe, Henry Kallock. *The History of Religion in the United States*. New York: Macmillan, 1924.

Schlesinger, Arthur Meier, Jr. *The American as Reformer*. Cambridge: Harvard University Press, 1950.

Scott, Nathan A. *The Broken Center; Studies in the Theological Horizon of Modern Literature*. New Haven: Yale University Press, 1966.

————. *Modern Literature and the Religious Frontier*. New York: Harper, 1958.

Selby, Thomas Gunn. *The Theology of Modern Fiction. . . .* London: C. H. Kelly, 1897.

Sheehan, Donald Henry. *This Was Publishing; a Chronicle of the Book Trade in the Gilded Age*. Bloomington: Indiana University Press, 1952.

Sheldon, Charles Monroe. *Charles M. Sheldon; His Life and Story.* New York: George Doran, 1925.

———. *The First Christian Daily Paper.* . . . New York: Street and Smith, 1900.

———. *New Opportunities in Old Professions. An Address Given at Washburn College Commencement, Topeka, Kansas, June 14, 1899.* Chicago: J. A. Ulrich, 1899.

———. *One of the Two.* Chicago and New York: Fleming H. Revell, 1898.

Slater, John Rothwell. *Recent Literature and Religion.* . . . New York and London: Harper and Brothers, 1938.

Smith, Hilrie Shelton. *Changing Conceptions of Original Sin; a Study in American Theology Since 1750.* New York: Scribner, 1955.

Smith, Timothy Lawrence. *Revivalism and Social Reform in Mid-Nineteenth-Century America.* New York: Abingdon Press, 1957.

Sprague, Philo Woodruff. *Christian Socialism. What and Why.* New York: E. P. Dutton, 1891.

Stead, William Thomas. *If Christ Came to Chicago. A Plea.* . . . Chicago: Laird and Lee, 1894.

Stewart, Randall. *American Literature and Christian Doctrine.* Baton Rouge: Louisiana State University Press, 1958.

Stigen, William LeRoy. *God in Literature.* New York: George H. Doran, 1925.

———. *The High Faith of Fiction and Drama.* Garden City, N.Y.: Doubleday, Doran, 1928.

Strong, Josiah. *The New Era; or, The Coming Kingdom.* New York: Baker and Taylor, 1893.

———. *Religious Movements for Social Betterment.* New York: League for Social Service, 1900.

Stuckenberg, John Henry Wilburn. *Christian Sociology.* New York: I. K. Funk, 1880.

———. *The Social Problem.* York, Pa.: Social Problem Publishing Co., 1897.

Sumner, Charles. *Prophetic Voices Concerning America. A Monograph.* Boston: Lee and Shepard; New York: Lee, Shepard and Dillingham, 1874.

Sutherland, A. *The Kingdom of God and the Problems of Today.* Nashville: M. E. Church, South, 1898.

Sweet, William Warren. *Religion in the Development of American Culture, 1765–1840.* New York: Scribner, 1952.

———. *The Story of Religion in America.* 2d ed., rev. New York: Harper, 1950.

Taylor, Walter Fuller. *The Economic Novel in America.* Chapel Hill: University of North Carolina Press, 1942.

Thompson, Robert Ellis. *De Civitate Dei. The Divine Order of Human Society.* . . . Philadelphia: J. D. Wattles, 1891.

Tolman, William Howe. *Municipal Reform Movements in the United States.* New York and Chicago: Fleming H. Revell, 1895.

Toulmin, Harry Aubrey, Jr. *Social Historians.* Boston: R. G. Badger, 1911.

Tyler, Alice Felt. *Freedom's Ferment; Phases of American Social History to 1860.* Minneapolis: University of Minnesota Press, 1944.

Underwood, John Curtis. *Literature and Insurgency; Ten Studies in Radical Evolution: Mark Twain, Henry James, William Dean Howells, Frank Norris, David Graham Phillips, Steward Edward White, Winston Churchill, Edith Wharton, Gertrude Atherton, and Robert W. Chambers.* New York: M. Kennerley, 1914.

Urmy, William Smith. *Christ Came Again*. . . . New York: Eaton and Mains; Cincinnati: Curts and Jennings, 1900.

Waffle, Albert Edward. *If Christ Were King; or, The Kingdom of Heaven on Earth*. Philadelphia and Boston: Griffith and Rowland Press, 1912.

Wagenknecht, Edward Charles (ed.). *The Story of Jesus in the World's Literature*. New York: Creative Age Press, 1946.

Wiggins, James B. (ed.). *Religion as Story*. New York: Harper and Row, 1975.

Wilson, Edmund. *Patriotic Gore; Studies in the Literature of the American Civil War*. New York: Oxford University Press, 1962.

Wilson, Samuel Law. *The Theology of Modern Literature*. Foxcroft, Pa.: Foxcroft Library Editions, 1976.

Woodress, James Leslie. *Dissertations in American Literature, 1891–1955*. Durham, N.C.: Duke University Press, 1957.

Wright, Lyle Henry. *American Fiction, 1851–1875; a Contribution toward a Bibliography*. San Marino, Calif.: Huntington Library, 1957.

ARTICLES AND PERIODICALS

Boyer, Paul S. "*In His Steps*: A Reappraisal." *American Quarterly* 23, no. 1 (Spring 1971): 60–78.

Brooks, Obediah. "The Problem of the Social Novel." *Modern Quarterly* 6 (Autumn 1932): 77–82.

Cawalti, John G. "Changing Ideas of Social Reform as Seen in Selected American Novels of the 1850's, the 1880's, and the Present Day." *Social Service Review* 35 (September 1961): 278–89.

Davies, Wallace Evan. "Religious Issues in Late 19th Century American Novels." *Bulletin of the John Rylands Library* 41 (1959): 328–59.

Erskine, John. "American Business in the American Novel." *Bookman* 83 (July 1931): 449–51.

Fox, Arnold Benjamin. "Howells as a Religious Critic." *New England Quarterly* 25, no. 2 (June 1952): 199–216.

Glicksbert, C. I. "Proletarian Fiction in the United States." *Dalhousie Review* 17 (April 1937): 22–32.

James, M. M., Brown, D., and Dunn, G. M. (eds.). *The Book Review Digest*. New York: H. W. Wilson, Published annually.

Jones, Claude E. "Modern Books Dealing with the Novel in English: A Check List." *Bulletin of Bibliography* 22 (1957): 85–87.

Moss, Mary. "Contemporary Themes in Fiction." *Outlook* 84 (1906): 774.

Nicholl, Grier. "The Christian Social Novel and Social Gospel Evangelism." *Religion in Life: A Christian Quarterly of Opinion and Discussion* 34 (Autumn 1965): 548–61.

Perry, H. Francis. "The Workingman's Alienation from the Church." *American Journal of Sociology* 4 (March 1899): 621–29.

Rahv, Philip. "Proletarian Literature." *Southern Review* 4 (January 1939): 616–28.

"Religious Fiction." *Protestant Episcopal Quarterly* (January 1856): n.p.

Rezneck, Samuel. "Patterns of Thought and Action in American Depression, 1882–1886." *American Historical Review* 61 (January 1956): 284–307.

Ripley, John W. *"In His Steps." Kansas Historical Quarterly* 34, no. 3 (1968): 241–65.

Roohan, James E. "American Catholics and the Social Question, 1865–1900." U.S. Catholic Historical Society *Historical Records and Studies* 43 (1954): 3–26.

Rose, Lisle Abbott. "A Bibliographical Survey of Economic and Political Writings, 1865–1900." *American Literature* 15 (January 1944): 381–410.

Schlesinger, Arthur Meire. "A Critical Period in American Religion, 1875–1900." Massachusetts Historical Society *Proceedings* 64 (June 1932): 523–47.

Sheldon, Charles Monroe. "Work with Humanity at First Hand." *The Commons* 5, no. 53 (December 1900): 6–7.

Stansell, Christine. "Elizabeth Stuart Phelps: A Study in Female Rebellion." *Massachusetts Review* 13, nos. 1 and 2 (1972): 239–56.

Strauss, Harold. "Realism in the Proletarian Novel." *Yale Review* 28 (December 1938): 360–74.

Suderman, Elmer F. "Criticisms of the Protestant Church in the American Novel: 1870–1900." *Midcontinent American Studies Journal* 5, no. 1 (Spring 1964): 17–23.

———. "Jesus as a Character in the American Religious Novel: 1870–1900." *Discourse: A Review of the Liberal Arts* 9 (Winter 1966): 101–15.

———. "Religion in the Popular American Novel: 1870–1900." *Journal of Popular Culture* 9, no. 4 (Spring 1976): 1003–9.

———. "The Social-Gospel Novelists' Criticism of American Society." *Midcontinent American Studies Journal* 7, no. 1 (Spring 1966): 45–60.

Taylor, Walter Fuller. "On the Origins of Howells' Interest in Economic Reform." *American Literature* 2 (1930): 3–14.

Webber, Christopher L. "William Dwight Porter Bliss (1856–1926) Priest and Socialist." *Historical Magazine of the Protestant Episcopal Church* 28 (1959): 9–39.

Wilkinson, Hazel. "Social Thought in American Fiction, 1910–1917." *University of Southern California Studies in Sociology* 3, no. 2 (1918): 18–24.

UNPUBLISHED MATERIAL

Bludworth, Rosa L. "A Study of the Biblical Novel in America, 1940–49, with a Survey of the Biblical Novel in General in the 19th and 20th Centuries." Ph.D. dissertation, University of Texas, 1955.

Dusenberry, Robert B. "Attitude Toward Religion in Representative Novels of the American Frontier, 1820–1890." Ph.D. dissertation, Washington University, 1952.

Hallenbach, John. "Economic Individualism in the American Novel, 1865–1888." Ph.D. dissertation, University of Wisconsin, 1941.

Koerner, James D. "The Triumph of the Dinosaurs: A Study of the Politico-Economic Novel of Protest in America, 1888–1906." Ph.D. dissertation, Washington University, 1952.

Laubenstein, Paul L. "A History of Christian Socialism in America." Ph.D. dissertation, Union Theological Seminary, 1925.

Nicholl, Grier. "The Christian Social Novel in America, 1865–1918." Ph.D. dissertation, University of Minnesota, 1964.

Ransom, Eilene. "Utopus Discovers America." Ph.D. dissertation, Vanderbilt University, 1947.

Rose, Lisle Abbott. "Unpublished Bibliographic Material on Social Problems of the Nineteenth Century." Washington, D.C.: George Washington University.

Shuck, Emerson C. "Clergymen in Representative American Novels, 1830–1930: A Study in Attitudes Toward Religion." Ph.D. dissertation, University of Wisconsin, 1943.

Shurter, Robert LeFevre. "The Utopian Novel in America, 1865–1900." Ph.D. dissertation, Western Reserve University, 1936.

Suderman, Elmer. "The American Religious Novel, 1870–1900." Ph.D. dissertation, University of Kansas, 1961.

Whitfield, Josephine W. "American Social Movements 1873–1885 as Reflected in Contemporary Novels." Master's thesis, University of Illinois, 1933.

Index

About the Author

ROBERT GLENN WRIGHT was Professor of English at Michigan State University. His earlier works include the *Author Bibliography of English Language Fiction in the Library of Congress Through 1950.*